Exquisite Wickedness

Two Murders and the Making of Poe's "The Tell-Tale Heart"

ANDREW AMELINCKX

AMERICA
THROUGH TIME®
ADDING COLOR TO AMERICAN HISTORY

America Through Time is an imprint of Fonthill Media LLC
www.through-time.com
office@through-time.com

Published by Arcadia Publishing by arrangement with Fonthill Media LLC
For all general information, please contact Arcadia Publishing:
Telephone: 843-853-2070
Fax: 843-853-0044
E-mail: sales@arcadiapublishing.com
For customer service and orders:
Toll-Free 1-888-313-2665

www.arcadiapublishing.com

First published 2021

ISBN 978-1-63499-303-6

Typeset in 10pt on 13.5pt Sabon
Printed and bound in England

PREFACE

"The Tell-Tale Heart," one of Edgar Allan Poe's most famous short stories, has inspired artists, filmmakers, and writers since its first publication in 1843. Yet it was two murders a decade apart that helped inspire Poe to write his macabre masterwork of psychological fiction.

In Salem, Massachusetts, in April 1830, someone bludgeoned and stabbed an old and rich sea captain named Joseph White while he slept in his mansion. A decade later, in December 1840, in New Brunswick, New Jersey, a wealthy banker named Abraham Suydam mysteriously disappeared.

While there is no direct evidence—Poe never came out and said he based his story on these two cases—several Poe experts believe he used these infamous nationally publicized crimes as source material for his story.

The eminent Poe scholar Thomas Ollive Mabbott states in *The Collected Works of Edgar Allan Poe* that the speech given by the prosecutor in the 1830 White murder case probably caught Poe's attention. The prosecutor's final summation appeared in the August 21, 1841, edition of *Brother Jonathan*, a weekly New York City illustrated newspaper that described it as "the most thrilling speech ever made in this country." Poe quoted directly from the article in another of his stories, "The Mystery of Marie Rogêt," just a week later.

The American literary critic David S. Reynolds writes in his book *Beneath the American Renaissance: The Subversive Imagination in the Age of Emerson and Melville* (1988) that Poe used elements of the White murder that popularized the "cool criminal, the detached and manipulative murderer" in "The Tell-Tale Heart." Reynolds also believes Poe found inspiration from the Suydam case, especially in relation to the details of the killing.

Isabelle Lehuu details in her book *Carnival on the Page: Popular Print Media in Antebellum America* how Poe used elements of the Suydam case but "focused on the psyche of the criminal rather than on the gruesome criminal act."

Other sources for the story, according to Mabbott, were the long-held superstitions concerning the "evil eye" and a short story by Charles Dickens, "A Confession Found in a Prison in the Time of Charles the Second." In that story, published in 1840, a murderer describes how he killed his nephew, buried him in the garden, and sat in a chair over the spot while entertaining two acquaintances. In a May 1841 review Poe wrote for *Graham's Magazine,* he praised Dickens' book that included the story.

Still another source for the story is much more personal. A childhood friend of Poe recalled how Poe had a recurring nightmare in which he was being watched by dark and forbidding figures as he lay in bed.[1] While possibly apocryphal, it gives a tantalizing glimpse into Poe's personality.

Poe's short story—and I mean short; it comes in at barely over 2,000 words—made a splash when first published in the Boston-based literary magazine *The Pioneer* in January 1843. Various newspapers and magazines (sometimes with Poe's name removed) quickly reprinted the story, including *The Sun,* a hugely popular penny newspaper from New York City. That summer, periodicals in England and Canada reprinted it. Due to lax copyright laws, which Poe fought hard against in his lifetime, he did not see any royalties from these unauthorized reprints.

Another official version of the story with some slight modifications appeared in the August 23, 1845, edition of *The Broadway Journal,* where he was the editor. The story continued to resurface in various publications in his lifetime, but it really took off after his death in 1849. The first official anthology of Poe's work after his death, *The Works of the Late Edgar Allan Poe,* published in 1850, included the story. From there, "The Tell-Tale Heart" gained more and more fame, eventually being transformed into various radio and film adaptations, and even comic books. Nearly 180 years later, the story is still with us, as haunting as it was when first published in 1843.

Since "The Tell-Tale Heart" is the glue that holds this book together, I felt it necessary to include it in its entirety.

"THE TELL-TALE HEART" BY EDGAR ALLAN POE

True!—nervous—very, very dreadfully nervous I had been and am; but why will you say that I am mad? The disease had sharpened my senses—not destroyed—not dulled them. Above all was the sense of hearing acute. I heard all things in the heaven and in the earth. I heard many things in hell. How, then, am I mad? Hearken! and observe how healthily—how calmly I can tell you the whole story.

It is impossible to say how first the idea entered my brain; but once conceived, it haunted me day and night. Object there was none. Passion there was none. I loved the old man. He had never wronged me. He had never given me insult. For his gold I had no desire. I think it was his eye! yes, it was this! He had the eye of a vulture—a pale blue eye, with a film over it. Whenever it fell upon me, my blood ran cold; and so by degrees—very gradually—I made up my mind to take the life of the old man, and thus rid myself of the eye forever.

Now this is the point. You fancy me mad. Madmen know nothing. But you should have seen me. You should have seen how wisely I proceeded—with what caution—with what foresight—with what dissimulation I went to work! I was never kinder to the old man than during the whole week before I killed him. And every night, about midnight, I turned the latch of his door and opened it—oh so gently! And then, when I had made an opening sufficient for my head, I put in a dark lantern, all closed, closed, that no light shone out, and then I thrust in my head. Oh, you would have laughed to see how cunningly I thrust it in! I moved it slowly—very, very slowly, so that I might not disturb the old man's sleep. It took me an hour to place my whole head within the opening so far that I could see him as he lay upon his bed. Ha! would a madman have been so wise as this, And then, when my head was well in the room, I undid the lantern cautiously-oh, so cautiously—cautiously (for the hinges creaked)—I undid it just so much that a single thin ray fell upon the vulture eye. And this I did for seven long nights—every night just at midnight—but I found the eye always closed; and so it was impossible to do the work; for it was not the old man who vexed me, but his Evil Eye. And every morning, when the day broke, I went boldly into the chamber, and spoke courageously to him, calling him by name in a hearty tone, and inquiring how he has passed the night. So you see he would have been a very profound old man, indeed, to suspect that every night, just at twelve, I looked in upon him while he slept.

Upon the eighth night I was more than usually cautious in opening the door. A watch's minute hand moves more quickly than did mine. Never before that night had I felt the extent of my own powers—of my sagacity. I could scarcely contain my feelings of triumph. To think that there I was, opening the door, little by little, and he not even to dream of my secret deeds or thoughts. I fairly chuckled at the idea; and perhaps he heard me; for he moved on the bed suddenly, as if startled. Now you may think that I drew back—but no. His room was as black as pitch with the thick darkness, (for the shutters were close fastened, through fear of robbers,) and so I knew that he could not see the opening of the door, and I kept pushing it on steadily, steadily. I had my head in, and was about to open the lantern, when my thumb slipped upon the tin fastening, and the old man sprang up in bed, crying out—"Who's there?" I kept quite still and said nothing. For a whole hour I did not move a muscle, and in the meantime I did not hear him lie down. He was still sitting up in the bed listening;—just as I have done, night after night, hearkening to the death watches in the wall.

Presently I heard a slight groan, and I knew it was the groan of mortal terror. It was not a groan of pain or of grief—oh, no!—it was the low stifled sound that arises from the bottom of the soul when overcharged with awe. I knew the sound well. Many a night, just at midnight, when all the world slept, it has welled up from my own bosom, deepening, with its dreadful echo, the terrors that distracted me. I say I knew it well. I knew what the old man felt, and pitied him, although I chuckled at heart. I knew that he had been lying awake ever since the first slight noise, when he had turned in the bed. His fears had been ever since growing upon him. He had been trying to fancy them causeless, but could not. He had been saying to himself—"It is nothing but the wind in the chimney—it is only a mouse crossing the floor," or "It is merely a cricket which has made a single chirp." Yes, he had been trying to comfort himself with these suppositions: but he had found all in vain. All in vain; because Death, in approaching him had stalked with his black shadow before him, and enveloped the victim. And it was the mournful influence of the unperceived shadow that caused him to feel—although he neither saw nor heard—to feel the presence of my head within the room.

When I had waited a long time, very patiently, without hearing him lie down, I resolved to open a little—a very, very little crevice in the lantern. So I opened it—you cannot imagine how stealthily, stealthily—until, at length a simple dim ray, like the thread of the spider, shot from out the crevice and fell full upon the vulture eye. It was open—wide, wide open—and I grew furious as I gazed upon it. I saw it with perfect distinctness—all a dull blue, with a hideous veil over it that chilled the very marrow in my bones; but I could see nothing else of the old man's face or person: for I had directed the ray as if by instinct, precisely upon the damned spot. And have I not told you that what you mistake for madness is but over-acuteness of the sense?—now, I say, there came to my ears a low, dull, quick sound, such as a watch makes when enveloped in cotton. I knew that sound well, too. It was the beating of the old man's heart. It increased my fury, as the beating of a drum stimulates the soldier into courage.

But even yet I refrained and kept still. I scarcely breathed. I held the lantern motionless. I tried how steadily I could maintain the ray upon the eve. Meantime the hellish tattoo of the heart increased. It grew quicker and quicker, and louder and louder every instant. The old man's terror must have been extreme! It grew louder, I say, louder every moment!—do you mark me well I have told you that I am nervous: so I am. And now at the dead hour of the night, amid the dreadful silence of that old house, so strange a noise as this excited me to uncontrollable terror. Yet, for some minutes longer I refrained and stood still. But the beating grew louder, louder! I thought the heart must burst. And now a new anxiety seized me—the sound would be heard by a neighbour! The old man's hour had come! With a loud yell, I threw open the lantern and leaped into the room. He shrieked once—once only. In an instant I dragged him to the floor, and pulled the heavy bed over him. I then smiled gaily, to find the deed so far done. But, for many minutes, the heart beat on with a muffled sound. This, however, did not vex me; it would not be heard through the wall. At length it ceased. The old man was dead. I removed the bed and examined the corpse. Yes, he was stone, stone dead. I placed my hand upon the heart and held it there many minutes. There was no pulsation. He was stone dead. His eye would trouble me no more.

If still you think me mad, you will think so no longer when I describe the wise precautions I took for the concealment of the body. The night waned, and I worked hastily, but in silence. First of all I dismembered the corpse. I cut off the head and the arms and the legs. I then took up three planks from the flooring of the chamber, and deposited all between the scantlings. I then replaced the boards so cleverly, so cunningly, that no human eye—not even his—could have detected any thing wrong. There was nothing to wash out—no stain of any kind—no blood-spot whatever. I had been too wary for that. A tub had caught all—ha! ha! When I had made an end of these labors, it was four o'clock—still dark as midnight. As the bell sounded the hour, there came a knocking at the street door. I went down to open it with a light heart,—for what had I now to fear? There entered three men, who introduced themselves, with perfect suavity, as officers of the police. A shriek had been heard by a neighbour during the night; suspicion of foul play had been aroused; information had been lodged at the police office, and they (the officers) had been deputed to search the premises. I smiled,—for what had I to fear? I bade the gentlemen welcome. The shriek, I said, was my own in a dream. The old man, I mentioned, was absent in the country. I took my visitors all over the house. I bade them search—search well. I led them, at length, to his chamber. I showed them his treasures, secure, undisturbed. In the enthusiasm of my confidence, I brought chairs into the room, and desired them here to rest from their fatigues, while I myself, in the wild audacity of my perfect triumph, placed my own seat upon the very spot beneath which reposed the corpse of the victim.

The officers were satisfied. My manner had convinced them. I was singularly at ease. They sat, and while I answered cheerily, they chatted of familiar things. But, ere long, I felt myself getting pale and wished them gone. My head ached, and I fancied a ringing in my ears: but still they sat and still chatted. The ringing became more distinct:—It continued and became more distinct: I talked more freely to get rid of the feeling: but it continued and gained definiteness—until, at length, I found that the noise was not within my ears. No doubt I now grew very pale;—but I talked more fluently, and with a heightened voice. Yet the sound increased—and what could I do? It was a low, dull, quick sound—much such a sound as a watch makes when enveloped in cotton. I gasped for breath—and yet the officers heard it not. I talked more quickly—more vehemently; but the noise steadily increased. I arose and argued about trifles, in a high key and with violent gesticulations; but the noise steadily increased. Why would they not be gone? I paced the floor to and fro with heavy strides, as if excited to fury by the observations of the men—but the noise steadily increased. Oh God! what could I do? I foamed—I raved—I swore! I swung the chair upon which I had been sitting, and grated it upon the boards, but the noise arose over all and continually increased. It grew louder—louder—louder! And still the men chatted pleasantly, and smiled. Was it possible they heard not? Almighty God!—no, no! They heard!—they suspected!—they knew!—they were making a mockery of my horror!-this I thought, and this I think. But anything was better than this agony! Anything was more tolerable than this derision! I could bear those hypocritical smiles no longer! I felt that I must scream or die! and now—again!—hark! louder! louder! louder! louder!

"Villains!" I shrieked, "dissemble no more! I admit the deed!—tear up the planks! here, here!—It is the beating of his hideous heart!"[2]

ACKNOWLEDGMENTS

This book would not have been possible without the help of my wife, Kara Thurmond, a hard but excellent editor and the perfect partner in crime (writing) and life.

A huge thanks to the staff at the Phillips Library at the Peabody Essex Museum in Rowley, Mass., and the New York State Library in Albany, NY., for their time and patience with me.

The Edgar Allan Poe Society of Baltimore was a massive help to me in writing about Poe's life. The organization's website is an incredible storehouse of information on everything you would ever need to know about the author (at times, it was overwhelming in its scope).

Thanks as well to everyone at Fonthill Media for seeing the vision for this book through. I hope I have done Poe proud.

CONTENTS

PART III: ALL THINGS IN HEAVEN AND EARTH 145

PART I

BLOOD, BLOOD, BLOOD

1

A TALE

Edgar sat down to write. As usual, he was desperate for money. He was so desperate he was considering bankruptcy as an option for trying to get out from under the mountain of debt that included bills for books, his wife Virginia's piano lessons, and even the paper he was using—the lifeblood of a writer. He looked much older than his thirty-three years, as much to do with his money woes as both he and his wife's fragile health. Yet he was still handsome, with his broad forehead, thick dark, wavy hair, and piercing gray eyes.

They rented a home on Coates Street in Philadelphia. The castle-like Eastern State Penitentiary loomed over the neighborhood, a constant reminder of man's darker nature. He sat at the kitchen table as Catterina, his beloved tortoiseshell cat, nuzzled his legs; his mother-in-law's birds chirped in their cage.

The year 1842 was coming to a close. It had been a year marked by violence in Philadelphia. That summer saw severe storms and three days of rioting by Irish Catholics, who looted and burned several African-American churches, businesses, and homes with no real repercussions against the culprits. As the heat of summer dissipated, so had the city's enmity. Autumn had been mild, as was the city's general mood following the outburst of violence. The start of November was warm, but as Poe sat contemplating a new story, an icy wind whipped the city. The thermometer plunged into the teens, presaging a long and bitter winter ahead.

Poe had been thinking about a tale from the perspective of a murderer and how the killer's soul would turn against him, usurp his very will to survive, and force him to admit his guilt. It was to be a tale of the terror of the soul, a realistic depiction of psychological horror that did not rely on the phantasmagorical or antastic.

Poe used true stories to draw from for his tale. There was the murder of old Captain Joseph White in Salem in 1830, recently featured in *Brother Jonathan*, the New York newspaper that Poe often read. It called Senator Daniel Webster's final summation from when he prosecuted the case "the most thrilling speech ever made in this country."

Poe also relied on details from a second killing that took place three years earlier, in 1840, to the north of Philadelphia, in New Brunswick, New Jersey. The New York City press covered the story, especially the *Herald,* as did many of the Philadelphia papers. A rich banker named Abraham Suydam disappeared under mysterious circumstances. It turned out he had been murdered and buried in a cellar in a home he had sold to the killer.

Poe took out his penknife and sliced off a bit of the quill's tip to give it a sharp edge, dipped it in the ink, put pen to paper, and plunged into the mind of a killer.

"True!—nervous—very, very dreadfully nervous I had been and am; but why will you say that I am mad?"

He focused on only the essentials for this tale from the perspective of a psychotic killer with no other motive than his aversion to an old man's milky, film-covered "vulture" eye. He excised everything he deemed unnecessary to drive the story forward as he labored towards its end.

The final version would come in at just over 2,000 words, but they were all the words he needed to create his masterpiece. Poe did not understand what a sensation his lurid tale would make, not only in his time but for years and years afterward.

2

NIGHTMARES

The clouds hung low in the night sky on April 6, 1830, as the dark figure quietly made his way through the garden towards the back of Captain Joseph White's house, guided by the intermittent light of the full moon as it broke through the gray sky. The window on the right side at the back of the house was unlocked, as promised. Slowly, he raised it and then slipped into the house. All was darkness. All was quiet. The intruder crept through the back room into the long front hall and then up the stairs, each creak of the floorboards sending a rush of adrenaline through his body. Finally, he made it to the second floor. The door to the room he wanted was to the left. The man grasped the handle and slowly opened the door just enough to slip through. The room was all black. No light burned. The curtains were all drawn tight. As his eyes slowly adjusted to the darkened room, an outline of the old man sleeping in his bed came into focus.

Captain Joseph White, an eighty-two-year-old widower, lay asleep in his bed wearing a flannel nightgown and cap to keep warm on the chilly Salem, Massachusetts, night. He was lying on his right side, facing away from the door, and appeared to be fast asleep. The bedding covered his aged frame.

Until now, the timing had not been right. The killer had waited days for this moment to arrive. He had considered stabbing the captain to death on the street, but he never got the chance. The moment was now at hand. He raised the heavy wooden club he had made himself and swung it hard against White's head, the impact making a heavy thud as it slammed hard into flesh and bone. He knew that on the floor above them, two servants—Lydia Kimball and Benjamin White—slept, he hoped, and remained unaware of what was going on. To finish the job, the killer pulled out a dirk, an elegantly tapered double-edged dagger with a 5-inch blade. Slipping back the bedcovers, he began striking at the body, the blade easily penetrating the loose flesh. He felt for a pulse—there was none— and threw the covers back over the old man. His job done, the killer quickly retraced his steps and exited out of the house and onto Essex Street.

He walked to Brown Street, which paralleled Essex, and saw a figure. It was his friend who was standing by a post, looking jumpy and impatient. His friend rushed over. They stood in the mist-shrouded street, greeted each other, and walked up the roadway arm-in-arm talking in low whispers, their breath coming hard in the cold.

"Did you find any money?" his friend asked.

"No, but I fixed him," he answered.[1]

They parted then. The killer ran up Howard Street, ending up near a church where he found the perfect hiding place for the murder weapon. He went home and slept. Yet unfortunately for him, this brief meeting in the street that night did not go unnoticed.

Benjamin White, a distant relative of Captain Joseph White, woke up about 6 a.m., as he did every morning, and headed down to the kitchen. He had been the captain's servant for many years. The night before, his employer had gone to bed just before 10 p.m.—his usual time.

Having a little time before the captain would need him, Ben shook off sleep and busied himself with his morning routine, starting with opening all the shutters around the house. As he slid them apart on the east-facing windows, he noticed something strange. From his vantage point, he could see the back part of the house through the pane. One window was wide open, like a man's mouth at a full scream. They never kept them open at night. Then he noticed a wooden plank below the window.

"Someone's broken in," he thought with a start. He rushed to the back room and found the iron bar used for securing the window lying on the floor. "Miss Kimball, someone's been in the house," he called loudly to the housekeeper as he made his way to her room on the third floor directly above Captain White's bed-chamber.

Ben explained what he had seen to Miss Kimball, her expression changing from sleepiness to horror-struck. "You'd better tell Mr. White," she replied, her voice quavering.

He hurried to the captain's room; the door was slightly ajar. Inside the room, the captain lay in bed, his blankets pulled up around his fleshy body. His face was very pale. Ben leaned over the bed and touched the captain. He recoiled at the feel of the cold flesh. Then he noticed blood on the captain's flannel nightgown.

Ben ran out of the room to get Miss Kimball, who had gone down to the main floor of the house. "He's gone to the eternal world," Ben stammered before rushing out of the house to report the shocking news.[2]

They sent for Stephen White, Captain Joseph White's nephew, and Dr. Samuel Johnson. Stephen arrived at the house first and asked Miss Kimball what had happened. She tearily stumbled through the explanation.

Stephen and his deceased older brother, also named Joseph, had grown up in the captain's home and had been more like sons than nephews. The news hit

Stephen like a ship run aground—a sharp contrast to the happy news he had received only days before that his fellow citizens had elected him as state senator.

Dr. Johnson arrived at the house next. At thirty-six, he was already one of the city's leading medical men. Salem often called on the Harvard-educated physician in cases involving apparent foul play. While he had been told someone had murdered the captain, he reserved judgment on that point until he could see the corpse for himself.

In the captain's room, Dr. Johnson bent down near the body and studied the wound on the victim's left temple. The doctor surmised that a violent blow from a heavy instrument that did not break the skin had made the injury. A trickle of blood seeping from the nose had dried into a dark blotch. The doctor pulled back the covers. The captain's body was at an angle, with the head towards the right of the bed and the feet to the left. His left hand was under his left hip, resting on the blood-stained sheets. The body was cool but not cold to the touch, retaining a modicum of heat, which helped the doctor surmise that the captain had been dead three or four hours. He had no doubt that the captain had been murdered. "We need to call a coroner's jury," he said to Stephen White, replacing the bedclothes over the body.

Stephen fetched Thomas Needham, a neighbor and the town coroner. As was customary at the time, other neighbors came to the house to form a coroner's jury, which would determine whether Captain White had met his death by the hand of another.

A second physician, Dr. Samuel Hubbard, showed up and assisted Dr. Johnson with the proceedings. All gathered in the captain's bedroom, now stuffy and crowded. As the proceedings began, the servants and a few rubber-necking neighbors came in and out of the room to catch a few minutes of the macabre scene.

Dr. Johnson pulled out a long metal probe from his equipment bag and began his explanation to the jury about the mass of stab wounds that had made a pincushion of the old man's chest. Some of the wounds were centered near the left nipple and others slightly further back, as if the killer had raised the arm to get at the spot. The doctor inserted the probe into the wounds and found that several were 3 inches deep. The head wound was not all that noticeable except by touch, but the doctor could feel the fractured bone beneath the skin when he ran his hand around it. He believed something like a cane weighted with lead probably caused the wound. There did not appear to be a struggle and death, Dr. Johnson believed, was instant. "It's my belief that either the wound on the head, or the stabs, would have caused death," he told the assembled crowd.[3]

At the insistence of Stephen White, the assemblage then went around the house trying to hunt up clues. In the days before police detectives, it was up to townspeople to do the work themselves. They first examined the iron chest that was, for many, the centerpiece of the captain's bedroom, for it was where, among other valuables, he usually kept his will, an ever-changing document that the old man used as both a carrot and a stick with his extended family.

They also found two muddy footprints made by the killer underneath the open back window facing the outside wall. The jury took little time in determining that "said White came to his death by a blow on the left temple, and by thirteen stabs in the left side, in and near the chest."[4]

The next day, Dr. Abel Peirson, Salem's leading surgeon, took charge of the autopsy, assisted by Dr. Johnson, and witnessed by some of Dr. Peirson's students and other spectators. He removed the victim's scalp to better examine the head wound. There was an oval fracture at the left temple, nearly 4 inches long and 2.5 inches wide. A spider's web of smaller fractures spread out from the wound, like a cracked window.

There were two groups of stab wounds. One group had six wounds a few inches from the left nipple that gaped slightly, Dr. Peirson observed. Some 6 inches further down, there were seven stab wounds grouped closely together that were mere slits and did not gape like the other set. When the doctor opened up the chest, he found that two of the stab wounds had penetrated the outer wall of the heart. There were three fractured ribs. Dr. Peirson believed there may have been two weapons used to make the stab wounds, and that one was a dirk—a heavy two-edged thrusting dagger used for combat—and that the killer applied so much force that the knife's hilt had fractured the ribs during the attack. He did not make a guess as to what the other weapon looked like. Dr. Johnson disagreed, feeling a single implement could have caused both sets of wounds.

The local newspapers gave a full account of the autopsy the next day. While the doctors could explain how White had died, they could not answer the one question everyone was desperate to learn. It would be a long time before Salem discovered who killed Captain White and why.

The city was in an uproar, and fear was rampant. Salem was a close-knit community with a gentry bound either by blood, marriage, or business, which was almost exclusively the business of the sea. The sea made old Captain White his fortune, and it made Salem one of America's richest and most important cities in the decades surrounding the Revolution.

Joseph White was the closest thing to royalty Salem had. Both praised and reviled in his long life, now that someone had murdered him, Captain White achieved near sainthood. While the newspapers and his old friends lionized him, there were others who knew him as a petty tyrant, especially with his family. He wielded his fortune as a cudgel, often changing his will when a relative fell out of favor.

Some of this money came from the lucrative but illegal African slave trade. Captain White once boasted to a clergyman he had "no reluctance in selling any part of the human race." Massachusetts had outlawed the slave trade in 1783, yet White and many other Salem ship owners continued to buy enslaved people in Africa and ship them in deplorable conditions to the Caribbean, where those who had not died in the brutal crossing were sold for gold. Humans were just one more commodity that helped make Salem rich, as did the opium trade, but the times were changing and the shipping business was not what it once was.

By 1830, the city's fortunes were waning, and with them, cracks in its genteel façade revealed previously hidden facets: prostitution, debauchery, poverty, and violence. Captain White's murder was just the latest, and greatest, earth-shaking episode that threatened to destroy the city's foundations. Salem needed to do something quick to shore up its reputation.

In the wake of Captain White's death, the city's selectmen—friends, relations, or business partners of the deceased—distributed handbills offering a $500 reward for the capture of the murderer. The victim's nephew, Stephen White, had also offered $1,000 (equivalent to $25,000 today).

On April 9, 2,000 citizens showed up at a meeting held at the town hall to form a Committee of Vigilance to oversee the murder investigation. In a time before a well-regulated police force, local citizens often took it upon themselves to investigate crimes hand-in-hand with local law enforcement and, in this case, with the state attorney general.

A full 15 percent of Salem's population crowded in and around the town hall that night. The number of citizens who had shown up shocked an *Essex Register* reporter. It was "a larger number of persons than were ever assembled on the floor of the town hall." The enormous crowd was "expressive of the horror and indignation of the citizens at the outrage perpetrated in our usually quiet town," reported the paper.[5] While the brutal and cold-blooded murder horrified the townspeople, the fact that the killer or killers had stolen nothing from the captain's home was even more terrifying. What was the motive? Was there one or was there a madman loose in Salem?

An executive committee chose twenty-seven men, seven from each of the four wards (the fourth ward included only six), "to be constantly vigilant and to be ready at all hours of the day to render any service for the accomplishment of the objects of the committee which circumstances may show to be important." The members swore "not to divulge to any person anything that transpires … in relation to the investigation" and to keep "all its proceedings a sacred and inviolable secret." They also doubled the meager police force and established a citizen's brigade charged with walking the streets at night on the lookout for evildoers.

Stephen White agreed to foot the bill for the investigation, putting up another $1,000 for the committee to use however they saw fit. White also offered his company's counting-room for their meetings. The committee was a who's who of Salem's elite, many of whom had close ties to the murder victim and his family. Dr. Gideon Barstow, who chaired the committee, was a close friend and political aid of Stephen's; William Fettyplace was Stephen's brother-in-law; and Stephen C. Phillips, the committee's secretary, was one of Stephen White's best friends.

Rumors that Stephen murdered his uncle floated around town. He stood to gain from the captain's death more than anyone. Most of the committee was made up of his friends who wanted to squelch this idle talk and clear Stephen White's name. They also wanted to clear the name of their beloved city.

The committee agreed to meet every evening until they had tracked down the killer or killers and brought them to justice. Barstow, the committee head, was a physician by training but a politician by inclination and understood the importance of delegating duties. He broke the committee into various subcommittees tasked with investigating and interviewing the many leads and witnesses. He and four others combed Captain White's house. The search was a bust, so much so that the sub-committee did not even bother to write up any notes.

In the following days, the committee interviewed various witnesses, including Captain White's servants, Benjamin White and Lydia Kimball. The two servants described a fairly typical night. Captain White had gone to bed around his usual time after spending the day at Cherry Hill Farm, in Wenham, 8 miles north of Salem. A few years back, he had given the property to his widowed niece, Mary White Beckford, who looked after the captain. Her adult children were living there while she continued to reside at Captain White's mansion where she was more of a companion than an employee. The night of the murder, Mary stayed at the farm while Captain White returned to Salem. His servant, Benjamin, drove the captain back and the old man was in bed by 9.40 p.m. that night.

The committee also interviewed a few townsfolk who had seen two shady looking characters near the White mansion on the night of the murder, but no one could give much in the way of usable details except that the two men were dressed in commonplace hats and cloaks.

Night after night, the committee met in what was becoming a futile search for answers. Soon, the committee's secretary filled the official minutes documenting their activities almost exclusively with lists of those in attendance and notes that "nothing of importance was to be laid before the committee."[6] The committee members worried whether they would ever solve Captain White's vicious murder.

Then, on April 27, twenty days after the murder, John Francis Knapp, known as Frank, and his younger brother, Joseph Jenkins Knapp, who went by Joe, reported a gang of robbers had attacked them just north of Salem.

The Committee of Vigilance summoned the brothers on April 30. The Knapps, it so happened, had close ties to the White family. Joe Knapp was married to the murder victim's grandniece—the daughter of Mary Beckford—and their father had business ties to the Whites. Frank and Joe described the events of the night of their assault for the twenty-four members of the committee in attendance.

Joe, who did the talking during the meeting, explained that he and his brother left Salem in a chaise heading north for Wenham at around 8.30 on the night of the 27th. About forty-five minutes into their journey, near Wenham Pond Hill, three bandits dressed like sailors and with painted-on mustaches stood in the middle of the road. While two of the bandits converged on the Knapps' wagon from either side with weapons drawn, the third ran up and grabbed the horse's bridle, pulled out a dirk, and smiled. "How do you do? Where are you going?"

"I'll let you know damned quick," Frank Knapp said, pulling out his sword cane. Joe Knapp struck the robber on the right with his horsewhip, lashing the tall, heavily muscled man across the right cheek. The bandit on the left rushed the carriage. Frank leaped at him and swung his sword in an arc, forcing the bandit back. Frank thrust his sword at him again and the robber turned and ran towards the pond, leaping over a stone fence like a hurdler. The other two bandits also turned and ran. As Frank clambered back into the carriage, he and his brother heard a sharp whistle—scouts signaling the others it was time to go, the brothers guessed.

The Knapp's descriptions of the men fit those of the two suspects seen in Brown Street on the night of the murder. A committee member handed the brothers a copy of the minutes to sign off on as being true to their statements. "Take care of yourselves," a committeeman called out as they left.

"We're prepared to give them cold lead if they attack us again," growled Joe as he exited the building.[7]

After the meeting, the *Essex Register* editor, who knew the Knapps, approached them, hoping to get a story for the paper. The brothers obliged and met the editor at the imposing Stearns building, on the corner of Washington and Essex Streets, that had once housed the East India Marine Society. Again, Joe did most of the talking. Afterward, the editor went back to his office and reduced the conversation to writing. They published the story on May 3, 1830, whipping the city into another frenzy of fear and anxiety. Would these brigands ever be brought to justice?

3

DEPARTURE

It was with a heavy heart Poe waved goodbye to the only father he had known as the steamer pulled out of the Richmond, Virginia, docks amid the noise of screaming gulls, the shouts of stevedores and enslaved people loading cotton and tobacco, and the whinnying of workhorses. John Allan had cared for Poe since he was about three years old and given Poe his middle name, but by May 1830, he had become as distant in his manner as he was now physically from Poe's vantage point on the ship's deck. The steamer swiftly pulled away from the dock and into the James River, destined for Baltimore. Allan was tiny compared to the looming warehouses interspersed with dingy saloons along the waterfront, always crowded with men, wagons, drays, and horses.

"I'm never going to see him again," Poe thought.[1] The twenty-one-year-old's heart was breaking. His foster mother, Frances, had been dead for less than three months. She had been the glue that kept the family together; with her passing, Allan and Poe's relationship frayed even more. It began to unwind while Poe was at the University of Virginia in 1826 due to Allan's refusal to give Poe enough financial support while he was at school in Charlottesville. Poe had accrued overwhelming debts at UVA, including gambling ones, in a futile attempt to make up for the funds his foster father had refused to give. When Allan found out how much money Poe owed, he exploded with such fury that Poe, just a year into his studies, dropped out.

Six months later, in May 1827, Poe ran away to join the army under the assumed name of Edgar Perry. He served two years, stationed in South Carolina and Virginia. A month before leaving the army, his foster mother, Frances, died. He missed her funeral by a day. Her death brought Poe and Allan closer, for a time, but their old animosities crept back and their relationship continued to wax and wane.

After leaving the army, Poe returned to Richmond to a home that no longer felt like one while he tried to get an appointment to the U.S. Military Academy at West Point. Poe suffered for two months under Allan's tyranny before bolting for Baltimore. He was back in Richmond by January, and it was worse than the last time. Staying at Moldavia, the stately home that Allan had purchased in 1825, only reminded Poe of his dead foster mother, Frances. It also dredged up the painful emotions about his first love, Elmira.

Her parents, not finding Poe a suitable partner for their only daughter, had derailed the relationship while Poe had been attending the University of Virginia and Elmira had married another man. It was just one of many wounds he had suffered of late. Allan's unfriendly attitude was yet another.

Their deep animosity was a blade that slowly sawed away at their connection. Poe could not forgive the affair Allan had carried on while Frances was still alive. Poe discovered it by accident, and his foster father's behavior disgusted him. Allan's drinking after his wife's death had exacerbated these tensions. Allan felt Poe was lazy, a spendthrift, and living off of his charity.

A few weeks before Poe shipped out for West Point, they had fought. They quarreled bitterly, dredging up all the rancor they had been building up against each other for years. Allan insulted Poe's birth family, which struck the vulnerable Poe to his core. Yet Allan begrudgingly provided his foster son the financial help he needed to get into West Point, and with some necessities, he would need while there. Yet as when Poe had attended university, Allan, tight-fisted, gave him the very minimum needed to get by, including four blankets, a little cash, and not much else. He did not provide enough money for school books or the dormitory furnishings the academy expected the cadets to pay for themselves. Poe hoped that Allan would send the money once he had arrived at West Point.

As the steamer headed down the James River towards the Chesapeake Bay, the landscape changed from a city of brick and stone and wood to the tobacco plantations flanking the river banks. Poe turned away from his troubled thoughts and focused on his new life as an officer and a poet. He was not due at West Point— nearly 400 miles to the north and a world apart—for a few weeks. He planned to stop in Baltimore to visit his older brother, Henry, his Aunt Maria, and his young cousin, Virginia. He would arrive not as a young cadet but as a conquering poet. That past December, Hatch & Dunning, a Baltimore publisher, released Poe's second book of poetry, *Al Aaraaf, Tamerlane, and Minor Poems,* to favorable reviews. In one, the reviewer likened Poe to the English poet Percy Bysshe Shelley, whom Poe greatly admired. The young man's achievement impressed his relatives in Baltimore, and Poe was looking forward to a joyful reunion.

Yet his mind kept drifting back to the letter. In the emotionally draining days before Poe left Richmond, he had responded to a letter from Sergeant Samuel "Bully" Graves, who had agreed to be his Army substitute when Poe left the service early. At the time, the military allowed soldiers to pay someone else to take their place; Poe had promised to pay Graves. The letter concerned debts Poe owed to Graves and another soldier.

The few lines Poe had dashed off to his old army friend would have devastating consequences and change the course of his life.

4

THREADS

While Poe was contemplating his life choices on a ship headed for Baltimore, the Committee of Vigilance gathered the threads of rumors, speculations, and vague talk of the shady characters seen near Captain White's home, trying to weave them into a coherent case.

Two family friends of the Whites from Boston who wanted to help in the investigation visited the state prison in Charlestown to enquire about recently released prisoners. They learned a man named Joseph Hatch had been released in December, four months prior to the murder. Hatch had been seen in Salem over the winter and was rumored to be part of a plan to break into Captain White's mansion to steal his iron chest, which supposedly contained vast riches. Where Hatch was now was anybody's guess.

The committee's first big break came when Stephen White received a letter from New Bedford's jailer. A prisoner had come across a newspaper account of the captain's murder and claimed he had information about the case. A representative of the committee interviewed him at the New Bedford jail. The prisoner was going by the name Joseph Hall, but during the interview, he admitted he was actually Joseph Hatch, the petty thief the committee had been searching for. He was back behind bars and willing to talk.

Hatch told the interviewer that after being released from prison, he and another ex-con began hanging out at a gambling den in Salem run by Richard "Dick" Crowninshield. They overheard Dick and his brother, George, talking with another man, Benjamin Selman, about stealing Captain White's iron chest. Further digging turned up a fourth man named Daniel Chase, also allegedly in on the plot. The plan was to sneak into the old captain's house in the evening after he had gone to bed, but before the servants had locked up the mansion for the night. One of them would bash the old man on the head, then steal the chest and lug it to a waiting boat. If they could not get a boat, then they would use a wagon. The plan was to wait until spring so no one could trace them by their footprints left in the snow.

Dick and George Crowninshield had been quietly building a multidimensional criminal enterprise under the noses of the gentry. Dick was a talented artisan by day who had his own machine shop in the nearby town of Danvers. By night, he was an equally talented criminal who, with his brother George, were thieves, robbers, and forgers, besides owning the illegal tavern and gambling house in South Salem that they claimed was a "reading room." They kept newspapers lying around the place, but the young men of Salem and even some of Boston's elite came there to drink, gamble, and carouse, not to read.

The Crowninshields were an old and noble Salem family of German descent who had made their fortune, like many a neighbor, in the shipping business and from there extended their reach into politics. Members of the family included a U.S. secretary of the navy. At one time, Crowninshield ships sailed to India, Europe, South America, and the Indies.

Richard, Sr., the boys' father, had been the black sheep of the family. While living in New York City, where he was looking over the family's shipping interests, he fell in love and married Ann Sterling, an Irish hotel maid and the widow of a sea captain. His snooty family did not approve of his choice in a mate from such a lowly station.

Richard, Sr., foreseeing that manufacturing, and not sea trade, would drive America's economy, got into the woolen business but did not have much luck. His first wool mill failed and fire destroyed the next two.

Dick, Jr., was born in 1804 and George in 1805. They grew up under a cloud of constant gossip about their parents' refusal to curtail the boys' unruly behavior. There were rumors that Dick, while still in his teens, had burned down his school to spite his teacher. His behavior at the boarding school where their father later sent him and George only got worse. There, he was known for his cruel psychological games and violent temperament. When the brothers returned home, they went full bore, with their wild behavior culminating in 1825 in a "riot" at a local tavern that they had instigated.

More than three weeks after the murder, the committee still did not have much to work with, and the pressure for answers mounted daily as the news of the murder spread across the country. In Salem, residents grew edgier with the killer or killers still on the loose. Between a baggage wagon hold-up just outside the city and the attack on the Knapp brothers by highwaymen, the committee needed results.

They were wary of any missteps involving the Crowninshield brothers. Yes, they had contemptible reputations, but they were still members of one of the city's elite families, the same class as the men who made up the committee, and so they proceeded cautiously. Following the attack on the Knapps and the testimony from Hatch, the committee decided, family name be damned, they would have to arrest the Crowninshield brothers.

On May 2, they arrested Dick and George Crowninshield along with Chase and Selman. The following day, prosecutors handed the grand jury, being held at Ipswich, about 13 miles due north, a case short on facts but long on the testimony of Hatch. He was the star witness and repeated what he had told the committee. Several others, mostly convicts, corroborated the story. Upstanding Salem residents who described seeing at least two men near the captain's house on the night of the murder rounded out the prosecution's case. Their descriptions were vague, and no one positively identified any of the defendants.

The prosecution did not have any evidence Dick was in Salem on the night of the murder. Even so, just three days later, the grand jury indicted the four men— Dick as the principal and the others as accessories who aided and abetted the murderer. They threw the four into Salem jail to await trial.

The news of the men's arrest whipped through the streets of Salem like a firestorm. Dick took his arrest in stride. Once settled into his cell, he spent his time writing poetry and visiting with friends who came to visit. He knew the authorities had no evidence against him. Dick would not swing from the end of a rope, he believed.

The letter confused Captain Joseph J. Knapp, Sr., even after he reread it. He did not recognize the name of the sender, Charles Grant, Jr., and knew no one from Belfast, Maine, where the letter originated, yet it was addressed to him in Salem:

Dear Sir,—I have taken the pen at this time to address an utter stranger, and strange as it may seem to you, it is for the purpose of requesting the loan of three hundred and fifty dollars, for which I can give you no security but my word, and in this case consider this to be sufficient. My call for money at this time is pressing, or I would not trouble you; but with that sum, I have the prospect of turning it to so much advantage, as to be able to refund it with interest in the course of six months. At all events, I think it will be for your interest to comply with my request, and that immediately—that is, not to put off any longer than you receive this. Then set down and inclose [*sic.*] me the money with as much despatch as possible, for your own interest. This, Sir, is my advice; and if you do not comply with it, the short period between now and November will convince you that you have denied a request, the granting of which will never injure you, the refusal of which will ruin you. Are you surprised at this assertion?—rest assured that I make it reserving to myself the reasons and a series of facts which are founded on such a bottom as will bid defiance to property or quality. It is useless for me to enter into a discussion of facts which must inevitably harrow up your soul. No, I will merely tell you that I am acquainted with your brother Frank, and also the business that he was transacting for you on the 2nd of April last; and that I think that you was [*sic.*] very extravagant in giving one thousand dollars to the person that would execute the business for you. But you know best about that, you see that such things will leak out. To conclude, Sir, I will inform you that there is a gentleman of my acquaintance in Salem that will observe that you do not leave town before the first of June, giving you sufficient time between now and then to comply with my request; and if I do not receive a line from you, together with the above sum, before the 22d of this month, I shall wait upon you with an assistant. I have said enough to convince you of my knowledge, and merely inform you that you can, when you answer, be as brief as possible.

Direct yours to

CHARLES GRANT, Jun. of Prospect, Maine.[1]

Knapp, a well-respected shipmaster and merchant, had received the mysterious letter on May 15, three days after Grant sent it. It was vaguely menacing, but it made no sense to him. Yet, given the recent murder of old Captain White and the thwarted attack by bandits on his two sons, Joe and Frank, it had him rattled. He showed it to his second oldest son, Nathaniel Phippen Knapp, who went by Phippen. The letter baffled him too. The next day, the pair drove out to Wenham to speak to Frank and Joe. The elder Knapp handed the letter to Joe, who read it over several times. "It's a devilish lot of trash," Joe told his father. "Turn it over to the Committee of Vigilance."

When Captain Knapp returned to Salem, he hand-delivered the letter to the committee of vigilance. The letter caused a stir among the men who passed it from one to another, studying it as if it was a rare artifact.

Two more letters arrived in quick succession. One was sent to Dr. Gideon Barstow, the committee's chairman, and again appeared to be from the mysterious Grant. The letter was addressed on the outside to the "Hon. Gideon Barstow, Salem," and was sent May 16, four days earlier. It was mailed from Salem, while the earlier letter had come from Maine.

Gentlemen of the Committee of Vigilance.

Hearing that you have taken up 4 young men on suspicion of being concerned in the murder of Mr. White I think it time to inform you that Steven White came to me one night and told me if I would remove the old gentleman, he would give me 5,000 dollars; he said he was afraid he would alter his will if he lived any longer. I told him I would do it but I was afeared to go into the house, so he said he'd go with me, that he would try to get into the house in the evening and open the window, would then go home and go to bed and meet me again about 11. I found him and we both went into his chamber. I struck him on the head with a heavy piece of lona then stabbed him with a dirk, he made the finishing strokes with another. He promised to send me the money next evening, and has not sent it yet, which is the reason that I mention this. Yours &c. GRANT.[2]

Someone named N. Claxton mailed the last letter to Stephen White. It was dated May 12, and it too was mailed from Salem at the same time as the letter sent to Barstow:

Lynn, May 12, 1830.

Mr. White will send the $5,000 or a part of it before to-morrow night, or suffer the painful consequences.

N. Claxton, 4th[3]

Who was this mysterious Grant? The letters spurred the committee to set aside both time and money to investigate Grant. They sent him an anonymous letter in care of the post office in Prospect, Maine. The letter contained $50 (equal to nearly $1,400 today) with a promise to send more. They also sent Joseph G. Waters, Captain White's attorney, to Maine and arranged for the postmaster to alert him when Grant showed up to collect the letter.

Meanwhile, the committee had the unenviable job of summoning Stephen White to his own counting-house to lay out evidence of his alleged role in the murder of his uncle the captain. White, unaware of what was about to unfold, appeared before the committee, dressed impeccably as always in a green coat and top hat. He assumed he was there for an update on the case since he had spearheaded and bankrolled the search for the murderers and offered a large reward for their capture. It soon became obvious this was no ordinary meeting; it was an outright ambush.

Waters did not have to wait long after arriving in Prospect, Maine. On May 24, a good-looking young man of medium height and build entered the post office. He had a light complexion and gray eyes. He inquired whether anything had arrived for Charles Grant. The postmaster hesitated and then answered that he indeed had a letter for him. After a lengthy delay, the postmaster returned with his mail. He held it out to the man, then hesitated. "Is this your name on the letter?" he asked. Grant answered it was, took the letter, and dropped it into his pocket.

Grant could not believe that Knapp had responded so quickly. He could tell by the heft that there was money inside. He was elated until Waters and a Boston constable by the name of Jones approached him and began peppering him with questions.

Jones forced Grant into a carriage and they went to the nearby Belfast jail where they grilled Grant for several hours. To no surprise, Grant was not his actual name. It was John C. R. Palmer, and he wanted to tell his side of the story. As he watched the lawyer record his words "like a man traveling in a whirlwind," his quill flying wildly across the paper, Palmer knew a whirlwind of trouble was coming for him, one created by his so-called friends—the Crowninshields. He wondered if he would survive it. He would not go in empty-handed, though. He extracted a promise from Waters that the government would not prosecute him for what he was about to divulge, to which the attorney readily agreed. Palmer became worried when Waters refused to put the agreement in writing. Palmer was even more troubled when they would not let his father see him, even before the authorities had charged him with a crime.

Palmer was a sailor by profession who had met George Crowninshield four years earlier in New Orleans in the fall of 1826, where they plunged into a world of vice together, from which they never emerged. He had latched onto George. They traveled to Charleston, then New York City, and finally Providence, Rhode Island, raising hell the whole way. Palmer eventually met George's older brother, Dick, a wily and dangerous rogue. Dick took Palmer under his wing and gave him a place to stay in their family home in South Danvers.

Palmer and another friend later went on a drunken gambling spree that started in Maine and ended in Manhattan. Palmer was arrested and served a two-year prison sentence after police caught him amid a store break-in.

After his release from prison, Palmer found his way back to the Crowninshields, who again put him up. He quickly fell back into crime, helping the two brothers in a forgery scheme and the theft of bolts of flannel—a valuable commodity at the time.

In the early spring of 1830, Palmer looked out from the window in his room at the Crowninshield home and watched Frank Knapp—whom Palmer had met the last time he had been in Essex County—ride up to the house and converse with his hosts. Later, Dick and George came up to his room and asked him for help in murdering old Captain White for a third of the $1,000 the Knapps would pay for the job. While it was a lot of money—$25,000 in today's terms—Palmer felt way out of his depth and was not about to get drawn into a murder-for-hire scheme. He made an excuse and left town. Palmer later claimed that the reason he sent the extortion letter was to draw out the Knapps, and perhaps Mary Beckford, who he believed was also involved, without getting dragged into or blamed for a crime involving Salem's elite. He intended to send the letter to Joe, Jr., not his father. Palmer denied he had sent the other two letters and said he knew nothing about them.

Palmer's story was believable enough to earn him a trip back to Salem in chains to testify before the grand jury, cementing fears he had about getting involved in the case. The committee issued arrest warrants for the Knapp brothers, vindicating Stephen White after the humiliation of being accused of murder by his friends in his own counting-house.

Joe and Frank Knapp stood before Squire Ezekiel Savage as he read the evidence against them. The authorities arrested the pair at Joe's home in Wenham like common criminals and brought them before the justice charged with murder and conspiracy.

Their brother Phippen did not believe his siblings were involved in the murder of Captain White; they had alibis, after all. On the night of the killing, Joe had been in Wenham with his wife and his mother-in-law, and Frank had been home and in bed by 10 p.m. Phippen listened with shock at the allegations. His brothers were seamen, not killers. Frank was working his way up through the ranks in the commercial shipping business. Joe was a shipmaster, having captained his father's ship, the *Governor Winslow*, and the *Caroline*, owned by Stephen White. That was until White sacked Joe for his poor performance commanding the *Caroline*. The relationship between Joe and the Whites got even more complicated after Joe married Mary White Beckford, Stephen's teenage cousin and the grandniece of Captain Joseph White, the man he was now accused of killing.

Captain White felt Joe was an opportunist and gold-digger. He tried his darndest to stop the marriage. When the old man did not get his way, he cut Mary out of his will and kicked her out of his house. Joe and Mary lived at Cherry Hill Farm in Wenham, given to her mother by Captain White. In the three years since the wedding, the family drama had reached a kind of equilibrium. Captain White was again on speaking terms with Joe and Mary and had spent the evening before his murder with them at the farm.

The Knapps were a large, close family; Joe, twenty-five, was the oldest. Phippen was a year younger, while Frank was not yet twenty. There were two younger brothers, William and Samuel, and two sisters, Ellen and Sarah. The most stolid of the boys, Phippen was his father's bedrock. Everyone regarded him as honest and dependable. Unlike Joe and Frank, he had not gone to sea, choosing Harvard Law School instead. The Essex County Bar Association had recently admitted Phippen as a full-fledged member. He never imagined that he would be having to use his Harvard connections to secure defense attorneys for his own brothers. Phippen needed to go to Boston, and soon, to make the arrangements.

This calamity was on top of the collapse of their father's merchant shipping business. On the night of the murder, Phippen had stayed up into the early hours finalizing his father's bankruptcy. Earlier that evening, he and his father had been hashing out the details with the lawyer who represented his creditors, the main creditor being Captain Joseph White, with whom his father had once owned a ship, along with Richard Crowninshield, Sr., and others. If all this was not bad enough, Mary, Joe's beautiful young wife, had tried to kill herself after her husband's arrest. It felt as if their lives were being torn apart like a sail in a hurricane.

5

CONFESSION?

Dick Crowninshield felt ill, his legs nearly gave way, and the sweat poured from his ashen face. The committee had arrested the Knapps, and Palmer was talking to the authorities. Dick thought he had planned everything perfectly, but everything was coming unwound. On the night of the murder, he began complaining of stomach trouble to his family, took some medicine, and went to bed. Two hours later, he again woke several family members with the same complaint, took more medicine, and went back to bed. It was a damn good alibi, and what had seemed to be a paper-thin case against him was quickly growing stronger and stronger as the committee continued its investigation. The mounting pile of evidence might soon suffocate him, but what could he do from inside a dank jail cell? He soon discovered that Palmer was in the cell below and he began tormenting his former friend through a crack in the floor.

Members of the Committee of Vigilance visited Palmer, and he again told his story. Palmer explained how he had learned of the plan to kill Captain White and that Joe Knapp destroyed the old man's will so his family would get a larger share of the inheritance. Palmer explained how he had left town after learning about the murder plans but came back to stay with the Crowninshields one last time. Dick loaned him some money gained as partial payment from the Knapps for killing Captain White. After that, Palmer left Salem for good.

During one of these jail visits, the members heard a shrill whistle and looking up saw Dick peeking through the crack. He called Palmer by name to get his attention. A scrap of paper and pencil tied to a string soon inched its way down through the crack. It was the beginning of a poem: "Tho' rocky walls enclose me round/And fetters soothe the prisoner's groans…"

Palmer was to supply the next two lines, as part of a popular word game called Crambo or Capping the Rhyme. Palmer backed away towards the corner, his face pale as he stared at the note hanging in the air.

The jailer quickly moved him to another cell. Dick also sent notes to his brother and Joe Knapp through a crack in the ceiling. The brothers were worried. If Palmer told the committee everything he knew, it could go hard on them. Dick needed a new plan.

On Friday, May 28, the Rev. Henry Colman went to see Joe Knapp's wife, Mary. He was the pastor of the Independent Congregational church where the Knapps, all except Frank, attended. Colman had married Joe and his wife, Mary White, whom Colman thought of like a daughter.

They sat in the parlor chatting when the reverend asked Mary if her husband had been home on the night of the murder. She said he had. "Well, I'm very much relieved by what you tell me, for I have been asked the question repeatedly and have not been able to answer it." He then turned to Samuel Knapp, Joe's younger brother, and asked him what time Joe had returned home the night of the murder. "I know that he was at home and went to bed before 10.30." After his visit, Colman headed to the jail.

Besides his relationship with the Knapps, Colman was a dear friend of Stephen White and the now-dead Captain White. He was tall and handsome, with a charismatic personality and a kind heart. Yet beneath the exterior, there were darker urges—vanity, conceit, and a violent temper. Colman had been snooping around for clues in the murder case.

The reverend ran into Phippen Knapp near Salem jail. They greeted one another and headed in to see Joe. Phippen thought Colman had not seen his brother yet, but as the reverend spoke to Joe, it was becoming clear this was not the first conversation they had shared that day. This alarmed Phippen, who did not want his brothers talking to anyone without legal representation.

Phippen was having a hard time following the conversation. It was like starting a book in the middle with no idea of what the previous chapters contained. Colman mentioned something about a club of some sort, but Phippen was not clear about the details. He realized it was likely the murder weapon. From these snippets of conversation, Phippen gathered that Colman was orchestrating a plan to save Joe from the gallows, only it involved turning state's evidence against his brother, Frank. Colman was trying to exact a written confession from Joe without giving Frank any say in the matter. Phippen interrupted the reverend, telling them it would be unfair for Joe to accept immunity unless Frank would consent to the plan. Joe agreed. Phippen insisted they go straight to Frank's cell.

Colman stopped Phippen just outside Joe's cell door. "On your honor, don't disturb the club. I will get a witness and go and get it myself. For my own security." Phippen hesitated, still unsure of exactly where the club even was, but he knew it would be an important piece of evidence. He assented to Colman's plan, hoping it could save his brothers. The two men walked down the short hall to Frank's cell. The reverend hesitated in the doorway, looking anxious.

"Are you coming in?" Phippen asked.

"Yes," Colman answered, following Phippen into the cell. Phippen greeted his brother, whom he had not seen since his arrest, sat down next to him, and got straight to the point:

> Mr. Colman says that the committee have evidence enough to convict both you and Joe. He says the only salvation is for you to confess. Palmer's applied for a pardon on condition of his being a witness.
>
> A promise of pardon has been sent out from the offices of the government. The messenger is to pass through town tonight on the mail stage. If you or Joe don't confess before the mail stage comes through, it will be too late. If either of you confess, the committee will stop the message and will apply for a pardon for whichever of you confesses first.[1]

Palmer knew everything and was telling his story to the committee. Either Joe or Frank had to confess if they hoped to save themselves. Phippen looked over at Colman. "Everything I've said is true, isn't that correct?"

Colman nodded his head and turned to Frank:

> I have made your brother these assurances and offered him a pardon in case he would be willing to confess. I also assured him that if he committed anything to me in confidence, it should never be revealed, unless he should choose to become a witness. I am authorized by the committee to offer this pardon to either of you.[2]

Phippen then broke in. "Mr. Colman thinks Joe ought to confess. If Joe is convicted, there will be no chance for him, but if you are convicted, you may have some chance for procuring a pardon." He then turned to the reverend. "Don't you think so?"

"Yes, undoubtedly," Colman responded. "Your youth will very much be in your favor. Your case will excite great sympathy, especially if it shall appear that you were persuaded to do what you did by your older brother. But I don't insist on preference. I leave that for you to settle between you."

Frank looked from his brother to Colman and back again, but said nothing. The reverend continued:

> You know the condition if you stand a trial … You both inevitably will be convicted. If either of you chooses to confess, he will save himself. If Joseph confesses, and you shall be convicted, you will have a good chance of pardon, but if Joseph should be convicted on your confession, his chance would not be so good. At all events, your chance will be greater if you stood a trial and were convicted on Palmer's testimony. You have but a few minutes to choose.[3]

Frank did not say a word for a minute. He stared hard at Colman. "I have nothing to confess. It's a hard case. But if it's as you say, Joseph may confess if he pleases. I shall stand trial." Phippen and Rev. Colman left Frank, who sat in his cell mulling over what he'd learned. As they left the jail, Colman told Phippen he was planning to go straight to the Committee of Vigilance. Phippen went back to his office. Colman turned up a few hours later. "I'm going to Boston at eight o'clock this evening with Mr. Treadwell to see the attorney general," he told Phippen.

The next day, around 10 a.m., Phippen headed south out of Salem for Boston with his friend, Henry Field. Colman came from the other direction and pulled up alongside Phippen's carriage. The reverend asked Phippen if he would not mind getting into his carriage so he could speak with him privately. Phippen assented, handed the reins to his friend, and got into Colman's buggy.

"I've seen the attorney general. Here's the promise of a pardon." He handed Phippen a document. It stated that the government would drop the case against whoever confessed first. It excluded Richard Crowninshield from the agreement.

"Won't you turn around and come back to Salem with me?" Colman asked. "I'm on my way to see your brother, Joseph."

Phippen's heart jumped. He was on his way to Boston to secure defense attorneys for his brothers. "I can't go back now but you must promise me you won't go see my brother without me."

The reverend hesitated, then agreed. "I will not go without you. I'll wait until you return." This relieved Phippen. Colman's insertion into the case was maddening. Phippen's father was angry Colman had been to see Joe alone. This had hastened Phippen's journey to Boston, which was now being delayed by Colman. Then the reverend said something that struck Phippen as odd. "I'm not sure I got the story of the club from Joseph or Frank, but I believe it was from Joseph."

"You didn't get it from Frank," Phippen replied curtly. "He said nothing about it."

"I don't know, but I believe Stephen White has misunderstood me on this. Would you take a note to him to correct this impression?"[4]

Colman pulled out a pencil and jotted down a message on a scrap of paper and handed it to Phippen. "You should find him in the Senate chamber."

Phippen returned to his own carriage and sped off towards the state capitol. He felt it was imperative to correct the impression that Frank had confessed as quickly as possible. If Frank was to stand trial, as he said he planned to do, the mistaken idea that he knew where the murder weapon was hidden would be used to convict him.

When Phippen arrived in Boston, he went to the senate chamber, but the senate was not in session. Phippen hurried over to the house chamber, but White was not there either. He had neglected to find out which Boston hotel Stephen

White was staying at and had to give up the search so he could nail down his brothers' defense counsel.

Through his Harvard connections, he got Franklin Dexter and William H. Gardiner, the leading defense attorneys in Boston, to represent his brothers. Phippen's close friend and former classmate, Robert Rantoul, would assist them.

Exhausted from lack of sleep, Phippen rushed back to Salem. He had a terrible feeling that Colman would go see his brothers alone. He did not trust the reverend. Neither Joe nor Frank had even spoken to a lawyer yet, and he needed to be there when Colman handed Joe the letter from the attorney general. As he rushed north to Salem, he saw a friend on the road with a fresh, smart horse. Phippen explained his dilemma and switched horses with his friend. Phippen was supposed to be at the jail by 3 p.m., but even with the faster horse, it did not appear that he would make it back in time.

Unbeknown to Phippen, Rev. Colman had been laboring tirelessly for days trying to get Joe's confession. The day after the Knapps' arrest, Colman waited for them to be arraigned so he could get in to see Joe in jail.

He told Joe he was "distressed" over the situation and offered to render him any service in his power. Joe wanted to know whether they could prove he'd been involved in the murder. Colman told him the committee had conclusive evidence provided by Palmer. Joe said he did not know anyone by that name.

"I do not know what can be done," Colman told the prisoner. "but if anything can be obtained for you, and if you see fit, and think you can rely upon my honor to make any disclosures to me, you may be sure they should never be divulged—I would die first, until I can obtain the security of the government."

His words seemed to bounce off Joe, who just kept asking whether they could prove the case. Colman gave up trying to wring a confession out of Joe, who spent most of the time silently staring at the floor. Later that afternoon, Colman returned to Joe's cell. He told Joe the evidence against him was overwhelming.

Joe would have a very hard time accounting for the two letters they had traced back to him, Colman told him. There was also the committee's letter to Palmer with the promise of a pardon if he would turn state's evidence. "If anything is to be done it has to be done today," Colman warned. He wondered if he would ever get the confession from Joe.

"I'm nearly exhausted—indeed, I am oppressed with grief and anxiety," Colman said. "I must leave you—I can do no more—can offer you no bribe—will not persuade you. You must act on your own responsibility. I have discharged my conscience."[5] There was nothing more to say. He got up to leave. Finally, Joe broke down and called Colman over to the corner of the cell. In a barely audible voice, he confessed, but a verbal confession was not enough—Colman needed it in writing.

The third interview, the one Phippen attended, got Colman no closer to a written confession, so he went to the Committee of Vigilance to find out what he should do next. They decided he had to go to Boston to speak with the attorney general to secure the paperwork for Joe's pardon. He left about 10 that night and arrived after midnight. He stopped at the Tremont House, Boston's newest and most luxurious hotel where Stephen White was staying, to tell him the news. He then met the attorney general, Perez Morton. It was nearly 1 a.m. by the time he secured the paperwork. Colman now had what he needed to get Joe to confess. He rushed back to Salem and ran into Phippen on the turnpike as he was heading to Boston to get a lawyer for his brothers. Colman was running out of time. If Phippen returned before he could get Joe's confession, it would ruin his plans.

The next day, Colman waited impatiently at the wooden steps leading up to the Howard Street Meeting House, a Puritan church across from the graveyard. Gideon Barstow, the chairman of the Committee of Vigilance, and William Fettyplace, another member of the committee, finally arrived. Colman at last had his audience. With a showman's flourish, the reverend got down on all fours and searched the bottom step for a rathole. He found it, thrust his hand in, and began blindly groping around. His heart skipped a beat when he patted nothing but earth. He pulled his hand out. It had to be there. He reinserted it and plunged it in deeper. His fingers felt something wooden—triumph. He grabbed the wood and pulled. It was the club. "This killed Captain White," Colman said, showing off the club like a prize he had won. The men examined the elegantly tapered weapon, which was made of hardwood, about 2 feet long, and ornamented with beads at the handle. It had a good heft to it, aided by the addition of lead. Whoever had made it had some skill at woodworking. The members of the committee secured the weapon.

Flush with his victory, the reverend decided it was time to get Joe's confession in writing. He had a whirlwind few days and was running on adrenaline. Colman arrived back at the jail on Saturday afternoon while Phippen was still away in Boston and showed Joseph the attorney general's letter of clemency. Then they slowly went through Joe's story. He sat down before the prisoner, dipped the quill in the ink, and asked Joe to recount his story as the reverend's pen flew across the page and took it all down in his slanted businesslike script:

I mentioned to my brother, John Francis Knapp, in February last, that I would not begrudge one thousand dollars that the old gentleman, meaning Capt. Joseph White, of Salem, was dead. He asked me why. I mentioned to him that the old gentleman had a Will, which if destroyed, half of the property would come on this side; that is, to my mother in law Mrs. Beckford; that with the present Will, the bulk of the property would go to Stephen White; that he had injured me in the opinion of the old gentleman, and I had no doubt had also prejudiced him against all the family, and that I thought it right to get the property if I could. I mentioned to him also in a joking way, that the old gentleman had often said he wished he could go off like a flash.[6]

In Colman's excitement and rush to get all of Joe's words down, he smudged some letters, and the ink pooled in spots. He had to scratch out and rewrite a few words. He stopped, took a breath, and encouraged Joe to continue:

> We then contrived how it could be done. One way was to meet him on the road, but the old gentleman was never out at night.—Another was to attack him in the house, but Frank said he had not the pluck to do it, but he knew who would. I asked him who, and he said he would see George and Dick Crowninshield. I told him, well, I did not think they would, but he could go and see.[7]

Dick readily agreed to kill Captain White for $1,000 (equivalent to $25,000 today). Dick met with Frank Knapp several times over the coming months to hash it out.

Joe Knapp met with Dick on the night of April 2, at the Salem Common, the heart of the city's communal life. Joe told Dick he had already stolen the captain's will so now all that was left to do was kill the old man. Dick pulled out the weapons he planned to use for the job. He handed Joe the club. It had a deadly heft to it. "I turned it myself," Dick bragged.

He next handed Joe the knife. It was sharp on both edges and tapered to a point. "Are you going to do it tonight?" Joe asked. "He goes to bed at ten or a little before."

"No, I can't do it tonight. I have to wait a little. I'm alone. George won't back me. I'll meet Frank again soon. I don't know what evening." Joe left and headed back to Wenham. He had secreted the will in a lockbox stashed in the hayloft at Cherry Hill Farm, where he lived. After the murder, he burned the will.

Colman was several pages into the confession when there was a loud knocking at the cell door. Colman, in a huff at being disturbed at such a pivotal moment, went to the door. He opened the scuttle and peered out. It was Phippen. He looked harried. "Can I come in?" he asked.

"No," came Colman's reply. "Not until I've finished my business." Phippen appeared shocked. Colman closed the scuttle and returned to his work.

Joe described how on the Friday before the murder, he had gone into Captain White's house, unbarred the windows, and closed the shutters to hide what he had done so that five days later, Dick could sneak into the mansion to kill Captain White.

On the day of the murder, Frank visited Joe at Cherry Hill Farm. While there, Joe let his brother know that Mary Beckford, Joe's mother-in-law, would not be staying at the Salem mansion that night. It was the perfect opportunity to go through with their plans.

"You'd better tell this to Dick," Joe said. Frank agreed and headed back to Salem in the afternoon. As Frank ascended the carriage, he looked at his brother. "I guess he will go tonight," he said.

The story, so long bottled up in Joe, had come bursting out with the promise of a pardon helping to loosen his lips. The reverend could not believe his luck. Now that he was getting it down on paper, it would be incontrovertible. Joe continued with his story.

"On Wednesday, 7th of April, my brother came to the farm about noon—he asked if we had heard the news; we told him yes, and how we heard it. After dinner he told me aside how it occurred," he recounted.

Frank described to his brother how Dick had murdered Captain White and the meeting afterward in Brown Street between Frank and Dick. He later told Joe something strange about the killing:

> My brother informed me that Richard Crowninshield having seen the accounts of the number of stabs in the Newspapers said he had stabbed him but four times, and Richard Crowninshield remarked that he really believed there had been another person in the chamber.[8]

Finally, Joe described to Colman how he had written the letters to the Committee of Vigilance and to Stephen White using two aliases, Grant and Claxton, and had asked a friend to mail them. He also told of how he made an initial payment of 100 five-franc pieces from Guadeloupe to Dick for murdering Captain White.

> Richard Crowninshield informed me that same evening, that he had put the club with which he killed Capt. White, under the Branch Meeting House steps; my brother went to look for it since, but could not find it. I know nothing of Chase or Selman in this business. I know nothing of Palmer or Carr nor ever heard anything until since I came into the Salem Gaol.[9]

Colman, confession in hand, bid the prisoner good afternoon and left his cell. The reverend brushed past Phippen, who was still waiting outside the cell. "I'm going to see the committee," he said. "I'll meet you at your office at five." Feeling angry and betrayed, Phippen rushed in to see his brother. He could not believe what Joe had just done.

It soon got worse. Colman had promised to show Phippen the confession, but after talking it over with members of the Committee of Vigilance, they decided it would not be proper. Instead, they leaked the confession to the press, helping to guarantee the Knapps would not be getting a fair trial. The committee wanted closure, not justice.

Two days later, Colman went back to see Joe. He got a further written confession based on answers to his specific questions. Among the various statements he made, Joe admitted that the January before the murder he snuck into Captain White's room and opened the iron chest and read White's will. He discovered the old man had left only a small portion of his estate to Mary White

Beckford, his mother-in-law and White's niece. This lit the fuse that would end in White's death and everything else that spun out from there. He replaced the will and left. Joe did not know that this was an older will and that the newest version, which was more equitable, sat at the office of Captain White's lawyer.

Other revelations from the second written confession were that Dick Crowninshield had melted down the knife he used to kill White the day after the murder at his shop in Danvers. The Knapps originally approached George Crowninshield with the proposal to kill White. George said he would be willing to stab the old man on the road to his farm or even on a Salem street, but he refused to do it inside White's house. His brother, Dick, had no such qualms.

Joe said Frank had tried to dissuade him several times from going through with the plan, but Joe would not hear it. While Frank saw the "great danger" of murdering White, Joe only saw the bright side of their plan. "I had weighed the consequences well," he told Colman. Even with all the planning and effort put into the scheme, Joe did not really expect Dick would go through with the murder, but he had.

6

WEST POINT

After leaving Richmond, Poe spent some time with his relatives in Baltimore, staying with his aunt, Maria Clemm. He got to reconnect with his brother, Henry, and also see his little cousin, Virginia, who he came to adore. The warmth of his blood relations and his aunt's cozy home were a stark contrast to Allan's grand mansion and chilly demeanor in Richmond. While in Baltimore, Poe also met with Nathan Covington Brooks to discuss including one of Poe's poems in an upcoming annual. Poe would not give up on his dreams of being a poet.

From Baltimore, he went to New York City and then West Point. The ferry from New York City docked below what looked like a sparse, irregular village perched atop an imposing cliff overlooking the Hudson River. It was the United States Military Academy—Poe's new home, at least until he graduated and received a military commission. Richmond and the troubles with John Allan were behind him, and Poe instead focused on his future. He hoped West Point would be a way to jumpstart his military career and help repair his strained relationship with his foster father.

He had gone as far as he could as an enlisted man in the First Regiment of Artillery, reaching the rank of sergeant major in less than two years. Yet from the moment he arrived at West Point in June 1830, he realized this would be harder than his earlier time spent in the army, although his spirits were high, believing his prior service would allow him to finish in six months.

After disembarking, Poe trekked up the winding road from the dock towards the parade ground, the academy's heart, surrounded by five imposing stone buildings, some administrative, others dorms and classrooms. Six brick buildings housed the officers and professors near the river. A few buildings dated back to the Revolutionary era, when the Americans had stretched a massive iron chain across the Hudson River to prevent British ships from traveling north, and where Benedict Arnold, a war hero turned traitor, had attempted to hand over West Point to the British. By 1830, these buildings were in disrepair and used for supplies and arms.

Poe walked through the doors into the headquarters building and registered as a cadet of the United States Military Academy for the year 1830. He was now on his way to becoming a "plebe," short for plebeian, the derogatory term used by upperclassmen for first-year students. Until he had made it through the various hoops required of him, the academy considered him a "candidate" and not a cadet.

After being assigned quarters, he headed to the cadet barracks and reported to the officer in charge of the recent arrivals. Poe's austere room was in the three-story-high, somber stone South Barracks. At only 11 sq. feet and shared with two other cadets, the quarters offered no privacy nor comfort. The room contained little more than the thin mattresses laid on the floor that the cadets had to sleep on.

Poe's first hurdle was an academic exam. Several hard-nosed professors sat at the back of the classroom and instructed Poe to go up to an empty blackboard and show his learning. The professors called out questions on grammar, geography, and arithmetic while Poe hurriedly scribbled the answers in chalk. He easily passed the entrance exam. His early education in England where he had lived for five years, his short time at the University of Virginia, and his own restless intellect served him admirably. Other candidates did not do as well. In Poe's first letter to Allan from West Point, he wrote that "a great many cadets of good families" had not passed the entrance exam, including Thomas Peyton Giles, the son of Virginia's governor, William Giles. Poe learned from the other cadets that on average about only thirty of the 130 who started at West Point each year graduated, the rest being dismissed for bad behavior or deficiencies. "The regulations are rigid in the extreme," he reported to Allan.[1]

Next came the physical examination at the hospital overlooking the Hudson River, where three different doctors examined Poe and the other candidates hoping for a spot at the academy. The doctors assessed overall health, including looking for signs of various communicable diseases, such as consumption, which were then common. They tested for vision problems by holding up a Capped Bust dime at fourteen paces and asking the men which side was showing, Lady Liberty or the American eagle. They had a fifty-fifty shot at getting the answer correct even if they had sight problems.

Poe, with letters of introduction in hand, then met with Captain Ethan Allen Hitchcock, a faculty member, and Lieutenant Edward C. Ross, a mathematics professor, who cordially received him. Poe had worked hard to get to this point. He had not gotten there alone. Frances had to plead with Allan on her deathbed before he would agree to help their foster son. He used his business connections to rally the support of U.S. Senator Powhatan Ellis to get Poe a recommendation to the Academy. Poe's superior officers in the army also backed his bid. Allan signed off on the plan in March 1830 in a letter to the U.S. War Department.

Following Poe's meeting with the West Point faculty members, there was a pleasant surprise waiting for him—a letter from Allan. Inside was a $20 bill (equivalent to about $550 today). While he was happy to receive the money, it was not enough to cover his expenses at West Point. Poe worried that this would be a repeat of what happened at the University of Virginia, where he had ended up in debt because of Allan's lack of promised financial support.

Each West Point cadet received a salary of $16 a month and two meal rations a day, but cadets' parents typically set up a deposit with the academy that the young men could draw from for necessities, such as school books, candles, and toiletries. Allan had not set up an account. For Poe, who was fastidious about his appearance and cleanliness, this was especially intolerable.

Not only had Allan not provided the necessary funds, but the letter also accused Poe of stealing several items when he left Richmond—books from Poe's own room and a brass inkstand, sand caster, and pen holder that Poe had had for years. Yes, they had Allan's name engraved on them, but Poe considered them his own since he had been using them since childhood.

In his return letter to Allan, Poe was cordial. He addressed Allan as "Dear Pa" and, although he defended himself of the theft charges, writing "As to what you say about the books, etc., I have taken nothing except what I considered my own property," the letter remained breezy in tone and included a smattering of West Point news.[2] Poe was there to make Allan, the only father he had ever known, proud, and he still had hopes for a return to a time when they had been close. Frances had doted on Poe and always kept the peace between him and his foster father. She made him feel a part of the family, but with her death, Poe felt like he had been cast out and set adrift.

It had not always been like that. When the family lived in London, from the time Poe was six to eleven, he and Allan had a tender relationship. In the flat on Southampton Row, the family—John, Frances, Frances' sister Nancy, and Edgar—would sit together by the fire while Edgar read his storybooks, the women would sew, and Allan wrote letters home. It was the picture of domesticity.

Allan in his letters to friends and family nearly always mentioned "little Edgar" and loved to tell of his capers. He also sent Poe to an excellent boarding school outside of London. He thought of Edgar as his son, but that was then. Time and temperament had created an increasingly greater distance between Allan and Poe. West Point was Poe's last lifeline thrown to the man he still considered his "dear Pa," a last attempt to bridge the chasm.

On June 23, Poe and the other first-year students headed to the Plain, the name given to the level 40-acre parcel of parade ground. It served as the summer residence for the cadets who hauled all their belongings from the dorms to the semi-permanent canvas tents erected for use during their tactical field training.

Their summer homes were laid out on the flat expanse of the Plain. This stood in stark contrast to the rest of the Point, which was hilly and included a deep ravine known as Execution Hollow because of its rumored use for military executions during the American Revolution. Near there, atop a knoll, sat the 15-foot-high white-marble obelisk dedicated to Eleazer Wood, an early West Point graduate who died during the War of 1812. It was a stark reminder of the price of duty.

On July 1, 1830, Poe took his oath, intoning the words:

I, Edgar Allan Poe, of the State of Virginia, aged nineteen years, five months, having been selected for an appointment as Cadet in the Military Academy of the United States, do hereby engage with the consent of my guardian in the event of my receiving such appointment, that I will serve in the army of the United States for five years, unless sooner discharged by competent authority. And I, Edgar Allan Poe, do solemnly swear that I will bear true faith and allegiance to the United States of America, and that I will serve them, honestly and faithfully against all their enemies or opposers whatsoever; and that I will observe and obey the orders of the President of the United States, and the orders of the Officers appointed over me, according to the Rules and Articles of War.

Poe lied about his age. He was twenty-one and five-months, but new West Point cadets had to be under twenty-one. This was the second time he had lied to the U.S. military. In 1827, when he had originally joined the army, he entered service under the assumed name of Edgar A. Perry, claiming he was a clerk from Boston, and gave his age as twenty-two, when he was actually nineteen. In a time before government-issued IDs or even certified birth records, they relied on a person's word regarding personal information. This time, Poe low-balled his age. After being sworn in, Poe and the other first-year cadets returned to the summer encampment to stay until the beginning of their classes in August.

The next morning after being sworn in, Poe awoke at 5 a.m. to the sound of reveille. Wearing his grey wool uniform, he headed out for the grueling military training with the other plebes. That summer, they drilled incessantly, bathed in the chilly Hudson River, and slept on bedrolls in canvas tents. At least they still got to eat in the mess hall, a small enjoyment in a summer of privation. Poe still kept his poet's sensibilities, luxuriating in the wild and majestic landscape surrounding the academy—the ever-changing tidal flow of the wide Hudson River abuzz with sailing vessels and the craggy beauty of Storm King Mountain, a glowering fortress-like peak and the Catskill mountains that rolled north into infinity.

He was used to the rigors of military life and had always been an exceptional athlete, but even after two years in the army, the summer encampment at West Point was especially tough as the military instructors attempted to beat the raw recruits into soldiers. Their days began at 5 a.m. and ended at 10.30 p.m. That did not include guard duty, which was mandatory throughout the summer encampment. The cadets learned the valuable lesson of catching naps whenever they had a few minutes free, a trick soldiers throughout history have used during wartime where sleep was a luxury.

Life at West Point was a lot harder than Poe's first go-round in the army, and he had not even begun his classes yet. Duty at Fortress Monroe, on the southern tip of the Virginia peninsula near Hampton, had been a vacation by comparison. There, Poe did not have much to do besides guard duty at the massive fortress that bristled with hundreds of cannons. He spent a lot of time writing poetry and chatting with the other non-commissioned officers.

He had left the army with the highest rank available to non-commissioned officers. At West Point, he was starting from scratch. It was a hard path, but Poe hoped that his ambition to become a commissioned officer would please Allan. Repercussions from the letter he wrote to his old army friend Bully about his foster father would soon throw all his well-intentioned plans into chaos.

7

DECISIONS

While Poe settled into life at West Point, Dick Crowninshield was weighing his options and the consequences for himself, his brother, and his friend, Frank. It seemed Joe was looking after himself and would turn state's evidence. Dick read the newspapers daily and was up on all the news about the case. It was already the middle of June, and he had been in jail for more than a month. Overall, the time he had been in jail had not been that bad. A steady stream of friends had visited. He read books on mathematics and mechanics and worked on his poetry. Being stuck in a jail cell allowed for these kinds of pursuits.

Yet his mind kept returning to the conversation he had shared with the Knapps' attorney, Franklin Dexter. Dick had an inkling of how the law worked regarding principals and accessories, and the lawyer had confirmed it. He had asked Dexter what would happen to the prosecution's case against the others if he were to die suddenly. Dexter answered that you could not prosecute an accessory to a crime without first having a principal tried and convicted. "Are you sure?" Dick had persisted. Yes, Dexter was sure. It had been on the books for a decade after the state's Supreme Judicial Court ruled in Commonwealth *v*. Phillips that because the law presumes suspects innocent until proven guilty, they could not try you as an accessory until they had convicted someone as the principal in the crime.

The state considered Dick the principal in the murder, and the others accessories. Dexter warned that if they did not convict Dick of the crime, the prosecution could go after one of the others as a principal. Dick was not going to give the government the satisfaction of executing him, and he did not plan on spending the rest of his life in prison. There was only one solution.

On the afternoon of June 15, 1830, Nehemiah Brown, the man in charge of the jail, left his home next door and went to Dick Crowninshield's cell to deliver a note he had received for the prisoner from the elder Crowninshield. He called out the prisoner's name twice but received no response. He looked through the tiny window in the cell door. With a shock, he called for a turnkey, who came running at the voice of his boss. He inserted the key, swung the door open, and the two men rushed into the cell.

While Dick Crowninshield had escaped the hangman, he had not escaped a hanging. Using two silk scarfs in his possession, he had fastened a noose and hanged himself from a window grate by kicking away a chair that he had been standing on. His feet were touching the ground and his knees were bent upwards and less than 1 foot off the ground. They took the prisoner down and laid him on his bed. The two men stared at Dick. They surmised that he had been hanging for fifteen or twenty minutes. He looked dead. His face had a purplish hue. They went to find a doctor. Two arrived. Initially, they believed Crowninshield was still alive, though they could not find a pulse or detect a heartbeat. They tried some crude medical procedures then in use. The doctors cut some veins at the wrist and neck and blood flowed freely, which they believed showed he was alive. One physician had a galvanic battery that he attached to Dick's body, hoping to reanimate him. There was no reaction.

After these failed attempts at reviving him, Brown summoned the coroner. They immediately held a coroner's jury and determined that Crowninshield had eaten his lunch as normal at 1 p.m. When the turnkey came to collect Dick's dishes a short time later, everything seemed fine, but when Brown showed up just before 2 p.m., Dick was dead. The jury read two brief letters found in the cell. One was to Richard's father, the other to his brother George, who was just down the hall in his cell awaiting the outcome of the case. While neither of the letters contained anything like a confession, they dwelled on his feelings of hopelessness of escaping justice if he were to stand trial.

Dick wrote to his father apologizing for being an "undutiful son" who had disregarded his father's "chaste, moral precepts." He asked him to give him a decent burial and to save his body "from the dissecting knife."[1]

To his brother, George, Dick wrote that he prayed that God and his innocence would guide him through his coming trial. Dick admitted that had he listened to his brother, he would "still enjoy Life, Liberty, and a clear conscience." He explained the reason for taking his own life.

"I have come to the determination to deprive them of the pleasure of beholding me publicly executed, as after I am condemned they will not give me the opportunity, and may God forgive me," he wrote. The letter contained a warning to George and others to steer clear of vice or end up suffering a similar fate. Dick apologized to his brother for what he had "caused you and others to suffer on my account."[2] He ended the letter with a poem:

> *Ungrateful wretches; why do ye crave?*
> *The life our heavenly maker gave*
> *Why confine us in the gloomy cells?*

Where nothing save grief and sorrow dwell's
Detested fiends: be banished hence,
Among your Kindred go [boast] your sense,
Where imps of hell, and Devils [roam],
Go and seek out your native home.[3]

Dick's suicide would have ripple effects in the murder case for months and years to come. The attorney general scrambled to save his case against the Knapps and Dick's brother, George. They needed a principal, and they decided Frank Knapp would do. Since there was no evidence that he had had a hand in the actual murder, it would take some prosecutorial gymnastics to make it stick.

On Tuesday, July 20, a little more than a month after the suicide, the grand jury assembled at the Salem courthouse for a special session of the Supreme Court. At the time, the state's highest court oversaw all murder trials. The justices traveled to the various counties to hear these capital cases at set dates throughout the year. The Supreme Judicial Court was not scheduled to be in Essex County until November, but the court granted the prosecution a special session for this case.

The state attorney general, Perez Morton, figured out how to circumvent the law and charge Frank as the principal in White's murder by alleging he had stabbed and bludgeoned Captain White even though there was ample evidence to the contrary. Hoping to guarantee this outcome, he also charged Frank as aiding and abetting Dick Crowninshield, a move that would be easier to prove at trial if their witnesses could identify Frank as one of the mysterious men seen near the White mansion on the night of the murder. The prosecution would not only have to convince the jury Frank was there that night, but that he was there to help in the murder by "co-operating in the act, watching to prevent relief, or to give alarm, or to assist his confederate in escape, having knowledge of the purpose and object of the assassin." If the defense could prove Frank had gone there out of curiosity or even to find out if Dick had gone through with the killing, the prosecution's case would sink.

Chief Justice Isaac Parker, a straight-shooting jurist in his seventies whose bald pate fringed with greying hair and hooked nose made him look like a surly vulture, delivered his charge to the grand jury, explaining the points of law related to the case and ordering them to "divest themselves of prejudice and preconceived opinions." This was easy to ask for but hard to enforce in an atmosphere filled with righteous indignation that the murder was not just the killing of one old man, but an act that could upend Salem's entire social system and blacken its good reputation forever if left unchecked.

They sequestered the twelve grand jurors to hear the prosecution's evidence. For everyone else involved, it was a waiting game. Three days later, on Friday, July 23, the court was back in session. The grand jurors returned a series of indictments. The circus was about to begin.

James Gordon Bennett, the associate editor for the *Morning Courier and New-York Enquirer,* came from New York to cover the trial. Bennett had not been in New England for years, although he once considered it home. After moving to the United States from Scotland in 1819, at twenty-four, he became a schoolteacher near Portland, Maine. He then went to Boston, where he was a bookseller, before finally finding his true calling in the newspaper business.

The thirty-four-year-old journalist was an arresting presence. Long and lean, with hair curling at his temples and down his neck, he had severely crossed eyes and a cantankerous manner. He was just one of many journalists there to cover the proceedings.

In 1830, sending reporters to cover national news was still a novelty. Newspapers typically just reprinted stories taken from the local paper where the incident had taken place. Crime reporting was in its infancy. In the coming decade, a new breed of New York City newspapers would thrive on lurid crime stories, with Bennett helping to lead the way.

The newspapermen were in Salem to give readers a blow-by-blow account of the trials, so it was a great shock when the Chief Justice proclaimed the court would not be allowing daily coverage. Parker spoke from his bench:

> The court were decidedly of the opinion that the proceedings ought not to be published from day to day, as they would give only imperfect information ... What passes one day may essentially be modified by the doings of a subsequent day. There may be no objection to publish the state of the case as it advances, but there must be no publication of evidence until the trials are concluded.[4]

Bennett scoffed at the idea. He would not allow the court to dictate how he reported the case. The court paid no heed to the disgruntled murmurings of the reporters as there was business to attend to. The grand jurors filed into court as the guards hustled the prisoners—Frank and Joe Knapp and George Crowninshield—to the bar to hear the indictments read.

They also brought in Benjamin Selman and Daniel Chase, the Crowninshield's friends who had been arrested along with Dick and George back in May. They too had been languishing in jail for three months as their cases slowly made their way through the system. The prosecution declined to pursue the charges against Chase and Selman as accessories and the court released them.

The other prisoners pleaded not guilty to the charges. Besides Frank being charged for murder, they charged the other two, Joe Knapp and George Crowninshield, as accessories. To give a catch-all at trial, there was another indictment charging the now dead Dick Crowninshield as the principal and Frank Knapp as "being present, aiding, and abetting" the murderer.

Franklin Dexter and William H. Gardiner, the Boston lawyers hired by Phippen, appeared for the Knapp brothers. Salem lawyers Ebenezer Shillaber and

John Walsh represented George Crowninshield. The three defendants received separate trials. The court set Frank's trial, the first of the three, for July 27.

Chief Justice Parker returned to Boston, awaiting the next court session in Salem. He and a few of his friends met up at the home of Nathan Dane, a lawyer and statesman who had served in the Continental Congress. The men sat together chatting, speaking rather loudly so Dane, who was almost completely deaf, could hear them. They spoke about days gone by and their careers, now nearly at their end. Parker, in a buoyant mood, spoke up.

"During the twenty-four years I have held my seat, I've never been prevented by ill health for a single day, from being in the place where my official duty called me, in every part of the Commonwealth."[5] The other men took this statement not as a boast but with a sense of his humble gratitude at being so healthy for a man in his early sixties.

Parker spent part of the next day in the state law library, then went for a carriage ride, and enjoyed the evening out with friends. It had been a pleasurable day. On Sunday morning, he woke up and could barely speak. Parker fell into a coma after suffering a stroke from which he never regained consciousness. Twenty hours later, he was dead.

Daniel Webster was enjoying what seemed like the first break he had had in a long time. He was at his family farm in Franklin, New Hampshire, which he considered the sweetest spot on earth. He was playing checkers with his son as a storm raged outside, the wind and rain whipping the farmhouse. There was a sudden banging at the door. Webster got up from his chair and answered it. A man, more like a drowned rat, stood in the doorway dripping wet.

After drying himself by the fire, the visitor got straight to the point. It was a time-sensitive business proposition he delivered from Webster's friend Stephen White. Webster balked at the thought of more "business." He told his visitor he was too busy to take on anything new but agreed to hear what he had to say.

White wanted Webster to aid the attorney general in prosecuting the Knapp brothers for his uncle's murder and would pay $1,000. Webster was very much aware of the Knapp case. He had first been told of the murder by his friend Judge Joseph Story, a U.S. Supreme Court justice with ties to Salem, days after it had occurred. Webster followed the newspaper reports and general gossip of the goings-on in Salem that had landed the Crowninshield and Knapp brothers in jail.

Throughout his law career, Webster had fought on the side of the accused, not for the state. It was a hard decision. He was extremely busy, but $1,000 was impossible to refuse. He had debts that always seemed to grow rather than diminish, and there was the political capital that he would get from helping his friend Stephen White and the other power players involved.

Private prosecution was not unheard of, especially in young Western states with little bureaucratic infrastructure, but Massachusetts was different. There was not a lot of case law on the practice, but Webster knew the defense would fight to prevent him from joining the case. His only chance was to convince the justices to allow his involvement. Webster took his chances and agreed to take the job on. They left the next day for Salem.

Securing Webster for the prosecution was a major coup for Stephen White. Webster was considered the greatest orator of his generation, and while he had not achieved his ultimate goal of becoming president, he was still regarded as the most important statesmen in the country. As a U.S. senator—he was a sitting senator for Massachusetts at the time—Webster was unequaled in his debating ability. Only months before, in January, he had given his most famous Senate speech, known as the "Second Reply to Hayne" against the ideology of "Nullification." Some Southern politicians, including Senator Robert Hayne of South Carolina, supported the doctrine that a state could annul an act of Congress if it believed the national government had overstepped its authority. It was an issue revolving around slavery and a precursor of sorts to succession, the political ideology that led thirty years later to the Civil War.

Hayne and his cohorts, led by Vice President John C. Calhoun, believed the states were only a loose confederation that had the right to ignore federal laws they deemed not in their best interest. In his booming voice, Webster thundered against Hayne and nullification, receiving wave after wave of applause when he had finished his speech that ended with the famous line: "Liberty and Union, now and forever, one and inseparable."

Thomas Carlyle, the British historian and essayist, in a letter to his friend Ralph Waldo Emerson, the philosopher-poet, said that as a "logic-fencer, advocate, or parliamentary Hercules" one would incline to back Webster "at first sight against all the extant world." He described him as having an "amorphous crag-like face," eyes like "anthracite furnaces only needing to be blown" and "a mastiff-mouth." Carlyle wrote, "Webster is not loquacious, but he is pertinent, conclusive; a dignified, perfectly bred man."[6]

Now, Webster was going to Salem to get justice for his friend, no matter what.

8

THE TALE OF SILVER

As the sun rose over Salem on the morning of Tuesday, August 3, 1830, vendors erected their stands and readied their wares to cash in on the crowds coming for Frank Knapp's murder trial. A carnival atmosphere bubbled up as people started milling around, hoping to snag a good seat when the courthouse opened.

In the town square, the authorities stretched heavy chains across the road to prevent carriages and riders from entering. On the outside of the courthouse, they strung up tanbark, a spongy material made from trees and used in the tanning business, in a vain attempt to deaden the crowd noise so that the court could do its work.

Bennett, the New York reporter, showed up early, pushing his way into the courtroom with the other newspapermen. He found a seat before the mad rush of the public crammed into the chamber that was too small to accommodate such an enormous crowd. Bennett thought the surging throng looked like the tide boiling up the rocks of Nahant, the tiny North Shore beach community on a spit of land in Essex County, southeast of Salem. The people continued to push their way into the room with fierceness, levity, rudeness, and roughness, Bennett felt. Some attempted to sit in the jury box, and the benches reserved for the attorneys.

Just before the justices arrived, Webster walked to the back of the courtroom. To Bennett, "the Great Orator" looked good, comfortable, at ease. In contrast, the defense attorneys, who made no real impression on him, seemed ill at ease. "In the hands of such a man as Webster, a dozen of them are a mere mouthful," Bennett concluded. He was underestimating the prowess of the defense, led by two well-respected high-powered Boston attorneys, Franklin Dexter and William H. Gardiner, assisted by Robert Rantoul, Jr. All three were from prominent Boston families. Dexter was a Harvard-educated lawyer, politician, and artist, whose father, Samuel, had served as U.S. secretary of the treasury under John Adams. Gardiner attended Cambridge and was an exceptional orator, but he paled in comparison to Webster. His father, John, had served as the rector of

Trinity Church. Rantoul, another Harvard man, was twenty-five and a relatively new lawyer. He had been admitted to the bar a year earlier and had set up his practice in Salem. He would one day replace Webster in the U.S. Senate.

The unexpected death of Chief Justice Parker, who only two weeks before had presided at the case, had thrown the court system into disarray. His death delayed the trial for a few days, which allowed the prosecution to secure Webster's help.

As the Associate Justices Samuel Putnam, Samuel Wilde, and Marcus Morton, Sr., entered the court, a hush fell over the crowd. Putnam, square-jawed and grandfatherly, had ties to Salem, having once practiced law there, and had served in both houses of the state legislature before ascending to the State Supreme Court sixteen years earlier. Wilde, stern, and pugnacious, had an encyclopedic mind that was a trove of both the intricate and more obscure aspects of the law. Morton, the former lieutenant governor, with his feline-like face and unflagging belief in Jacksonian democracy, took his seat last.

Next came the prisoners. Frank Knapp moved with a spring in his step, practically bounding to the front of the courtroom. Joe Knapp, the next in line, moved languidly, and George Crowninshield, with a quiet and easy air, brought up the rear. They were all well-dressed and looked refined in their frock coats and cravats, especially for having spent two months behind bars awaiting trial.

The clerk of court read the document that alleged Frank had murdered Captain White and the other two had "counseled, hired and procured the said J. F. Knapp to commit the said felony and murder." To clarify, the court referred to Frank Knapp as J. F. Knapp and Joe Knapp as J. J. Knapp, Jr.

Another count laid the murder at the feet of Dick Crowninshield, who "afterwards, before any conviction, feloniously committed suicide, and so can be no farther prosecuted." The indictment accused Frank Knapp of being present, aiding and abetting Dick. Yet another count alleged "a person unknown to the Jurors" committed the murder and that "J. F. Knapp was present, and that J. J. Knapp, Jr. and George Crowninshield did hire and counsel." The grand jury was being thorough in its indictments, hoping to guarantee a conviction.

Frank pleaded not guilty. The court decided the other men did not have to plead until after Frank's trial since if the jury acquitted Frank, the prosecution would not be able to try the other two. They returned to jail, leaving Frank to face justice alone.

Attorney General Perez Morton, a distant cousin of Justice Morton, asked the court whether "the honorable Daniel Webster be permitted to take part in the case on behalf of the government." The defense counsel remained silent on the request.

"The court is happy to have so distinguished a gentleman take part in the trial," Justice Putnam responded. The trial began with jury selection, a hard-fought battle involving nineteen peremptory challenges and eleven for cause. Eventually, the attorneys agreed on twelve men as jurors and the trial began in earnest.

Attorney General Morton gave his opening address focusing on Joseph Knapp's confession to the Rev. Colman and Joe's refusal to testify before the grand jury "on the advice of his counsel."

> But as the inquiry before the grand jury may not be considered as calling him as a witness upon the trial, I shall in the course of the examination of evidence again call him as a witness, and if he again refuses to testify, everyone will acknowledge that the pledge of the government will be completely redeemed, and his promised protection will be forfeited.[1]

Refusing to testify was a dangerous move on Joe's part. He was risking his life for his brother, and if the prosecution could get his written confession into evidence, it would be a moot point.

Morton continued his opening, telling the court that even if Joseph refused to testify, he would "prove it by other testimony in the case." He said they would show there had been a conspiracy and then could legally use any evidence against one defendant to prove their case against the others. Morton hoped he could convince the court to allow Joe Knapp's written confession into evidence.

Webster took the lead in examining the prosecution witnesses. He started with the testimony of Captain White's staff, who were in Captain White's mansion when he was murdered. Webster focused on Joseph Knapp's free access to the house in the weeks and days before the murder. From there, it was on to Dr. Johnson's gruesome testimony of the autopsy. The doctor believed the murder had taken place between three and four hours before they found the captain in bed. When Webster pushed the doctor, he wavered on the time of death, saying he supposed there was "nothing to prevent it having been done six or eight hours" earlier.

Webster wanted to stretch the murder's timeline. Exactly when the murder took place would be crucial since there were witnesses who swore Frank had been home and in bed around ten on the night of the murder. When Webster finished with Dr. Johnson, Morton stood up and proclaimed the prosecution had proven a murder took place based on the witnesses' testimony. They were now ready to prove there was a conspiracy behind it. He turned towards Joe Knapp, who sat in the gallery and called him to the witness stand. Joe reluctantly came forward. When asked whether he would testify, he shook his head back and forth. Morton asked him why he refused to testify, but the defense attorney, Franklin Dexter, cut him off with a loud "objection."

While Dexter and his team were defending Joe's brother Frank, they also represented Joe, who would go to trial next if the jury found his brother guilty. The court agreed with Dexter that Joe was "not obliged to state his reasons." The judges then concluded that the "government say they have pledged themselves not to proceed against him if he would testify; he does not testify, and now that pledge is recalled."

Joe's chance for saving himself was extinguished, and it was his own sense of loyalty that had blown out that flame. As he was being led away, Morton, angry that Joe had backed out, called after him: "The peril remains on your own head."

Dexter told the court that Morton had misspoken when he said that Joe's lawyers advised him not to testify. "I feel it my duty to state distinctly that I have never given such advice," he said. The other lawyers on the defense team made similar pronouncements.

With Joe refusing to testify, Rev. Colman became the prosecution's star witness and took full advantage of the spotlight. He told the jury that along with Joe, Frank had also confessed to him. The defense attempted to mitigate Colman's damaging testimony by keeping most of Frank's alleged confession with Colman from coming into evidence, but the prosecution still struck a fatal blow to Frank's case. Colman told the jury he had learned where Dick Crowninshield had stashed the murder weapon from Frank, a direct contradiction to what he told Phippen a few months earlier. The reverend was lying under oath. He went further and claimed that Frank had said: "I told Joseph when he proposed it that it was a silly business and would only get us into difficulty."

Later, Webster recalled Colman to the stand and again asked him about Frank's alleged confession. While Dexter again objected, the court reversed itself and allowed Colman to tell the jury that Frank had confirmed Joe's story about murdering Captain White. Colman's lie would bury Frank Knapp.

Palmer was the next witness. Webster led him through his testimony. The witness reiterated the story he had told so many times already it had nearly become rote. He told the jury Dick Crowninshield had offered him a third of the pay if he helped murder Captain White.

Palmer told of how he had seen Frank Knapp scheming with the Crowninshields and that the murder revolved around destroying Captain White's will. Against the defense's objections, the court allowed Palmer's letter into evidence. The two letters Joe Knapp wrote to Stephen White and Gideon Barstow, the head of the Committee of Vigilance, using the aliases Grant and Claxton, also came into evidence.

Gardiner, one of the Knapps' defense attorneys, spent a lot of time cross-examining Palmer about his shady past, including his time in prison for theft. Dexter, the other defense attorney, focused on Palmer's mistreatment at the hands of the Committee of Vigilance—how they brought him from Maine in chains, refused to let Palmer see anyone, and held him in Salem jail for months.

Webster angrily objected to Dexter's line of questioning. Dexter answered that he "expected to show that the witness had been harshly used." The court allowed the questioning to continue. It was a dead end as Palmer denied the committee had railroaded him into testifying or promised him anything in return. Palmer also denied that money was his chief motivation for writing the note to Joe Knapp. "I didn't think it ought to be concealed," Palmer said, before eventually admitting, "perhaps I thought I should have some part of the reward."

Benjamin Leighton, a seventeen-year-old farmhand who lived at Joe Knapp's home in Wenham, was another important prosecution witness. The attorney general had dismissed the teen's story and did not plan on including him on the witness list. Webster insisted on getting him on the stand. Leighton's testimony was vital in proving the Knapp's involvement in the conspiracy. Leighton told the jury about overhearing a conversation between the two Knapp brothers just before the murder. According to his testimony, he was hiding just on the other side of a stone fence when he heard the conversation:

"When did you see Dick?" Joe asked his brother.

"I saw him this morning."

"When is he going to kill the old man?"

"I don't know," Frank answered.

"If he does not kill him soon, I will not pay him," Joe said.[2]

Leighton did not particularly like Frank since the older teen liked to tease him by jabbing him with the dagger he carried. Leighton told the jury he feared that the Knapps would kill him if they were acquitted.

There was also testimony from various townspeople who saw two shadowy figures near Captain White's mansion on the night of the murder but were uncertain of who they had seen. One witness, John Southwick, believed it was Selman and Chase, the two co-defendants who had just been released from jail without charges, that he had seen that night.

On Monday, August 9, the fifth day of the nine-day trial, Phippen Knapp took the stand for the defense. He contradicted Rev. Colman on several counts, the most important being that it was Joe, not Frank, who had told Colman about the murder weapon's hiding place. Phippen also contradicted the testimony about Colman's conversation with Frank. Colman alleged Frank said it was not fair "that Joseph should have the advantage of making a confession, since the thing was done for his benefit." Colman was trying to make it appear as if Frank had admitted his guilt, but this was not the case. According to Phippen, the only statement Frank made to Colman was that he thought it was "a hard case, but if it be as you say, Joseph may confess if he pleases. I shall stand trial."

Under a withering cross-examination by Webster, Phippen became nervous and stumbled through his answers. It was unnerving to be at the receiving end of Black Dan's questioning. Webster's stern countenance had scared off a legion of rival Congressmen over the years. Webster forced Phippen to admit that he could not remember every detail of Colman's conversations with his brothers. On several points, Phippen refused to swear to minute details that Webster questioned him on. It made Phippen look like he was obfuscating when he was just trying to testify accurately. Bennet, the New York reporter, taking notes on

Phippen's testimony, felt that "notwithstanding the torture of the situation in which he was placed," Phippen "gave his evidence with great self-possession."[3]

Frank was the one person who was not allowed to take the stand. This was a time before defendants could testify in their own defense. It would be up to his lawyer, Dexter, to lay out his version of the facts and his interpretation of the law, hoping to get a not-guilty verdict for his client.

Dexter, in the small overheated courtroom, planted as much doubt in the minds of the jurors as he could during his final summation. He focused on whether there was enough evidence that Frank Knapp had been "aiding and abetting" Dick Crowninshield in the killing, the key factor in whether the jury could find Frank guilty of second-degree murder. None of the prosecution's witnesses could positively identify Frank as one of the men seen near Captain White's mansion. Even if Frank had been in the street that night, was he there to help in the murder or just to see if Dick Crowninshield had gone through with the killing? If the jury determined it was the latter, then they could not find him guilty of the crime.

Dexter spent a good deal of time tearing apart the Rev. Colman's testimony, pointing out that Colman had gone to see Joe Knapp not to offer succor but "in deadly animosity" to wring a confession out of him. He reminded the jury that "when a clergyman steps out of the sphere of his duty, he becomes a man amongst men and should be treated as such and no otherwise."

The defense attorney emphasized that Webster, a U.S. senator, came into the case as a paid special prosecutor and tried to rush the jury "beyond the evidence and against the law." "The whole evidence is before you," Dexter told the jury. "Try him by the testimony, and as you truly try him, so may his God and your God judge you." Dexter's speech was forceful and eloquent. Most watching agreed he had done a fine job. Yet Webster—Black Dan—was up next. If he could use his famed skills to sway the jury in his favor, Frank Knapp would not escape the noose.

The courtroom fell silent as Webster stood to give his final summation to the jury on August 11. His physical stature—standing 5 feet 10 inches and weighing about 200 lb—was imposing, but it was his dark, piercing eyes, contrasted with his white and wild eyebrows, set into a massive head that gave him his true dynamism. He scanned the courtroom and then the jurors individually before launching into one of his finest speeches in a lifetime filled with them. The small courtroom was packed beyond capacity, and an even larger crowd stood outside the courthouse trying to hear what was being said. In the trees surrounding the building, children sat on branches trying to get a glimpse of the action through the windows.

Dexter had spent six hours over two days giving his final summation. Webster would outdo him by two hours. Webster began by setting the scene of Captain White's last moments, the approach of the killer through the mansion into the victim's bedroom, and the killer's cold and calculating nature. The entire courtroom was rapt. His speech was slow, sometimes halting, his tremulous voice almost like a musical instrument.

It was a cool, desperate, concerted murder. It was neither the offspring of passion nor revenge. The murderer was seduced by no lionlike temptation; all was deliberation; all was skillful.

And now that all is known it appears more atrocious than was ever apprehended. The murderer was a cool, business-like man, a calculator, a resolute and determined assassin.

The object was money, the crime murder, the price blood. The tale of silver was counted out, the price fixed. Here is the money, there is the victim—grains of silver against ounces of blood.

Under our New England example, murder has received a new character. Let the painter beware how he exhibits the murderer with the grim visage of Moloch. Let him not paint the bloodshot eye beaming with malice and red with revenge, but the cool face of an infernal spirit of another stamp about his ordinary business. Let his features be smooth and unruffled—all calmness, coolness, and deliberation. Not human nature in despair nor in paroxysms—no rushing of the blood to the face, no fiendish distortions, but calm and unagitated smoothness.

At the blessed hour when of all others repose is soundest, the murderer goes to his work. In the silence and darkness, he enters the house. He does not falter, there is no trembling of the limbs, his feet sustain him. He passes through the rooms, treads lightly through the entries, ascends the stairs, arrives at the door. There is no pause. He opens it. The victim is asleep, his back is towards him, his deaf ear is uppermost, his temples bare. The moonlight plays upon his silver locks. One blow, and the task is accomplished!

Now mark his resolution, his self-possession, his deliberate coolness! He raises the aged arm, plunges the dagger to the heart—not once but many times—replaces the arm, replaces the bedclothes, feels the pulse, is satisfied that his work is perfected and retires from the chamber. He retraces his steps. No eye has seen him, no ear has heard him. He is master of his own secret, and he escapes in secret.

That was a dreadful mistake. The guilty secret of murder never can be safe. There is no place in the universe, no corner, no cavern where he can deposit it and say it is safe. Though he take [*sic.*] the wings of the morning and fly to the uttermost part of the seas, human murder to human vision will be known. A thousand eyes, a thousand ears are marking and listening, and thousands of excited beings are watching his bloodstained step.

The proofs of a discovery will go on. The murderer carries with him a secret which he can neither carry nor discharge. He lives at war with himself; his conscience is a domiciled accuser that cannot be ejected and will not be silent. His tormentor is inappeasable, his burden is intolerable.

The secret which he possesses, possesses him, and like the evil spirit spoken of in olden times leads him whithersoever it will. It is a vulture ever gnawing at his heart; he believes his very thoughts to be heard.

His bosom's secret overmasters him, subdues him—he succumbs. His guilty soul is relieved by suicide or confession, and suicide is confession.[4]

Webster's lurid description of a murderer who could not help confessing to his crime was enthralling even a decade later when Poe would read the slightly altered version Webster had published.

It was one thing to stir the imagination of a writer, and quite another to convince the twelve jurors to send a fellow human to the gallows. This was especially true when the focus of his speech was on Dick Crowninshield, who was already dead, rather than on Frank Knapp, who was the one on trial.

Webster spoke for about six hours before court adjourned for the day around 7 p.m. He spent two more hours speaking the next morning, ending his speech in a homespun, easy-going tone, but with a veiled threat that if the jury did not make the right decision—finding Frank Knapp guilty—the choice would haunt them the rest of their days:

> It will follow you, gentlemen, it will follow us all, as duty accomplished or as duty neglected; and if there is anything which is at all times and everywhere present, it is the consciousness that we have discharged ourselves well of every important trust. This recollection will follow us in life and be with us in death. It will be with us in light, and ever near us when darkness covers us. At the close of life it will be with us; and at that solemn hour, the consciousness of duty discharged or duty neglected will be there to afflict us if disregarded, or to console us if under the will of the Almighty, it has been performed.[5]

On the afternoon of Thursday, August 12, after the court explained the pertinent points of law that the jury needed to do its job, the twelve men filed out to deliberate.

For hours, the jurors debated the ins-and-outs of the case but kept returning to whether it was Frank Knapp the witnesses had seen that night and if so whether he was "aiding and abetting" or only there out of curiosity. The next day, the jury reported being deadlocked and asked the court to explain the law once again.

The jurors went back to deliberating. Twenty-five hours later, the jury foreman told the court they were "nearly worn out" and there was no way the twelve men could agree on a verdict. The court reluctantly discharged the defeated jury. Frank and his defense lawyers did not have long to celebrate. The prosecution asked the court to impanel another jury right away on the same indictments and to move ahead with a second trial.

The defense argued that the court should postpone the new trial until the next regular court term in November. The "present state of public excitement" prevented Joe Knapp from getting a fair trial, Dexter said.

When the court determined that this was not a good enough reason to delay the case, Dexter changed tack and insisted the defense could not go to trial until one of their witnesses, Frank and Joe Knapp's brother, Samuel, who was then on a ship in South America, returned to Massachusetts. The prosecution stymied the delay by stipulating to what Samuel would have testified to: that he spoke with

Frank at their home at the time the prosecution alleged the murder took place. The defense's stalling tactic failed. The second trial would begin the next day.

Bennett stuck around for the second trial. The story was too good and the details too juicy to head back to New York before it was over. He had been taking notes throughout the trial and sending dispatches back to his editor in New York. His stories of Frank Knapp's trial strongly contradicted the prosecution's version of the crime and regularly appeared in the newspaper, despite the court's order barring daily coverage.

Bennett peppered his stories of the trial with his own insights and anecdotes about the various people involved, including Joe Knapp and the deceased Dick Crowninshield. He called Crowninshield:

> One of the most singular beings of his criminal profession, which history or fiction can show. Ever since his boyhood his deeds have been characterized with daring, hypocrisy, coolness, defiance of all law, and a calculation and ingenuity that would have raised him to eminence in society, if he had received a proper direction in his infancy.[6]

Of Joseph Knapp, Bennett wrote that "he managed his criminal concerns on his own hook," and was not part of Crowninshield's gang, being jealous of his friend's status among the other Salem rogues. "Knapp possesses, it is said, much vanity and superciliousness," he wrote. "His wife is considered one of the handsomest females in Essex county."[7]

Throughout the trial, the court had reprimanded Bennett for his coverage. At one point, Judge Putnam harangued the New York press, characterizing their news stories as incorrect and stupid, and warned the newsmen:

> If any one person was detected taking notes of the evidence in the Court House, for the purpose of sending them without the state for publication, previous to the conclusion of the trial, he would be proceeded against by the Court, as for a contempt.[8]

Bennett jeered at the court's threats, saying "it is an old, worm-eaten, and Gothic dogma of the Courts, to consider the publicity given to every event by the Press, as destructive to the interests of law and justice." He believed the honesty, purity, and integrity of "legal practice throughout this country, are more indebted to the American Press, than to the whole tribe of lawyers and judges who issue their decrees. The Press is the living jury of the nation."[9]

Judge Putnam never went through with his threats against the press since the court had no jurisdiction over the papers in adjoining states. Just before the lawyers picked a new jury for the retrial, several Boston publishers quickly put out pamphlets professing to be the most exact account of White's murder and Frank Knapp's trial, derailing the court order meant to stop the press from influencing jurors.

9

THE THREE RS

As autumn came to the Hudson Valley at the beginning of September 1830, West Point's summer encampment ended and the cadets were thrown headlong into academia. Poe took math and French, two subjects at which he excelled. His teachers covered material he was already familiar with, especially in French, and it bored him.

Each day, he woke to the spartan surroundings of 28 South Barracks, which held nothing more than cots, a washbasin, a small communal table, a few chairs, buckets, bookshelves, and a musket rack above the unadorned, open fireplace.

He shared the compact space with two other cadets, Thomas W. Gibson and Timothy Pickering Jones, who found their bunkmate standoffish. Gibson thought he had "a worn, weary, discontented look" about him and appeared to be much older than the other cadets.[1] When the two first became roommates, Poe saw a book by the Scottish poet Thomas Campbell sitting on the communal table. He picked up the book and leafed through it. "Campbell's a plagiarist," said Poe, tossing the book aside with contempt.[2] Poe's statement surprised Gibson, but he said nothing. Poe retrieved the book and again flipped through its pages until he found the passage he was looking for. He recited a line that he said Campbell had taken from the work of another Scottish poet, Robert Blair, telling Gibson that Campbell had ruined it in his efforts to disguise the theft. By his early twenties, Poe had already become obsessed with plagiarism. This preoccupation would lead to bitter animosity with other writers in the coming years.

Gibson and Jones' first impressions of Poe softened as they got to know him. Poe's wicked sense of humor, especially in lampooning their officers and faculty, went far in changing the boys' views on him. Soon, Poe's funny and pointed little poems and satires about life at the academy circulated from cadet to cadet, giving Poe a reputation as a wit and romantic with hints of genius.

This helped stave off hazing by upperclassmen, the bane of the plebes. Poe's having served a two-year term in the army, his aloof manner, and air of being much older also helped. A half-joking rumor began circulating around the academy that Poe had secured a position for his son who then died and that Poe then took the boy's place. Poe did not find it funny and fretted over jests made at his expense.

Poe cultivated an aura of mystery. He dropped hints of a dark and adventurous past filled with stories of sailing the Mediterranean and traveling through the deserts of Arabia and the jungles of South America after running away from his rich adoptive father. One cadet, David E. Hale, wrote about Poe to his mother after she had seen Poe's poem "*Al Aaraaf*" in a magazine. Hale recounted stories of Poe's adventurous life and how he had graduated from a college in England before becoming a soldier and entering West Point. "He is thought a fellow of talent here but he is too mad a poet to like Mathematics," Hale wrote to his mother.[3]

There was another rumor that Poe was the grandson of Benedict Arnold. A friend finally cornered him on this. Poe would neither confirm nor deny the rumor, adding to his mystery. It is possible that Poe believed he was related to the notorious traitor. He knew his mother's maiden name was Arnold, but he knew little else about her ancestry.

Poe's daily routine was rigid, more so than as an enlisted man. He woke at sunrise, attended lectures, lined up, and marched into the mess hall (as they did for every meal) for a light breakfast at 7 a.m. The food was awful—bland and nearly inedible. Then it was more lectures and then lunch. From there, it was a quick return to his barracks to change into his dress uniform for drills, known as the "parade," that lasted until sunset. Supper followed with more classes and then study time (although Poe spent a lot of his time writing instead) then a call to quarters at about 9 p.m. Taps signaled the end of the day and lights out. Sunday was the only day with no classes, but the cadets had to spend a lot of it at the chapel.

The academy was highly regimented under its superintendent, Major Sylvanus Thayer, a veteran of the War of 1812. Before taking charge of West Point in 1817, he had spent two years on a governmental mission in Europe studying the military arts. He instituted various changes, encompassing admission standards, a curriculum heavy on engineering, and a large dose of discipline that included a student-enforced honor system. The academy's motto, "Duty, Honor, Country," came from him.

The cadets had 304 regulations they had to abide by and officers liberally doled out demerits, known as "crimes," when they would randomly pop into the barracks for inspections. Cadets could earn demerits for everything from fighting to needing a shave to being tardy to class or roll call at meals. If a cadet racked up 200 in a year, he could be expelled.

Among the extensive list of regulations meant to police the cadets' behavior, there was no drinking, smoking, or gambling; cadets could not leave their rooms after lights out, and there was no cooking in the barracks. Then there was Regulation No. 173: "No Cadet shall keep in his room any novel, poem or other book, not relating to his studies, without permission from the superintendent." Poe just could not abide by this particular rule.

Yet this was a slight infraction compared to the one he and his roommates committed on a cold drizzly night in late November. They were out of brandy—having alcohol in the room was another of the regulations they broke—and Poe suggested they sneak over to see Old Benny Havens after lights out. Havens had once supplied the academy with provisions until the officers caught him smuggling liquor to the cadets one too many times. Thayer permanently banned Havens and his wife from West Point. Not one to be deterred, Havens opened a saloon about 1 mile south of the academy, where many a rebellious cadet had gone on a drinking spree.

That night, the three cadets drew straws to see who would make the run to Benny's. Gibson came up with the shortest straw. He started off a little after Taps, scampering in the dark toward the tavern carrying 4 lb of candles and Poe's last blanket. The cadets were short on cash and hoped to trade their goods for brandy. When Gibson arrived at the ramshackle saloon and grocery store, soaked to the skin and looking to barter, Benny was not too keen on the idea. He had already accumulated a pile of similar items for his chicken dinners and bottles of brandy and very little money. After Gibson begged and cajoled, the old man relented and the cadet made his way back with a bottle and an old gander he planned on cooking in their barracks, another "crime" in a long list of regulations the cadets violated that night.

The bird was squawking so loud Gibson asked Benny to dispatch it for him before leaving the tavern since he did not want to risk getting caught as he made his way back to the academy. Gibson, already hitting the bottle, carried the heavy bird first over one shoulder and then the other; he was soon awash in the goose's blood.

Poe was the designated lookout and waited for Gibson outside of the barracks. On seeing his friend streaked with blood, Poe thought he looked like a crazed killer and came up with a plan to scare their other roommate. They tied the bird's neck, feet, and wings together, the blood-soaked feathers standing up in all directions, until the creature was nearly unrecognizable.

Poe went back into their room and found Jones studying and another cadet from a separate barracks lounging as they waited for Gibson to return with the brandy. Poe sat down and began studying French as if all was normal. Gibson set the dead bird down outside the door and stumbled into the room, pretending to be drunk. Blood smeared his face and shirt front, horrifying the boys.

"My God! What has happened?" Poe gasped in mock surprise.

Gibson answered that a professor had surprised him as he was sneaking back into the academy. "He won't stop me on the road anymore," Gibson said, his eyes burning with feigned madness. He pulled out his knife, which he had stained in the gander's blood, and sliced the air. "I have killed him!"

"Nonsense!" Poe said, "you are only trying one of your tricks on us."

"I didn't suppose you would believe me, so I cut off his head and brought it into barracks. Here it is!"[4]

Gibson walked back outside, picked up the dead bird, and heaved it into the barracks. The bird crashed into the room's only candle, plunging everything into darkness. The visiting cadet leaped through a window and headed back to his own room, spreading the word to the other cadets that Gibson had murdered a professor. Gibson and Poe relit the candle and found Jones huddled in the corner, a look of horror on his face. They finally convinced him it had all just been a joke. They skinned the bird, chopped it into small pieces, cooked it in a tin washbasin over a fire, and made a meal of it, washed down with brandy. Gibson would recount the tale years later.

Even with Poe's adventures, his grades did not suffer. Out of a class of eighty-seven students, he had the third-highest marks in French and seventeenth in mathematics. His life at West Point was going well, but his unanswered letters to his foster father were weighing on his mind. He had not heard from Allan since June, five months earlier, and Poe's letters home were becoming more desperate.

10

SECOND CHANCES

Frank Knapp's second trial began on August 14, 1830. During this trial, the attorney general stepped back and gave Webster full control of the prosecution. Webster would not let his reputation suffer by allowing Frank Knapp to be acquitted. Webster could consider the first trial a run-through for this one, which made it easier to shape the pace and structure of his second go round. Based on the previous trial, Webster knew the testimony from all the witnesses. He had hoped to get Joe's confession into evidence, but the court denied him that opportunity. Webster was thankful that during this second trial the judges agreed to let Rev. Colman freely discuss Frank's alleged confession. Dexter, the defense attorney, strenuously objected to the court's decision, but to no avail.

Colman was again the star witness and went further in implicating Frank than in his earlier testimony, even though there was no written proof. The defense brought Phippen to the stand to counter Colman, but a clergyman's word carried more weight than that of the defendant's brother. Like Colman, many prosecution witnesses seemed to have better memories and sharper eyesight than in the first trial. The townsfolk who had seen two unidentified men near Captain White's home now positively identified Frank as being one of them. Palmer, the blackmailer, and Leighton, the teenage farmhand, both stuck to their stories. The second trial was not looking good for the defendant.

In his summation, Dexter decried Webster's eloquence over his obvious lack of evidence and the bloodthirsty atmosphere of Salem:

If there is legal evidence against the prisoner, can there be a doubt that he will be convicted? And if there is not, is a verdict of condemnation to be wrenched from you by talent and eloquence which the ordinary course of a criminal trial would fail to procure? There is, however, a more dangerous influence in this case. We care less for the array of counsel than for the array of the community against him. We have greatly feared the effect of this hostile atmosphere on the testimony. We have feared, and found, that in such a state of excitement no man could take the stand an indifferent witness. He is to be esteemed a public benefactor on whose testimony the prisoner is convicted, and he who shrinks from the certainty expected of him, does it at the peril of public displeasure and reproach. If proof of this were needed, it might be found abundantly in the variance of the evidence on the two trials of this cause, and this last reinforcement of evidence is but proof of what had been done for the conviction of the prisoner.[1]

The defense attorney then launched into an attack on the key prosecution witnesses—Palmer, Leighton, and Colman. Of Palmer, he said that he was "a convicted thief" and blackmailer who the authorities initially arrested as part of the murder plot. Palmer testified in hope of getting the reward and being released from jail, the attorney said.

Dexter called Leighton's testimony nothing more than "gross improbabilities" and "the clumsiest contrivance of a play, where the audience is informed of what has taken place behind the scenes by the actors telling each other what they have been doing together." The attorney pointed out that without Leighton's testimony, there would be no proof of a conspiracy, which was the cornerstone of the prosecution's case.

Dexter saved his most vehement comments for Rev. Colman, telling the jury that "no man in the community has been so excited by this horrible event as Mr. Colman. No man has taken a more active part in inquiring into its mysteries," and that "whatever the government cannot otherwise prove, Mr. Colman swears the prisoner has confessed and nothing more."

The defense attorney finished up his final summation by begging the jury not to let what he was sure would be a powerful and eloquent speech by Webster sway them and to rely only on the facts in evidence. Dexter told the twelve men:

> Yield nothing to it but admiration, unless it convinces your understanding that the evidence you have here heard, without regard to anything said or written elsewhere, ought to satisfy you of the fact that the prisoner was where he could aid in this murder, and by such presence did aid in it.[2]

He warned the jurors that if they let the prosecution stretch the law to hang Frank, history would judge them harshly.

> The time will come when this trial will be coolly and impartially examined ... It is on record forever. The murmurs of applause that will follow a verdict of guilty from the multitudes that now surrounds you will soon subside and another and more enduring voice will then enquire whether you have been faithful to the law and your oaths and consciences.[3]

The sweltering courtroom was again packed to overflowing as Webster stood up to give his summation. A throng of women arrived to hear Webster's final summation and many of the reporters, including Bennett, lost their seats to the ladies. It was so packed that one reporter grumbled that if you were to lose a shoe or your hat "it is lost irrecoverably. To stoop is annihilation; bob your head and it is gone."

Webster's second attempt to get Frank's neck into a noose meant mustering every ounce of his oratory skills. Building on his final summation from Frank's earlier trial, Webster incorporated the slightly different testimony given by witnesses in the first trial and attacked Dexter's argument.

Webster pushed aside the rush to judgment by the people of Salem and especially the Committee of Vigilance; the push to have the trial early; and his role in the prosecution as a hired gun as unimportant to the case. He did the same with Dexter's "complaints" about the believability of the prosecution's witnesses. Webster told the jury:

> This style of complaint had been carried to great extent against disinterested and respectable witnesses, as if it were as bad to have had a hand in the detection of the murderers, as in the perpetration of the crime; as if to have known anything of the murderers were an act of the most flagitious and exquisite wickedness ... And it would seem that because the crime has been detected by extraordinary exertions, the man accused ought to be mildly and calmly judged.[4]

Webster defended the people of Salem and the committee, saying that it was not a "zeal for blood to the head of the defendant," but a desire "that men may not be exposed to murder in their own houses unarmed, and that they should be quiet in the pursuit of their daily toil."

He stressed that if the jury did not find Frank Knapp guilty as the principal, they could not convict any of the other defendants of participating in the crime. It was a clear signal to the twelve men that if they did not convict Frank Knapp, no one would pay for the murder of Captain White.

"The fate of the whole depends upon this verdict; and it is for you, gentlemen, to determine whether this and the other prisoners are guilty and should suffer according to the law," he told them. He summarized the jury's three options for finding Frank guilty as the principal: as the person who committed the murder; as an aider and abettor to Dick Crowninshield who committed the murder; and third, as an aider and abettor to another, unknown, killer.

He admitted the case depended mainly on circumstantial evidence, but defended this by telling the jury that "secret crimes ever do, midnight assassins take no witnesses," so it was not surprising there was no direct evidence.

"It shall be my business to weave this stuff into a web, and see what may be made of it," Webster said, before walking the jury through the facts as he saw them: someone with access to Captain White's house had unlocked the window and had given the killer a detailed layout of the house; there was a conspiracy between the Knapps and Crowninshields; Joseph Knapp tried to pin the murder on Stephen White through the two letters he sent; Joseph Knapp stole Captain White's will; the Crowninshields told Palmer about their plans to kill Captain White; Leighton heard the Knapps discussing the murder; several townspeople had seen Dick and Frank near the captain's house that night; and both Joe and Frank Knapp had confessed to the Rev. Colman. Whether Webster had actually proven these facts did not matter as he wove them into a lurid tale with Frank Knapp at its center.

He then defended the prosecution witnesses that Dexter had spent several hours tearing down during his final summation. Webster admitted Palmer wasn't the most stolid citizen, but Palmer's story had held up. Webster said:

> I shall not attempt to purify his reputation or uphold his character either as a man or as a witness … He stands, of all the witnesses in this case, the most entirely absolved from contradiction, either in his own story or by the testimony of other witnesses. His story is throughout consistent and credible; no one has attempted to detect any, the slightest inconsistency in its details.[5]

Of Leighton, Webster admitted he was "a very bad witness" but if the jury believed him "his testimony has a momentous weight in this case." Leighton did not want to take the stand and his testimony was "simple, clear, distinct," which showed its truthfulness, Webster told the jury.

Rev. Colman, he said, was "a gentleman of high and well-known character, and of unquestionable veracity; as a clergyman, highly respectable; as a man, of fair name and fame," according to Webster. The prosecutor conflated good standing with truthfulness and hoped the jury would too. He wrapped up his summation by stating what he believed he had proven.

> Gentlemen, I shall detail you no longer. I think you can have no more doubt that the two Crowninshields and the two Knapps were conspirators for the murder of Joseph White. I think you cannot doubt that the murder was committed between ten and eleven on Tuesday evening of the sixth of April; that it was perpetrated by the hand of Richard Crowninshield; that somebody was in Brown Street to aid in the murder of Captain White; that that person must have been the defendant. He could not have gone there to expose himself for any idle motive of curiosity. He went there to abet the murderer, by appointment and agreement. He did abet; he did follow his agreement; and thus has exposed himself to public justice.[6]

He ended by reminding the men of their duty to God and country, their community, and "the public law," even if it meant that Frank Knapp would hang:

> Gentlemen, your whole concern should be to do your duty, and leave consequences
> to take care of themselves ... Your verdict, it is true, may endanger the prisoner's life,
> but then it is to save other lives. Towards him, as an individual, the law inculcates
> no hostility; but towards him, if proved to be a murderer, the law, and the oaths you
> have taken, and public justice demand that you do your duty.[7]

Webster finished his speech, Judge Putnam explained the law to the jury, and the men filed out to begin deliberations.

Bennett, the New York reporter, felt Frank Knapp's defense team had bungled the second trial, telling his readers that based on Dexter and Gardiner's performances, he found it "problematical that they will ever rise above the mediocrity of the profession." Bennett was not being fair. The lawyers were up against a famous orator and U.S. senator willing to twist the evidence to fit into his narrative and prosecution witnesses whose testimony during this trial was more damning to Frank Knapp than in the first one. It was up to the jury whether they would go with Webster's well-spun, dramatic version of Frank's role in the murder or Dexter's analytical reading that provided enough doubt to acquit his client.

The first trial had taken ten days, the second only six. The jury spent about five hours deliberating before returning its verdict. The twelve men solemnly entered the courtroom that suddenly went from a noisy clattering akin to a barroom to the silence of a church. The verdict—guilty of murder. Frank Knapp involuntarily grimaced at the words, but he made no further show of emotion. The judge ordered the prisoner to be held overnight and brought back at 9 a.m. for sentencing.

The next morning, before Judge Putnam pronounced the sentence, he asked Frank Knapp if he had anything to say. "I have only to say that I am innocent of the charge alleged against me," Frank replied, his eyes locked on the judge's, his jaw set.

Judge Putnam urged Frank to repent his sins, then he passed the death sentence. He ordered the prisoner to "be carried from hence to the prison from whence you came, and from thence to the place of execution and there be hanged by the neck until you are dead. And may God in his infinite grace have mercy on your soul."

Frank kept staring at Judge Putnam until the emotion of the moment overtook the judge, who burst into tears. Frank's eyes dropped, and he seemed like he too would give in to his despair. His body went rigid, and he forced himself to regain control. He dug a plug of tobacco out of his pocket, put it in his mouth, and started chewing it slowly and deliberately as his eyes once again went to those of the judge.

After being taken back to Salem jail, Frank joked with his guards and seemed unworried by his situation. He was nearly giddy, as if he had been acquitted rather than heading to the gallows in a few short weeks. Frank, who had just turned twenty, said he would rather hang than spend even a year in prison. He told a friend:

> No, I do not wish to live—from the first moment I awakened and found the murder had been committed, I have been wretched and have no desire to prolong my life …
> I endeavored to dissuade Joseph from it, and told him that though the side he was looking on was bright, there was also another side, black, black as hell.[8]

Throughout the following days, his mood swung wildly between nonchalance and desperation. He wrote letters to the court, pleading for his life and denying his guilt. His sister-in-law, Mary, had again tried to hang herself after learning of Frank's guilty verdict. She did not succeed. His father, Captain Knapp, had also attempted suicide during Frank's trial, but he survived thanks to Phippen, who cut him down from a rafter before he was strangled to death.

Salem's citizens, who had been enthralled by the murder and then Frank Knapp's two trials, got back to their normal lives. Author Nathaniel Hawthorne, then a twenty-six-year-old unknown writer who lived in Salem with his mother, wrote to his cousin's husband, John Dike, following Frank's trial. Hawthorne wrote that the city "now begins to grow rather more quiet than it has been since the murder of Mr. White, but I suppose the excitement will revive at the execution of Frank Knapp."

There was a brief flareup of intense interest when a rumor began circulating that Frank had escaped from jail—even making it into the newspapers—but the rumor turned out to be false.

Just outside the jail, workers erected a tall wooden scaffold in sight of the graveyard and the church where Dick Crowninshield hid the club used to kill Captain White. The Saturday before the execution, the jailer brought Joe Knapp from his third-floor cell to see his brother in the jail's lower level. It was the first time they had seen each other since the state had called Joe as a prosecution witness and he had refused to testify. Compared to his brother, Frank had changed little, remaining stolid, but Joe was a mess. Gaunt and pale, nearly incoherent, the hardy seaman looked nothing like he had only a few months earlier. He was not eating much, and he had a hard time sleeping. Joe asked Frank if he was doing as well as he appeared to be.

"Yes, I can sleep as sound now on the soft side of a plank as I ever could," he replied. They chatted like they always had, but their banter was draped in a death shroud. Frank mentioned that his lawyers had petitioned the governor for a pardon, but he had denied the request. There was nothing more to do.

The day before the execution, a Monday, the jailer took Joe to see Frank for the last time. Joe broke down during the visit, but his younger brother remained somewhat detached. Their father also visited that day. Captain Knapp's world was crumbling. He had just lost his shipping business and was still suffering from the death of his steadfast wife three years before. Now his twenty-year-old son was going to be hanged, and his eldest son was facing trial. It was nearly too much for him to bear. Finally, it was time to leave. He hugged his son for the last time.

Frank told Sheriff Joseph Sprague he wanted to be alone on his last night on earth, but the sheriff decided two guards should stay in the cell. No one wanted a repeat of the Crowninshield incident. Frank slept heavily for five solid hours, woke up, and had a cup of coffee; he then returned to bed for an hour longer. He got up and ate his breakfast as usual. He then washed and got dressed. He hoped he would be able to keep his nerve for the next few hours. The execution was scheduled for around 9 a.m. on Tuesday, September 28.

Rev. Alexander Griswold came to visit, as he had several times after Frank's trial. Frank wanted to get the religious services out of the way in his cell rather than at the gallows, which was the common practice, because he did not want to draw out the time he spent on the platform waiting to die. He broke down and cried during his meeting with Griswold, but by the time the sheriff told him they had to go, he had gotten his emotions in check.

Close to 4,000 spectators were there to watch Frank die. It seemed more like a fair than an execution with the hubbub of the massive crowd overseen by several police officers and extra constables tasked with keeping the gawkers in check.

The sheriff and his men escorted Frank—looking handsome in a dark-colored frock coat, blue pantaloons, and light-colored vest—through the jail and up the steps to the waiting noose. Griswold came with them. Frank Knapp walked with a firm step, neither hesitating nor appearing scared. He looked like he could have been taking a walk through the woods on a cool evening, except that they pinioned his arms behind his back. He walked up the stairs and onto the platform, putting one foot on the trapdoor as if to test whether it could hold his weight before making his way behind the noose so the executioner could adjust it around his neck.

As he stood on the platform, he took a deep ragged breath, the only sign of the inner turmoil he was experiencing as death quickly approached. They untied Frank's hands and bound his feet as they made the final preparations for the execution. Frank did not want to draw it out and had asked the sheriff to allow him to drop his handkerchief as a signal that he was ready to die. They placed the noose around his neck. Frank pulled the white handkerchief from his breast pocket and held it tightly in his hand.

The sheriff read the death warrant in a loud voice as much for the massive crowd as for the prisoner. "Do you have anything to say?" The sheriff asked the prisoner.

"No," was his simple reply. It would be the last words Frank Knapp ever spoke. The executioner slipped the hood over Frank's head and adjusted the noose. Frank dropped the handkerchief before the men were ready. It fluttered to the ground. A few seconds later, the platform he was standing on dropped. Frank shot down and bounced at the end of the rope. His chest heaved and his hand went up convulsively and then dropped at his side. In three minutes, he was dead. A sense of horror overtook the crowd at the sight of Frank's death struggle.

The body hung there for nearly an hour before finally being cut down and placed in a casket that workers carried inside the jail. The crowd dispersed.

The jailer allowed Joe Knapp to see his brother's body that day. He hugged his younger brother's corpse, knowing he might soon join him in the grave. When he returned to his cell, he fainted.

His family buried Frank next to his mother in the graveyard just over the fence from the jail. All of Salem wondered if they would need another grave next to the one that had been freshly dug for Frank Knapp.

11

HAUNTED

The trial of Joseph Knapp for the accessory before the fact in the murder of Captain Joseph White began on Tuesday, November 9, 1830, and saw many of the same players as his brother's trial. It was the same three-judge panel made up of Putnam, Wilde, and Morton. Dexter and Gardiner were now defending Joe after losing his brother's case. That memory haunted the defense attorneys. It looked like it haunted Joe Knapp, too. He was gaunt, ghostly pale, and had a hunted caste to his eyes.

By this time, he knew that if he had testified at his brother's trial, Frank would probably still be alive and Joe would not be in court facing the gallows. Joe's testimony would have shown that Dick Crowninshield committed the murder by himself and that Frank had only snuck out of the house to find out if he had done the deed and not to "aid and abet." The jury could have found Frank not guilty, and without a principal in the murder case, Joe Knapp and George Crowninshield could have gone free. Webster admitted as much. Joe Knapp's terrible blunder had cost his brother's life and possibly his own.

Webster was back as a private prosecutor for the state. Attorney General Perez Morton again asked the court to allow Webster to help in the prosecution. Yet this time, Dexter spoke up and objected to Webster's presence, having seen first-hand what the brilliant orator could do:

> I'm sorry to be obliged to object to the appearance of that distinguished gentleman in my place where he himself thought it proper to appear … But this is introducing a new principle of jurisprudence and subjecting every person brought to the bar to a danger not contemplated by the law. No case can be cited, I believe, where a private prosecutor has been allowed to be employed and paid by counsel to assist in the conviction of a prisoner.[1]

Webster jumped in and told the court that he was only there at the behest of the attorney general and that "no other inducement has had the least influence on me." Considering Stephen White had given Webster $1,000 at the beginning of Frank Knapp's trial, Webster's statement was a half-truth, if not an outright lie. The money was indeed an "inducement." The court allowed Webster to once again assist in prosecuting the case.

Webster needed to convince the court to allow Joe Knapp's confession into evidence if he had a chance of winning this case. When Colman first showed up at Joe's cell after his arrest, he came in the guise of a minister, not a prosecutor. Joe thought he was confessing to a priest and believed what he had told him was privileged information that could not be used against him. When Joe gave his written confession, it was under the promise he was being granted immunity from prosecution. Typically, a confession given because of an inducement, threat, or promise is not admissible at trial.

Webster argued that Joe was only promised immunity if he testified, not for his written confession, and so when he refused to take the stand at his brother's trials, he gave up those rights. Dexter countered that his client gave his oral and written confessions under the same promise of immunity, so neither should be allowed in evidence.

The court gave a written decision the next morning, Thursday, November 11. Everyone knew how important the confession would be to the case, and townspeople thronged the courthouse before it even opened, hoping to be there for the court's decision. The judges agreed with Webster that the promise of immunity was tied to Joe Knapp testifying in court and not to the confession. Judge Putnam said that by allowing Joe to "trifle with the government by making or retracting his agreement at pleasure," he had squandered the opportunity to save his brother's life, since Frank could have taken the promise of immunity for himself. Putnam's statement tortured Joe, who felt responsible for his brother's death. He knew that with his confession in evidence, he too was a dead man.

The prosecutor read Joe's confession to the jury. The defense knew this was massively damaging to their case, but Dexter had an idea. He argued that Joe's confession proved that Frank was not with Dick Crowninshield during the murder, so Frank should not have been convicted as the principal. If there was no principal, then Joe could not be charged as an accessory. This argument fell flat, making no impression on the judges.

The prosecution called Rev. Colman to the stand. He described how he had convinced Joe to confess and walked the jury through the confession. The court also allowed the two letters Joe Knapp sent as Grant blaming Stephen White for the murder to come into evidence. As the defense's case crumbled, Dexter pleaded with the court for an adjournment so they could strategize. The court denied the request.

During the defense's opening, Gardiner, Knapp's other attorney, tried to convince the jury that Joe's confession proved Frank Knapp could not be the principal and that Joe Knapp therefore should not be prosecuted as an accessory.

The defense brought in several witnesses who testified that it could not have been Frank Knapp who was seen near the White mansion on the night of the murder. It was a rather listless counter to the prosecution's case, but there was little they could do.

Dexter gave the final summation and spent more than three-and-a-half hours trying to save his client's life. He flattered the "impartial and intelligent" jury, telling the twelve men that he did not feel the "tremendous weight of prejudice" he had felt when defending Joe's brother, Frank Knapp, during the earlier trial. He asked for justice for his client and nothing more. As in his previous closing arguments, Dexter derided the prosecution's hiring of Webster to do their bidding.

Webster closed for the prosecution on the fourth and final day of the trial. He once again gave an eloquent speech, holding the courthouse spellbound:

> We have arrived to the second, and would to God it were the last act, of a dark and bloody tragedy, which for its enormity finds no parallel in the long history of crime … The prisoner at the bar has already caused the death of three individuals; first, the aged victim of this conspiracy—second, Richard Crowninshield, who perished by his own hands—and thirdly, John Francis Knapp, his younger brother.[2]

Webster reviewed his interpretation of the evidence and relevant laws, before, as in his previous two closing arguments, he used his power of scene-setting and eloquent phrasing to describe White's murder "within this quiet town, which for coolness and cold-blooded barbarity, stands alone in the calendar of human depravity."

He described Joe Knapp as "an unhappy man encompassed in a sea of blood" and then launched into a vivid description of the night of the murder. Each version of this speech became more refined and descriptive, from the moonlit "gray hairs of the sleeper, visible in the breeze" to the "smoothing of the bed clothing" by Dick Crowninshield following the murder.

Joe Knapp's confession was the coffin; Webster's final summation, the nails that sealed the lid. The jury spent four hours deliberating before returning a verdict. The twelve men quietly filed into the courtroom. The clerk asked them whether they had agreed upon a verdict. In unison, they answered "yes."

"What say you, mister foreman, is Joseph Jenkins Knapp, the prisoner at the bar, guilty or not guilty?" the clerk asked.

"Guilty," replied the jury foreman. Like his brother Frank had done, Joe grimaced when he heard the verdict. As they led him to jail to await his sentencing in two days, he appeared stoic, resigned to his fate.

The jury in Joe Knapp's trial was still deliberating when George Crowninshield's trial before the same judges began on the afternoon of November 12, 1830. Two guards brought Crowninshield into the courtroom. The defendant was tall and muscular, with high cheekbones, grey eyes, and pale, yellow, curly hair. George, twenty-five, had become somewhat flabby during his time in captivity. He pleaded not guilty to the charges and sat next to his attorneys, Samuel Hoar (who had replaced John Walsh) and Ebenezer Shillaber. George appeared relaxed.

Hoar was a well-known lawyer and politician from Concord, Massachusetts. He came from a prominent political family and had been a state senator. Hoar would go on to be a U.S. congressman and an important anti-slavery advocate in the decades leading up to the Civil War. Shillaber, a local attorney, assisted.

The state solicitor general, John Davis, who had taken a back seat during the previous trials, gave the opening address. It would be only him and the attorney general handling Crowninshield's trial as Webster had business elsewhere. Davis' opening lacked Webster's panache and verbosity but got the point across: George Crowninshield, while not present at the actual murder, knew about the conspiracy to murder Captain White and took part in it.

Palmer, who had brought down the entire plot, was the first witness. The prosecution had not needed him during Joe Knapp's trial, but he had a starring role in Crowninshield's trial. Palmer described how the Crowninshields had offered him one-third of the money if he helped kill Captain White; how he had left town and later returned to borrow money from Dick Crowninshield; and how he had written the first blackmail letter to Joe Knapp under the assumed name Grant.

Under cross-examination, Palmer tried to explain why he had gone by an alias by saying he simply preferred it. He admitted that after he left the Crowninshields, he ran up a debt at an inn and gave his name as George Crowninshield to avoid paying the bill. He did not appear to be a very reliable witness.

The prosecution also called Mary Weller, a local brothel owner, to tell how one of her girls, Mary Bassett, had discovered George's dagger tucked under her pillow. The witness ended up providing Crowninshield with an alibi for the night of the murder. She told the jury George had spent the entire night in Bassett's bed, as he often did.

At the end of the prosecution's case, Hoar, Crowninshield's lawyer, lambasted the government's case, calling it "absurd" and asked the court to throw it out. "There is not a tittle of evidence to criminate the prisoner, except that given by Palmer, which was altogether unworthy of credit," he told the court. "It was not a case badly made out; but it was one not made out at all." However, the court allowed the case to continue.

The defense entered Palmer's criminal record into evidence, and the innkeeper testified about Palmer stiffing him on the bill and giving his name as George Crowninshield. That was the defense's entire case. After closing arguments and an explanation of the relevant law by Justice Putnam, the jury left the courtroom to deliberate. As the jury filed out, they brought in Joe Knapp for sentencing.

When Judge Putnam asked Joe whether he had anything to say before passing judgment, Joe did not answer. When Putnam again asked him, Joe still could not articulate what he wanted to say and instead broke down crying. He could barely stand and nearly passed out.

Judge Putnam then launched into a verbal assault on the prisoner in which he dragged Joe through the muck and mire of his crime. In Joe's state, it was akin to a physical assault. Putnam described how Captain White had been generous to Joe and his wife over the years and how Joe had repaid him for that kindness. He said:

> The aged sufferer was a near relative of your wife … She was nurtured at his house and loved and cherished by him as a child. You were admitted to partake of his hospitality—you availed yourself of the opportunities to visit at the house of the deceased, to prepare the way for the entrance of your hired assassin to the bedchamber of the victim. You were for months deliberately occupied with devising the ways and means of his death. Horrible to think! While you were eating his bread, at his own table, you were plotting against his life.[3]

The judge continued, telling Knapp that if this crime had been a work of fiction, no one would have believed it, finding it "too absurd and unnatural for public endurance. Who would have imagined that young, well-educated men—having respectable connections and means of living—could have been found in our cultivated society, ready to join in such a fearful conspiracy?"[4]

Justice Putnam beseeched Knapp to beg God's forgiveness before uttering the terrible words that end all such speeches:

> Our last duty remains to be performed, which is to pass the sentence of the law, for the crime of which you have been convicted, which this sentence is, and this court accordingly adjudge, that you are to be taken from hence to the prison from whence you came, from thence to the place of execution, and there to be hanged by the neck until you shall be dead. And may God of his infinite grace have mercy on your soul.[5]

Afterward, Crowninshield returned to court. He stood in the spot just vacated by Knapp. He seemed unconcerned, a slight smile playing across his face, humming tunelessly as he waited to hear his fate.

The jury returned in just over an hour. The verdict—not guilty. A cheer went up in the courtroom from Crowninshield's friends. A stern rebuke from the court quickly extinguished the noise. Judge Putnam told the crowd that "a repetition of the offence would be followed by the severest punishment the court could inflict, upon as many of the offenders as could be detected."

George Crowninshield was saved as much by his penchant for prostitutes as the public's apparently waning interest in retribution. Bennett, now back in New York, noted that readers had grown tired of hearing about the Salem murder.

Crowninshield had another charge against him, misprision of felony for "having had knowledge of a conspiracy to murder Captain White" and keeping it a secret.

That trial came on November 27. It lasted a single day, and the jury took all of half an hour deliberating before returning a not-guilty verdict. Crowninshield appeared to enjoy his time in court. George was the only defendant to escape the noose. He was free. His old friend, Joe Knapp, was not so lucky.

In the weeks following Joseph Knapp's sentencing on November 15, 1830, he spent long hours reading the Bible and speaking with clergy while he awaited an answer from Governor Levi Lincoln, Jr., about a hoped-for pardon or a commutation to life in prison that his lawyers had requested. They alleged someone else was behind the crime. Joe's wife and his father also pressed the governor, hoping to save Joe from the gallows.

Rumors circulated around Salem that others had been involved in the murder plot, specifically, Mary White Beckford, Joe Knapp's mother-in-law. It did not help that Mary Beckford had sent a letter to Stephen White asking him not to help save Joe, if he had been so inclined. She thought it better if they hanged him.

"Suspicions, as horrible as they are, have almost become certainty," Stephen wrote in a letter to Webster, in which he called Beckford a "wretched woman," and the "very devil," who seeks Joe's "life to smother further investigation."

Even *The Salem Gazette*, without naming Beckford, intimated she had been the mastermind behind the murder plot and may have attempted to carry out the murder herself by poisoning Captain White before the Knapps hired Dick Crowninshield to kill the old man:

> Both Knapps have intimated as much; and all that are acquainted with them, know it was not in character for them to have planned it; they were too passive and inert to have conceived, or to have executed, such an enterprise of their own heads.[6]

The *Rhode Island American,* reprinted the *Gazette* article and then laid into its editors, opining that "one would suppose that the Salem people were glutted with blood, and yet their editors are crying for more," linking Salem's supposed bloodlust with its notorious witch trials of nearly 150 years earlier:

> Three lives for one would not satisfy them, and they really seem to long for a female subject to harrow up the public feeling with. The Salem Gazette, in an article which we publish today, has let slip the dogs of suspicion against some one bearing the form of woman. The fact is that an attempt is making to damn the house keeper of Mr. White in public opinion, and drag her before the gaping multitude; and all because Joe Knapp wishes to save his own life by taking that of a woman. In God's name let us be spared this horror in the Salem tragedy. Even if the woman be guilty, let her go and sin no more. We do not believe it, we will never believe it, even of the vilest population of Salem, where they seem to have acquired an extraordinarily high relish for public executions. Must we on opening their papers forever find them stained with blood, blood, blood.[7]

Newspapers as far away as Arkansas and North Carolina published these rumors and alleged Beckford had been arrested. The story was untrue.

Joe's days slowly slipped away in a swirl of memories of better times, the mental anguish of his many sins, and the hope of a miracle. The night before Joe was to die, he slept fitfully. He woke early and read a few passages from the Bible. He ate and dressed. Rev. John Cleaveland, who had been there the previous evening, returned, and the two spoke about the afterlife. His former pastor, Henry Colman, had not been to see Joe since the day he wrung a confession out of him. Joe had become penitent and resigned to his fate. No last-minute commutation was coming from the governor. He asked Cleaveland to warn others of what awaited those drawn to a life of sin.

Joe recalled the heartbreaking scene the last time he saw his wife the night before. She was inconsolable. When she left, Joe's father held her up to keep her from collapsing.

On Friday, December 31, 1830, at 8.53 a.m., Joe walked to the gallows. It was a bitterly frigid day, but whether he shivered from the temperature or his impending demise was anyone's guess. His ragged breath came in bursts of steam as he stood with a guard to his left and right who held him up as the sheriff read the death warrant.

The crowd was slightly smaller but even less subdued than the one who witnessed his brother Frank's execution. Joe looked haggard and dejected but otherwise composed. At 9.10 a.m., they placed the noose around his neck, then the hood. Seconds later, the trapdoor flew open. He dropped and bounced back into the air, his body jerking several times afterward, spinning on the end of the rope. The crowd stared at the body as it convulsed for five minutes before going still. Joe hung there for thirty minutes before they cut him down, placed his body in a coffin, and took him into the jail. Joe's family buried him next to his brother, within sight of the jail where the brothers spent their final months and where they paid with their lives for a murder plot that began on a whim but quickly spun out, dragging down families, reputations, and shaking Salem to its core.

12

AFTERMATH

On July 24, 1888, George Crowninshield died at his home in Roxbury, Massachusetts, 30 miles south of Salem. It had been nearly sixty years since he had gone to trial for Captain White's murder. George had not heeded either his brother's or Joe Knapp's warning to turn away from vice, and he suffered not a whit for it. Hawthorne, writing to a friend in September 1831, said, "George Crowninshield still lives at his father's and seems not at all cast down by what has taken place. I saw him walk by our house, arm-in-arm with a girl."[1]

George later moved to Boston and retired in Roxbury, a fashionable suburb that was being transformed by Irish and German immigrants before Boston annexed it in 1868. He traveled extensively and spent his time studying science as a hobby. He married and had a daughter who took after him as far as flouting tradition went. She married a Boston haberdasher against her father's will, and George cut her off for defying him. She got her revenge by opening a candy store near his home so he would be forced to see her every time he left his house. Her daughter likewise married below what the blue bloods considered her station. When George died, he left an estate totaling more than $2 million in today's terms.

In a cosmic joke of sorts, a year before Crowninshield's death, police arrested Jimmie Halfpenny, a teenager who ran errands for George, for bilking the old man out of several thousand dollars. The young rogue spent some of the stolen money renting the fastest horse and buggy in town. Halfpenny roared around Roxbury, sending pedestrians scurrying, as George Crowninshield once did in Salem.

George's old friend, John Palmer, the man most responsible for revealing the murder plot, stuck around Salem after his release from jail. He attempted to get the reward money Stephen White had put up in April 1830 but to no avail. The money went to the Committee of Vigilance. Palmer was a pariah because of his association with the Crowninshields, so he attempted to vindicate himself by publishing a book detailing his role in the case; *Explanation: or 1830; being a series of facts connected with the life of the author, from 1825 to the present day* was part adventure story and part rant against the justice system. The book did nothing to rehabilitate Palmer's reputation.

Joe Knapp's widow, Mary, and her mother, Mary White Beckford, continued to live at the farm in Wenham under a constant cloud of malicious gossip that Beckford was the real mastermind behind Captain White's murder. Four years later, Mary remarried. Her new husband was a Boston lawyer. Her mother died several years later at seventy-nine.

Following the upending of the Knapp family, Phippen left Salem and moved to nearby Marblehead to practice law. Most of the rest of the family moved to Manhattan. The emotional strain of that terrible year of 1830—the execution of two of his brothers and the obliteration of his father's shipping business— pushed Phippen away from the law and towards the cloth. He became an Episcopal priest in 1833 and befriended Bishop Griswold, who had been there for his brother Frank before his execution. Griswold ended up buying Captain White's mansion after the murder.

Phippen moved to New York to be nearer to his family and soon married. His father, Joseph, Sr., remarried and opened a small cigar-making business. When Phippen's wife died suddenly, he moved to Alabama as a missionary before serving at Christ's Church in Mobile in 1843 during a raging yellow fever epidemic. He would later return to become the rector there. His second wife, whom he married in 1844, was a genteel Southerner named Ellen McMaken Lee; she was Robert E. Lee's cousin. Phippen died of yellow fever when he was forty-five in 1854.

Stephen White stayed in Boston, giving up on his hometown of Salem. He continued his close friendship with Webster, which became even closer when White's daughter, Caroline, married Webster's son, Fletcher. He bankrolled Webster's political campaigns and paid a second cousin of the Knapps to write Webster's memoir. The book included a section on Captain White's murder that helped solidify Stephen's version of the case. White would be a prime mover in developing the neighborhood of East Boston. He attempted to create a vast timber and shipbuilding empire, among other endeavors, but fell into financial trouble and died in 1841. He was fifty-four.

Webster never achieved his dream of becoming president, but he served three presidents as secretary of state—William Henry Harrison, John Tyler, and Millard Fillmore. He focused on consolidating federal power when the Southern states were pushing states' rights; expanded foreign trade that helped boost the young nation's international standing; and helped calm long-standing problems with England through an 1843 treaty that settled the border of Maine with Canada.

His attempt to forestall the U.S. Civil War through his support of the Compromise of 1850 that strengthened the Fugitive Slave Law was a dark blot on his legacy. The Compromise was a package of bills that opened up slavery in the new territories of Utah and New Mexico, brought California into the Union as a free state, prohibited slave-trading in the nation's capital (but not slave-owning), and bolstered the Fugitive Slave Law. The law allowed for the capture and return of runaway enslaved people anywhere in the United States and required citizens to help in apprehending them, levying heavy punishments for those who did not. It also denied enslaved people the right to a trial by jury.

Webster, as a U.S. senator for Massachusetts, gave his powerful support to the Compromise through his famous "Seventh of March" speech to the chamber that helped the series of acts pass. He believed the Compromise would help keep the country together, but it only slowed the inevitable rending of the nation a decade later at a heavy cost to enslaved people.

Webster did not have to wait for history to judge him harshly for this stance, for all of New England immediately reacted with anger and disgust. They accused him of attempting to gain the support of Southern politicians for a presidential run and of moral treason against New England. He lost his senate seat over his decision. A heavy drinker his whole life, he died of liver cirrhosis in 1852 while serving as Fillmore's secretary of state. He was seventy.

A year after the Salem murder, Rev. Henry Colman left the church. He had been interested in agriculture for a long time and threw himself headlong into the subject after buying a farm in Western Massachusetts, where he grew corn and raised pigs. He wrote extensively on alternative methods of production and served as Massachusetts's first agricultural survey commissioner. Besides writing about American farming methods, he also looked into European agricultural systems and rural economies, with his two-volume book on the subject running through six editions.

In 1845, he moved to England, where he ingratiated himself with the nobility, becoming an intimate friend of several royals, including Charles Gordon-Lennox, 5th Duke of Richmond, a well-known Conservative politician. He was among only a few Americans, especially those without a lofty position or fame, who was so well-received by the English nobility. The British philosopher Thomas Carlyle, writing to the American poet Ralph Waldo Emerson, called Colman "a kind of Agricultural Missionary, much in vogue here at present."

He returned to Salem in the fall of 1848 and published a book of the letters he had written to his wife and friends while in England called *European Life and Manners*. Colman should have probably stuck to agricultural subjects, for the books' gossipy content about the rich and famous he had known did not go over well with the subjects he had written about.

The British press was not kind. The writer Charles Dickens wrote an essay, "An American in Europe," that appeared in London's *The Morning Chronicle*, excoriating Colman's book for its obsession with the nobility.

Why an honest Republican, coming from the United States to England on a mission of inquiry of ploughs, turnips, mangelwurzel, and live stock, cannot be easy unless he is forever exhibiting himself to his admiring countrymen, with a countess hanging on each arm, a duke or two walking deferentially behind, and a few old English barons (all his very particular friends) going on before, we cannot, to our satisfaction, comprehend.[2]

Dickens said that if Colman ever wrote anything similar again, "he may rely upon it that the nearest fire will be its fittest destination."

Other London periodicals had similar reviews. "We promise him that should he return to this country, he will never be asked to their houses again," one reviewer wrote. The prediction was correct. Colman returned to England, and as the newspapers predicted, the nobility he had courted for so long shunned him. He died of typhus in the London suburb of Islington on August 17, 1849. He was sixty-four. Lady Byron, the English mathematician and widow of the poet Lord Byron, paid for his funeral. He was buried in London's Highgate Cemetery.

Whether Poe was aware of Captain White's murder and the subsequent trials of the Knapp brothers and George Crowninshield at the time they occurred is not known, but at some point, he came across Webster's speech and learned about the murder. Webster's description of Dick Crowninshield as a calculating, ice-cold killer would help Poe create the nameless narrator of "The Tell-Tale Heart."

13

LEAVING (AFTER THE LETTER)

Poe read the letter from his foster father, and his stomach dropped. He had been excited to hear from Allan after receiving no letters from him for seven months, especially since it was the Christmas holidays. His joy was short-lived. Bully Graves, his old friend from his army days, had contacted Allan to recoup the money Poe owed him and a few other officers. Poe had accrued several debts during his stint in the army he had not been able to pay back.

Poe wrote to Graves in May 1830, a few weeks before he left Richmond to head to West Point, that he had not been able to get the money from his foster father even though he had tried many times. In the letter, he explained Allan "is not very often sober," a statement that was not altogether true. Graves forwarded Poe's letter to Allan in an attempt to collect the funds himself.

Allan was enraged by what Poe had written to Graves. He told Poe he never wanted to hear from him again. He would disinherit his foster son, Poe believed. To make it worse, Poe was just about to start his mid-term examination, a time when he should be focusing on his studies, which now seemed impossible. Angered by what he felt was Allan's unfair treatment of him, Poe launched into a four-page response. While all his previous letters from West Point had begun "dear pa" this one, which he sent in early January 1831, was much colder.

> Sir,
>
> I suppose (altho' you desire no further communication with yourself on my part,) that your restriction does not extend to my answering your final letter.

Poe lashed out, starting with his childhood. "Did I, when an infant, solicit your charity and protection, or was it of your own free will, that you volunteered your services in my behalf?" He alleged that his wealthy grandfather, General David

Poe, would have taken him in if Allan had not convinced the general that he and his wife would formally adopt Poe and give him a good education. "Under such circumstances, can it be said that I have no right to expect any thing [*sic.*] at your hands?"

On December 8, 1811, a month before Poe turned three, his mother, the actress Elizabeth Arnold Poe, died while performing in Richmond. His father, David, had died the same month after abandoning the family. It was only a few days later that John and Frances Allan took Poe in, while another Richmond family cared for his younger sister, Rosalie. Henry, the oldest sibling, went to live in Baltimore with relatives.

This letter played out like many of the arguments Poe and Allan had over the years, especially after Allan forced Poe to leave the University of Virginia only ten months into his studies. Poe had never forgiven Allan for not providing him with enough money for school and rehashed the incident from four years earlier. Poe went into minute detail of how Allan's stinginess, down to the dollar, forced Poe to borrow money, and resort to gambling as a final desperate act, to make up for Allan's lack of financial support while he was at UVA. He said the other students treated him like a beggar. Poe blamed Allan for his taking solace in drinking and hanging around with disreputable characters.

> Here you will say that it was my own fault that I did not return—You would not let me return because bills were presented you for payment which I never wished nor desired you to pay. Had you let me return, my reformation had been sure—as my conduct the last 3 months gave every reason to believe—and you would never have heard more of my extravagances. But I am not about to proclaim myself guilty of all that has been alleged against me, and which I have hitherto endured, simply because I was too proud to reply. I will boldly say that it was wholly and entirely your own mistaken parsimony that caused all the difficulties in which I was involved while at Charlotteville [*sic.*].
>
> It was then that I became dissolute, for how could it be otherwise? I could associate with no students, except those who were in a similar situation with myself—alho' from different causes—They from drunkenness, and extravagance—I, because it was my crime to have no one on Earth who cared for me, or loved me. I call God to witness that I have never loved dissipation—Those who know me know that my pursuits and habits are very far from any thing [*sic.*] of the kind. But I was drawn into it by my companions Even their professions of friendship—hollow as they were—were a relief.[1]

After leaving the university and returning to Richmond, Poe hoped Allan would give him a job. It never happened. Poe knew how to needle his foster father. He dredged up the memory of Frances' death as a weapon against Allan.

I came home, you will remember, the night after the burial—If she had not have died while I was away there would have been nothing for me to regret—Your love I never valued—but she I believed loved me as her own child.[2]

While it is true that Allan left his ward in an untenable situation at UVA and did not give him a position at his firm, Poe's self-indulgent whining did nothing to help his cause. He made it worse in the last passage of his letter from West Point. He ended with a melodramatic flourish, in which he claimed he would soon be dead because of ill health exacerbated by Allan's poor treatment of him:

> As regards Sergt. Graves—I did write him that letter. As to the truth of its contents, I leave it to God, and your own conscience.—The time in which I wrote it was within a half hour after you had embittered every feeling of my heart against you by your abuse of my family, and myself, under your own roof—and at a time when you knew that my heart was almost breaking.
>
> I have no more to say—except that my future life (which thank God will not endure long) must be passed in indigence and sickness. I have no energy left, nor health, If it was possible, to put up with the fatigues of this place, and the inconveniences which my absolute want of necessaries subject me to, and as I mentioned before it is my intention to resign. For this end it will be necessary that you (as my nominal guardian) enclose me your written permission. It will be useless to refuse me this last request—for I can leave the place without any permission— your refusal would only deprive me of the little pay which is now due as mileage.
>
> From the time of writing this I shall neglect my studies and duties at the institution—if I do not receive your answer in 10 days—I will leave the point without—for otherwise I should subject myself to dismission.
>
> E. A. Poe[3]

Poe had been unhappy with the academy for some time. He had quickly come to realize that there was no way he would graduate in six months. The incessant drilling, which he already knew by heart from his prior service, was an irritation that grew each day. In November, his roommate Timothy Jones was court-martialed for gross neglect of his academic and military duties. Jones wanted to leave the academy, but his parents refused to sign off on the move, so Jones stopped attending classes and military exercises, intending to get himself kicked out.

Poe did not hear back from his foster father and Allan did not write the academy giving his permission for Poe to resign his post. Poe, uncertain of what to do, followed Jones' lead, and on January 8, five days after writing the letter to Allan, he began purposefully neglecting his duties.

Three days later, he changed his mind and once again began attending formations. He somehow got away with it and suffered no direct punishment. The following week, still having heard nothing from Allan, he again stopped taking part in the world of West Point. He refused to attend evening parades, roll calls, class parades, and guard duty twenty-three times, and he stopped attending his academic classes. He stayed in his room eating little and waiting for the inevitable. It came on January 23 when he disobeyed a direct order to attend chapel and was arrested. A few days later, he again ignored a direct order to attend his classes. It was his last chance.

Allan received Poe's letter on February 10, and three days later, he wrote a note on the back of it:

> I do not think the Boy has one good quality ... He may do or act as he pleases, tho' I wd have saved him but on his own terms & conditions since I cannot believe a word he writes. His letter is the most barefaced one-sided statement.[4]

Allan never responded to Poe.

On January 28, 1831, Poe's court-martial began with Lieutenant Thomas J. Leslie of the Corps of Engineers, the academy's paymaster, overseeing the proceedings. Poe was charged with two counts of gross neglect of duties and disobedience of orders. He pleaded not guilty to one count of gross neglect and guilty to everything else. By pleading not guilty to easily provable charges, he guaranteed that they would kick him out of West Point. He had no lawyer representing him and only one witness, his friend and fellow cadet, John Henderson, who was a character witness and provided no help regarding the charges, of which they found him guilty.

Secretary of War John H. Eaton signed off on the decision, and Poe left West Point for New York City on February 19. Poe, who had turned twenty-two the month before, was free but at a torturous price. He was cut off from the only man he had known as a father; he had put a match to his military career that was now a smoldering ruin; and he had no place to live, no job prospects, and little money.

In a freezing New York winter, he left the academy without a heavy coat or other warm clothes. He had collected subscriptions from his fellow cadets for a forthcoming book of poetry. Nearly all the cadets chipped in, believing the book would contain the satirical verses he had become well-known for among his classmates.

He arrived in New York City, suffering from an ear infection and chest cold that laid him low. In a shaky hand, he wrote another letter to his foster father, begging Allan for money:

> In spite of all my resolution to the contrary I am obliged once more to recur to you for assistance—It will however be the last time that I ever trouble any human being—I feel that I am on sick bed from which I never shall get up ... I have no money—no friends—I have written to my brother—but he cannot help me—I shall never rise from my bed—I hardly know what I am writing—

I will write no more—Please send me a little money—quickly—and forget what
I said about you.[5]

Allan did not respond to this letter either. Poe recovered and prepared his book, *Poems by Edgar A. Poe, Second Edition*, and the New York publisher Elam Bliss released it that spring. The book received a decent review from the *New York Mirror*, but the cadets at West Point were less kind. The cheaply printed 124-page volume that Poe dedicated to "The U. S. Corps of Cadets" contained none of the funny poems about academy life they hoped it would. They felt Poe had cheated them with his "ridiculous doggerel," as one cadet recalled years later.[6]

The cadets may not have appreciated Poe's work at the time but in the coming years as Poe made a name for himself as a writer, especially for his dark short stories, they would boast about knowing him during his short stint at the academy. Many of his former classmates would recount their memories of the famous writer for the rest of their lives.

PART II

THROUGH TIME AND THROUGH ETERNITY

14

MISSING

December 2, 1840, was a frigid, windy day, and the ride from New York City to New Brunswick, New Jersey, on the steamboat *Raritan* was bumpy. The ship was full and John Brush grew tired of standing. He went to the forward deck to look for an empty seat. Just as he walked over, a passenger got up and he was able to sit down and rest. To his surprise, someone he knew occupied the seat next to him. Brush greeted Peter Robinson, a carpenter from New Brunswick. After saying hello to each other, they sat in silence for a few minutes before Robinson spoke. "I have a question to ask you."

"Yes?"

"I'm going to pay off the mortgage that Mr. Suydam has on my house. How should I do that?"

"Well, once you pay the money to Mr. Suydam, you have to get it receipted. Then you take it to the clerk's office and have it canceled."

"Yes, that is the way it ought to be done," Robinson answered after a brief pause. A worried look came over his face. "There's a good many people who say Mr. Suydam will have my house, but I want to pay it off and not let anyone know I've done it."[1] The conversation ended then. When the steamboat docked, they disembarked In New Jersey and went their separate ways.

The next morning, Abraham Suydam left his stately New Brunswick home after kissing his wife Caroline goodbye. It was Thanksgiving Day, and he had business to deal with before he spent the rest of the day with his family.[2]

"I have to go to the bank, but will be back shortly for church," he told her, slipping on his coat as he headed out the door. He walked to the Farmers' and Mechanics' Bank of New Brunswick where he was president, picked up some paperwork, and left. Lewis Carman, a cashier, gave the bank president a deferential nod as Suydam left the building. Suydam had told no one where he was going or when he would be back.

He did not return home that night. It was not totally out of character. He was an important man who had his hand in many business interests, some in adjoining states, but he had promised Caroline he would only be gone a few minutes. It was not like him to break his promises to his wife.

By the next afternoon, Suydam's family and business associates were worried. Suydam could be secretive about his business dealings. He would sometimes go to New York on business without warning, but he always let someone know if he was planning to be away overnight.

Suydam was not on the train from New York. Carmen, the bank teller, then assumed Suydam had gone to Philadelphia, where he had considerable business interests. On Monday, when the train from Philadelphia returned, Suydam was not on that one either. It had now been four days since anyone had seen him. Soon, all of New Brunswick was abuzz with the news.

Abraham Suydam was a man that his fellow citizens looked up to. He had been in the dry goods business for years before retiring and starting a second career in real estate speculation, a business in which he thrived. Suydam soon was the president of a bank and a deacon in his church. He bought an old 40-acre farm on the outskirts of New Brunswick, divided it into building lots, and pursued working men, laborers, mechanics, and craftsmen, who were interested in building and owning their own homes. Most people believed Suydam was doing it to improve the city and give workingmen a valuable opportunity, but there was talk that it was not out of good-heartedness that Suydam chose these men. Some believed it was a scheme to get houses built for free and then foreclose on the owners when they could not come up with the money to repay the burdensome loans. Suydam was known to drive a hard bargain and get what he wanted. He would sell the lot to the man, loan him the money for building materials, and then take a bond and mortgage for the entire loan amount. Suydam would then have the homeowner take out an insurance policy and transfer it to him. If anything went wrong, Suydam would end up with the property and a house built with free labor.

The worried citizens called a meeting and offered a $100 reward (more than $2,500 today) for information related to Suydam's disappearance. The consensus was that someone robbed and murdered him. There was little hope that they would find him alive. The mystery soon made it into newspapers as far away as Baltimore and Boston, and the question on the minds of readers along the East Coast became "what happened to Mr. Suydam?"

It was a few days after Thanksgiving when the man entered the jewelry store in Newark. He was plain-looking, about 5 feet 10 inches, with small features and hazel eyes, and Henry Evans could tell he was a working man by his clothing. Evans continued arranging the display as the man roamed the shop, looking at the jewelry cases. He came over to where Evans sat.

"I have this watch that's just too thick," he said, pulling out a superbly made pocket watch of French design. "I'm thinking of exchanging it for something thinner."

He handed it to Evans, who examined it with a cool professionalism. It was jeweled and had a steel screw balance. It was well crafted and expensive looking. "Where did you get it?"

"I bought it at auction in New York about nine months ago," answered the man, who gave his name as William Brower. Evans wrote the name down on a slip of paper and placed it in the watch case that Brower brought in, closing it.

"Where do you work?" Evans asked the stranger.

"I just finished a job out of town. I just finished putting up a hand railing. I'm a carpenter."

"A carpenter? I know a few. Do you know Ebenezer Condit?"

"No, can't say that I know him. I work for Mr. Brown. I've just finished the job and now I'm heading to Jersey City, but I believe I'm coming down with the ague. I feel quite sick."

Evans looked the man over and decided he looked a bit peaked. "I have a remedy I swear by, a little glass of porter every day."

Brower, looking off-put by the suggestion, answered. "I can't drink that as I'm a teetotaler."

Evans, feeling embarrassed, rushed on. "Well, you could drink it for medicine." There was an awkward pause before Evans walked the man over to a display case filled with watches of every variety. Evans pulled a few of the thinner pocket watches out so the customer could get a better look at them. The pair agreed on an exchange of $100 (nearly $3,000 today) for Brower's watch.

Brower chose a gold ladies' watch with a key for winding it. It had Evans' private mark and the date: "12th month, 1840." The cost was $70.

"I have a sister who's getting married in New York soon. I'd like to make her a present of some spoons." Evans walked over to another case, and the customer followed. Evans picked out a half-dozen silver spoons that Brower took.

The next day, Brower returned to the shop. "My new watch is two or three hours out of time," Brower said, handing Evans the watch.

Evans looked at it. "My guess is that you or someone else has tried the key and got it in the wrong hole."

"Yes, probably, that's it. My sister very much likes the spoons, but they're too light."

"You can return them, if they aren't scratched, and I'll exchange them for heavier ones. How about these?" Evans pulled out some heavier spoons that Brower liked.[3] He had them engraved with the initials P.A.R. Brower paid for them with the understanding that if he brought the others back, Evans would reimburse him for them. He never returned.

About a week after Brush saw Robinson on the steamboat, he ran into him at a shop on Burnett Street in New Brunswick. "Did you manage to settle your business with Mr. Suydam before he went missing?" Brush asked.

"I did. But it's no good for anything."

"Really? Why?"

"Well, the bond and mortgage wasn't receipted."

"That's a singular thing," Brush said, surprised. "A man who's done as much business as Mr. Suydam didn't receipt the mortgage."

"Yes, I know. But he was in such a hurry he didn't think of it. He did give me some other papers, though."

"How do they read?"

"I'm not sure. I can fetch 'em down to your brother-in-law's office for you on Monday. I paid the mortgage in gold and silver."[4]

Before Brush could respond, Robinson turned away and began talking to a man about doing some work at the house. Brush left. Robinson did not turn up on Monday as he had promised.

James Edmonds was in Van Arsdale's hat shop when Peter Robinson entered. Robinson looked happier than he had seen him look in some time, considering Robinson had sunk all of his savings into a house he was still building. Having known each other for years, they greeted one another cordially.

"What time do you have?" asked Robinson. Edmonds pulled out his watch and gave him the time. Robinson then pulled out his watch with a flourish. It was a beautifully crafted ladies' gold pocket watch. "What do you think of my watch?" Robinson asked with a smug smile.

"I'd say it's expensive for a man in your circumstances," Edmonds replied. "Where'd you get it?"

"Oh, I've owned it for two or three years. When I commenced building my house I was short on money so I went to New York and pledged it for $25. The year's been steady, so I went to New York and redeemed it. I was thinking about trading it for lumber."

"What do you want for it?"

"Well, it stood me in $75."

"I don't want it," Edmonds growled. "And I won't trade you lumber for it. A man who carries around a watch like that ought to pay his debts." Robinson owed him and his father for construction materials.

"I'm paying my debts," Robinson said haughtily. "I've just paid off Mr. Suydam the bond and mortgage he held on my property. I'll pay the rest of my creditors soon."

Edmonds looked doubtful but said nothing. Robinson explained that he had paid everything off eighteen months earlier but kept it secret, had not even told his wife or brothers, and had $300 in gold coin and the rest in paper money.

"I wish Mr. Suydam would return soon," Robinson rushed on. "He hasn't canceled my mortgage yet and I'm afraid to go to the clerk's office for fear they'll think I robbed Mr. Suydam. Do you happen to know how to go about getting a mortgage canceled in a case like this?"

Above left: Elizabeth Arnold Hopkins Poe, half-length portrait, facing front. Eliza Poe (1787–1811), Edgar Allan Poe's mother, was an actress who died about a month before he turned three. (*Photograph of lithograph, c. 1914. U.S. Library of Congress, Prints and Photographs division*)

Above right: Composite photo of a photo of Rosalie Poe (Poe's sister) and a halftone reproduction of a painting of Frances K. Allan (Poe's foster mother). After the death of Poe's mother, he went to live with John and Frances Allan, in Richmond, Va. The Allans never formally adopted him. Another family in Richmond adopted his sister. (*Photographic print, c. 1914. U.S. Library of Congress, Prints and Photographs division*)

Below: Composite of Fordham House, N.Y., and head-and-shoulders portrait of Edgar Allan Poe. Poe lived with his wife and cousin, Virginia, and mother-in-law, Maria Poe Clemm in Fordham, N.Y., in what is now the Bronx, between 1846 and 1849. (*Lithograph, c. 1908. U.S. Library of Congress, Prints and Photographs division*)

Left: An illustration of Poe's
"The Tell-Tale Heart." (Rackham,
Arthur. "Poe's Tales of Mystery
and Imagination." Colorplate,
1935. Wikimedia Commons. Public
Domain)

Below: Cadet's Monument at West
Point. Poe was a cadet at the U.S.
Military Academy at West Point,
N.Y., from 1830 to 1831. (Smith,
John Rubens. Etching and Watercolor,
1820. U.S. Library of Congress, Prints
and Photographs division)

West Point—a nineteenth century print of the ferry landing where Poe arrived in 1830 to enter the U.S. Military Academy. (*Photograph of lithograph. Edmund Foerster & Co., publisher, n.d. U.S. Library of Congress, Prints and Photographs division*)

Encampment at West Point. Poe spent the summer of 1830 at the academy's encampment for his tactical field training, where he put in grueling hours drilling daily. (*Smith, John Rubens. Watercolor, 1820. U.S. Library of Congress, Prints and Photographs division*)

The Tell-Tale Heart—one of countless artworks inspired by Poe's story. (*Clarke, Harry. Photographic reproduction of illustration, 1923. Wikimedia Commons. Public domain*)

June 1849 daguerreotype of Edgar Allan Poe. This photograph was taken four months before his death. (*Unknown photographer. Photograph, 1849. Wikimedia Commons. Public domain*)

Above left: Portrait of George Rex Graham. Poe edited *Graham's Magazine* from 1841 to 1842. (*Armstrong, W.G. Engraving. Butler & Jay, 1850. Wikimedia Commons. Public domain*)

Above right: Portrait of Rufus Wilmot Griswold. (*Unknown artist, engraving from the 1855 edition of his The Poets and Poetry of America. Wikimedia Commons. Public domain*)

Right: Daguerreotype of James Russell Lowell, who published Poe's "The Tell-Tale Heart" in his literary magazine, *The Pioneer*, in 1843. (*Unknown artist, 1844. Wikimedia Commons. Public domain*)

Left: The Tell-Tale Heart—late 19th century French artists and poets embraced Poe's work. (*Redon, Odilon. Photographic reproduction of a charcoal drawing, 1883. Wikimedia Commons. Public domain*)

Below left: Portrait of Edgar Allan Poe from the February 1845 edition of *Graham's Magazine*. (*Welch, Thomas B. Engraving, 1845. Wikimedia Commons. Public domain*)

Below right: The original planned design for Poe's magazine, *The Stylus*. (*Poe, Edgar Allan. Engraving, n.d. Wikimedia Commons. Public domain*)

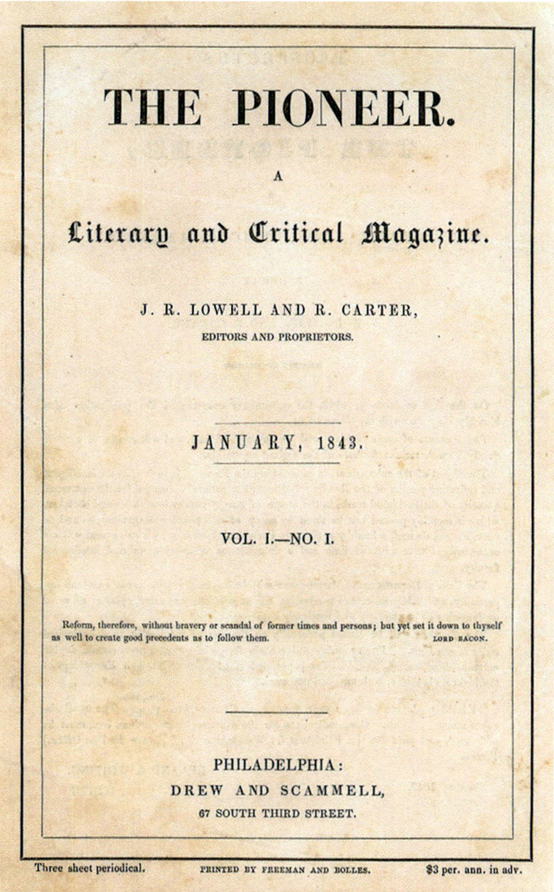

Cover for James Russell Lowell's *The Pioneer*, which featured Poe's "The Tell-Tale Heart." (*Engraving, 1843. Wikimedia Commons. Public domain*)

Tomb of Edgar Allan Poe, Baltimore. When Poe was buried in 1849, he had no gravestone. The grave remained unmarked until 1875 when a Baltimore school teacher, Sara Sigourney Rice, led a fund drive to create one for Poe, whose literary fame exploded after his death. (*Campbell, Alfred S., publisher. Stereographic print, 1896. U.S. Library of Congress, Prints and Photographs division*)

Portrait of Virginia Clemm Poe. Poe married Virginia, his first cousin, in 1836, when she was thirteen and he was twenty-seven. (*Artist unknown. Photographic reproduction of an oil painting, 1847. Wikimedia Commons. Public domain*)

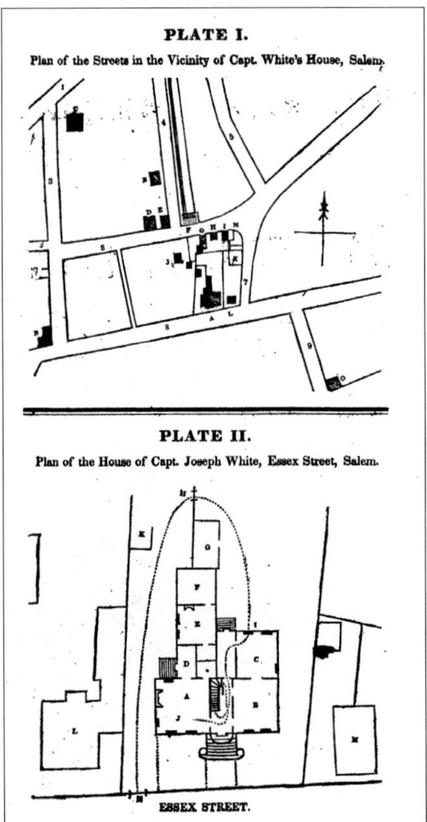

Diagrams of Captain Joseph White's Salem, Mass. mansion showing its location and how the killer entered the home. (*A Report of the Evidence and Points of Law, Arising in the Trial of John Francis Knapp, for the Murder of Joseph White, Esquire. Before the Supreme Judicial Court. Hathi Trust Digital Library, Salem, W. & S. B. Ives, 1830. Public Domain*)

Capt. Joseph J. Knapp, Jr., made his last voyage in the *Phoenix.* Knapp, like many of Salem's men, made a career of the sea. (*Trials of Capt. Joseph J. Knapp, Jr. and George Crowninshield, Esq: For the Murder of Capt. Joseph White of Salem, on the Night of the Sixth of April 1830. United States, Charles Ellms, 1830. Public Domain*)

Captain Joseph White spent the evening before his murder with his relatives at Cherry Hill Farm in Wenham, Mass. (*Frontispiece from Trials of Capt. Joseph J. Knapp, Jr. and George Crowninshield, Esq: For the Murder of Capt. Joseph White of Salem, on the Night of the Sixth of April 1830. United States, Charles Ellms, 1830. Public Domain*)

The club used to murder Captain Joseph White. (*A Report of the Evidence and Points of Law, Arising in the Trial of John Francis Knapp, for the Murder of Joseph White, Esquire. Before the Supreme Judicial Court. Hathi Trust Digital Library, Salem, W. & S. B. Ives, 1830. Public Domain*)

Daguerreotype of Daniel Webster, who was considered the finest orator of his generation. He was a lawyer and politician who served in both the U.S. House of Representatives and U.S. Senate and as U.S. Secretary of State under Presidents William Henry Harrison, John Tyler, and Millard Fillmore. (*Unknown photographer, n.d. Wikimedia Commons. Public domain*)

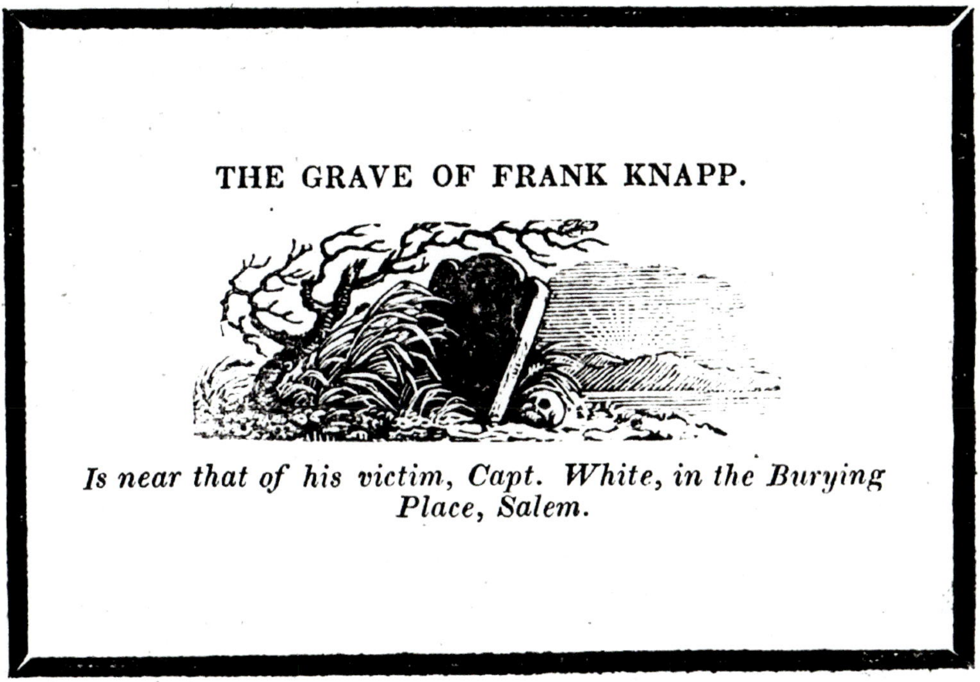

The grave of Frank Knapp. (*Trials of Capt. Joseph J. Knapp, Jr. and George Crowninshield, Esq: For the Murder of Capt. Joseph White of Salem, on the Night of the Sixth of April 1830. United States, Charles Ellms, 1830. Public Domain*)

Captain Joseph White's mansion today, showing the back of the house where his killer entered. Now known as the Gardner-Pingree House, it is owned by the Peabody-Essex Museum. (*Author's collection*)

Captain Joseph White's mansion. (*Author's collection*)

The old Salem jail. The building, originally built in 1813, was converted into luxury apartments in 2010. (*Author's collection*)

Above: Captain Joseph White's room where he was murdered on the night of April 6, 1830. (*Author's collection*)

Right: Portrait of Massachusetts Justice Isaac Parker (1768–1830), who died suddenly just before the start of the first trial in the Captain Joseph White murder case. (*Photographic reproduction of an oil painting, c. 1814. Wikimedia Commons. Public domain*)

Daguerreotype of James Gordon Bennett, Sr. Bennett (1795–1872), who covered the trials of Frank Knapp in 1830 and helped launch crime reporting a decade later through his newspaper, *The New York Herald*. (*Brady, Matthew B. Photograph, c. 1851. U.S. Library of Congress, Prints and Photographs division*)

Frank and Joe Knapp and George Crowninshield at the time of their trials in 1830. (*Trials of Capt. Joseph J. Knapp, Jr. and George Crowninshield, Esq: For the Murder of Capt. Joseph White of Salem, on the Night of the Sixth of April 1830. United States, Charles Ellms, 1830. Public Domain*)

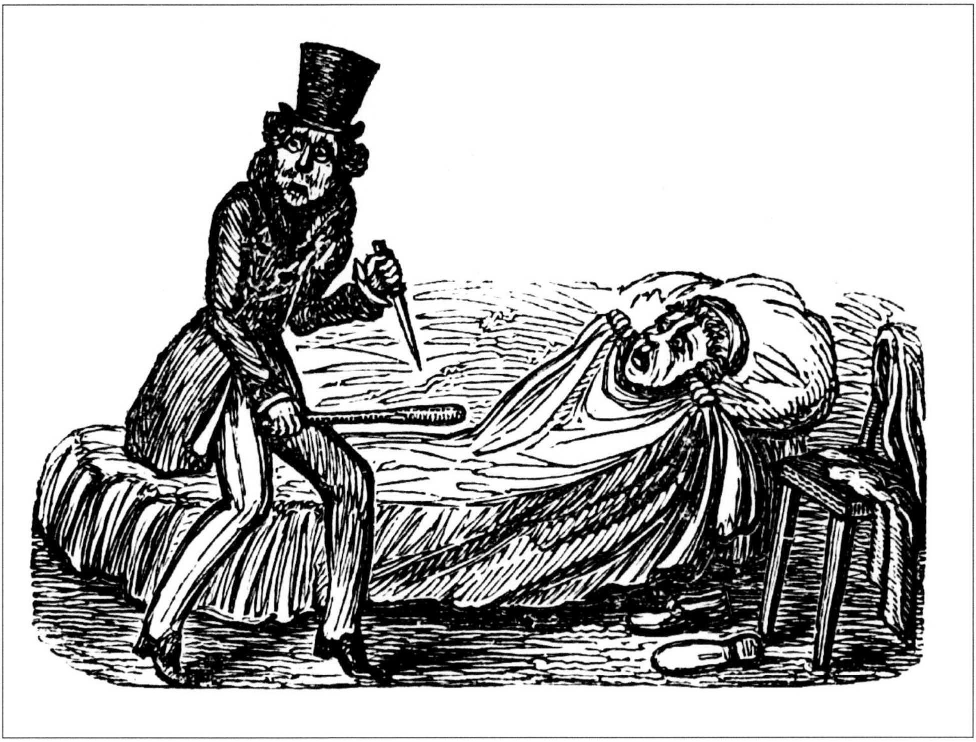

Above: Illustration of the murder of Captain Joseph White. (*Trials of Capt. Joseph J. Knapp, Jr. and George Crowninshield, Esq: For the Murder of Capt. Joseph White of Salem, on the Night of the Sixth of April 1830. United States, Charles Ellms, 1830. Public Domain*)

Right: Portrait of New Jersey Justice Joseph Coerten Hornblower (1777–1864), who oversaw Peter Robinson's trial for the murder of Abraham Suydam. (*Photographic reproduction of an etching. 1895. from the Semi-centennial Celebration of the Founding of the New Jersey Historical Society at Newark, N.J., May 16, 1895. Public domain*)

Plan of the city of New Brunswick, N.J. (*Roberts, J.M. 1829. U.S. Library of Congress, Prints and Photographs division*)

Above left: Frontispiece for *Trial, confession and execution of Peter Robinson for the murder of Abraham Suydam, Esq., of New Brunswick, N.J.* (*Unknown Artist, 1841. Public Domain*)

Above right: Portrait of Peter Robinson from the *New York Herald* of March 22, 1841. (*Unknown Artist, 1841. Public Domain*)

"I'm not experienced in these matters. I really couldn't say."[5] The conversation ebbed and there was an awkward, heavy silence between the men before Robinson bid Edmonds a pleasant day and left the shop.

The strange exchange stuck with Edmonds, considering the ever-present news that Suydam had disappeared without a trace more than a week earlier. It was all anyone in town was talking about. He went to see his father, Jacob, the next day and related what had passed between Robinson and himself.

Jacob walked over to Robinson's house on New Street the morning after his son told him of his conversation with Robinson. He found Peter working in the basement preparing mortar. Jacob could not help but notice the brand-new cellar floor. Even before they began chatting, the idea that Robinson had murdered Suydam was rolling around in his thoughts. "When did you lay down that floor?" he asked in a casual tone.

"A few days ago."

"Where's your wife?"

"She's visiting her sister in New York. She's been gone two weeks. I wanted to finish the house, so I let her go visiting while I finished."

"Have you been to New York lately?"

"Actually yes, just a few days ago."

Jacob steered the conversation to his unpaid debt. "Peter, there's an unsettled account between us and I want to have it settled. Can you do that?"

"I can."

"Let's take a walk outside and talk," suggested Jacob. Robinson agreed, and the pair walked out of the house towards a neighbor's property where a new well had been dug.

"I wonder if anyone's examined this well for the body of Mr. Suydam," remarked Jacob, looking at Robinson's face for any telltale reaction.

Robinson, looking shocked, stared at Edmonds. "Do you think Mr. Suydam is dead?"

"Yes. Don't you?"

"No. I think he's run away. I believe the well has been examined."

"My son tells me you've been getting along very well with Mr. Suydam. He says you've taken up that bond and mortgage."

"I have and paid him the money," Robinson answered. "Come with me back to the house and I'll show it to you."

"When did you pay Mr. Suydam?"

"I believe it was about four weeks ago."

"I can't go back to the house," Jacob replied as he stepped up to Robinson. Now nose-to-nose, Edmonds looked him in the eye. "Peter, Suydam is a murdered man, and the fact that you have his bond and mortgage, I charge you with being implicated in his murder."

Robinson's previously mild manner changed suddenly. "Do people suspect me of murdering him?" he stammered nervously.

"Peter, I've come here to tell you my own suspicions. Now, if you're an innocent man and have paid off the bond and mortgage honestly, tell me where you got the money. Do that and this stays between you and me."

"I had it out on interest and called it in."

"Who had the money?"

"I can't tell you that."

"I've made an awful charge against you, Peter. I'd think you'd be willing to tell me who had the money. If you don't tell me, I'll have you arrested and force you to tell."

Robinson tried to change the subject, mumbling something about looking at the window sashes and frames Edmonds had previously discussed selling him. As they walked over to Edmond's home a quarter of a mile away, Robinson was quiet. He spoke up. "Mr. Edmonds, would you suspect me of murder?"

"I suspect you of murdering Mr. Suydam to get that bond and mortgage. I hope you'll satisfy me and cause me to think otherwise."

They arrived at Edmond's house where he had the sashes. Robinson bought them and prepared to leave. "I need to hurry back to the house," he said.

"Peter, you still haven't told me where you got the money to take up the bond and mortgage."

"I've got a mason and carpenter at the house I need to attend to. You have to let me go," he said, cutting off Edmonds. "But I'll meet you at any hour you name."

"You name the hour but don't disappoint me."

"One o'clock, then."

"Meet me at the lumberyard and bring your account and we'll settle your debt."

Robinson returned to Jacob Edmonds' house at noon, an hour earlier than they had agreed. Edmonds was surprised to see him there so early. "You've got along, have you, before the time," Edmonds commented as Robinson came inside.

"Yes, I didn't want to be late." They walked over to the lumberyard through the icy streets that afternoon, not speaking. Their breath rolled out in misty clouds. At the lumberyard, they went into Edmond's office and settled the account. Robinson owed $16 (equivalent to about $475 today). He paid in banknotes. Edmonds stashed the money away. He got up and closed the office door.

"Now, sir, I hope you're ready to tell me where you got the money to take up that bond and mortgage."

"I've had it for about eighteen months."

"This morning you told me you had it out on interest and called it in?"

"I said no such thing," Robinson said, his voice rising.

"Sir, we will contend about that. You say you've had the money for eighteen months. You've had $300 in gold and $400 in state banknotes, by you, have you?" Edmonds said. Robinson could tell Jacob did not believe him.

"I have."

Well, Mr. Robinson, do you recall last spring when you came to me to purchase lumber and you said every last dollar you had in the world was invested in that house? And that you had two hundred dollars that you'd laid out at Mr. Acken's yard for lumber and then came to me asking me to trust you for forty dollars for lumber after you'd been to Acken's yard? You'd asked him to trust you for forty dollars' worth of lumber and he told you he'd trust you just as long as you could stick your hand in your pocket and take the money out. And then I said it's hardly fair to lay your money down at one yard and then come to me for trust. But I asked when will you pay me? Now, was this when you had all this money laying [*sic.*] around?[6]

The sarcasm dripped.

"That's a fact," said Robinson. "I had it lying about me and was considering putting on an addition to the house."

"Your statements only go to strengthen my suspicion," Edmonds said.

Robinson lost his cool. "If you suspect me of murdering Mr. Suydam, have me arrested."

"I intend to," came the cold reply.

15

PHILADELPHIA

Poe was sick again, brought on by the strain of worry and overwork. By December 1840, he was thirty-one, married to his eighteen-year-old cousin Virginia, living in Philadelphia, and had not had a steady job since June when he left as the editor of the Philadelphia publication *Burton's Gentleman's Magazine*.

The intervening years since launching his literary career following his embarrassing departure from West Point had been a hand-to-mouth existence. Allan had cut Poe off completely and provided nothing in his will after his death in 1834. That chapter of his life was over, and he wished to burn away the memory of it. He focused on his new family and his literary career.

After leaving the academy in 1831, Poe had lived in Baltimore and then again in Richmond, where he worked on the editorial staff of the *Southern Literary Messenger,* a periodical that became the most important in the South and launched his career as an editor and critic. Poe greatly increased the magazine's circulation and prestige. He left as editor in January 1837, feeling stifled by his pedestrian publisher, Thomas Willis White, and his paltry salary.

From there, Poe, Virginia, and his aunt, and his mother-in-law, Maria Poe Clemm, whom they called "Muddy," moved to New York City before settling down in Philadelphia in the summer of 1838. Philadelphia remained one of the country's principal publishing centers. He hoped the smaller but still cosmopolitan city would serve his purposes until he could once again give New York another, more successful, go.

Along with the disappointments and setbacks of the decade, there had been some happy milestones, besides his marriage in 1836 to Virginia who was just thirteen, Poe twenty-seven. In July 1838, the New York company Harper and Bros. published *The Narrative of Arthur Gordon Pym*, and that fall, the novel came out in London by the British publishers Wiley and Putnam. He received excellent reviews on both sides of the Atlantic, but he learned they did not put bread on the table. Poe focused on short stories he could sell to the magazines for cash, instead.

In the spring of 1839, Poe badly needed a steady source of income. He befriended the English actor William E. Burton, who had launched *The Gentleman's Magazine*, two years earlier. Poe offered his services, which Burton accepted, proposing to pay Poe $10 a week (equivalent to $238 today). Burton rebuffed Poe's counteroffer, and so with a measure of trepidation, Poe took the job. His fears were well-founded, for by June 1840, after pouring all his energies into the magazine, his relationship with Burton became untenable.

Poe had to seek out articles, stories, and poetry from writers across the country, edit them, and lay out the magazine. Poe was also filling its pages with some of his finest short stories, including "The Fall of the House of Usher," along with reviews and general interest articles.

During this time, Poe had another book published, but his hope of financial independence went unrealized. In November 1839, twenty-five stories, his entire output up to that time, were collected in two volumes, in his *Tales of the Grotesque and Arabesque*, put out by the Philadelphia publishers Lea and Blanchard. The publishers were upfront about who would get any profits from the book's sales:

> As your wish in having your *Tales* printed is not immediately pecuniary, we will at our own risk and expense print a small edition, say 1,750 copies … This sum if sold—will pay but a small profit which if realized is to be ours—The copyright will remain with you, and when ready a few copies for distribution among your friends will be at your service.[1]

The volumes did not sell that well. They printed only 750 copies, 1,000 less than they had planned. Hoping to see a measure of financial gain from the venture, Poe offered the publishers the copyrights to the stories. They rebuffed his offer, telling him it would be "of no value to us."

It was another financial setback in what seemed like an endless succession of them. For all his work at *Burton's*, Poe was getting second billing and meager wages from Burton. The publisher did little work, took most of the credit, and then lost interest in the publication as he began focusing his attention on a new theater he was about to open. Burton was also mad at Poe for attempting to start his own journal.

Burton attacked Poe in a letter claiming he owed him a sizable amount of money and that Poe had been slacking at his editorial duties. Poe's cutting response all but guaranteed their relationship was at its end:

> In the first place, your attempts to bully me excite in my mind scarcely any other sentiment than mirth … When you address me again, preserve, if you can, the dignity of a gentleman. If by accident you have taken it into your head that I am to be insulted with impunity I can only assume that you are an ass.[2]

Poe, always fastidious about his accounting, laid out what he owed Burton to the penny and the exact number of pages he had filled as editor.

After Poe left, Burton spread malicious gossip about his drinking. Poe was so incensed that he considered suing his old boss. Instead, he focused on launching his own journal, *The Penn Magazine.* That December, Poe tried to secure promises from other prominent writers for their stories and drum up enough financial support to launch what he believed would be the premier literary journal in America. He wrote the following to a cousin, seeking support for the new endeavor:

> If I fully succeed in my purposes I will not fail to produce some lasting effect upon the growing literature of the country, while I establish for myself individually a name which that country 'will not willingly let die.'"[3]

His health continued to decline, a hard thing for someone who had always been an exceptional athlete who had excelled at swimming, running, and boxing. He spent most of December 1840 working from bed.

His intermittent intemperance made things worse. He did not consider himself "debauched" since he knew it was his peculiar reaction to alcohol that was to blame. Where some men could have three or four drinks and not even show it, one sip that passed between Poe's lips made him nearly insane and uncontrollable. Once he started, he could not stop. He was able to stay sober for long stretches of time. By December 1840, it had been more than a year since he had succumbed. The ever-watchful Virginia and Muddy helped keep him sober.

Poe worshipped Virginia and wanted her to have the best of everything. If he could get *The Penn Magazine* off the ground, he could finally give her all that she deserved. He had by then built up a national reputation and was trying to parlay that into his own magazine. Poe had not yet put out a single issue, but he was quickly gathering subscribers and getting positive notices by the country's press. His dream seemed within reach.

16

CROSSHAIRS

On Monday, December 14, Andrew D. Mellick, a prominent merchant, was on an afternoon walk with his friend, Samuel Cooke, when they ran into Jacob Edmonds just in front of the Baptist church. Their friend was carrying a coiled rope attached to an iron grappling hook. Edmonds sheepishly admitted he had been looking for Suydam's body in a well. The other two men joked that Edmonds was after the $500 reward. Mellick and Cooke chuckled, but Edmonds did not think it was funny.

"Can I see you in private?" Edmonds asked Mellick. Mellick broke away from Cooke and walked up the street with Edmonds; they strolled as Edmonds spoke:

> There's a man who lives in the western suburb. His name is Peter Robinson. He's poor, a carpenter, and not worth a damn … Mr. Suydam took him by the hand, sold him a lot, and furnished him with money to build a house.
>
> He took a mortgage on it for seven-fifty. I've just seen Robinson with a handsome gold watch. And I heard him say he'd paid off and taken up his mortgage. He seemed to have plenty of money.[1]

Edmonds hesitated, then rushed on. "I think he may have murdered Mr. Suydam."

Edmonds had been ruminating over what to do since his confrontation with Robinson earlier in the day. Edmonds boasted he would go straight to the authorities, but he had not. While he believed Robinson probably murdered Suydam, there was no evidence. If he had found the body in the well near Robinson's house, that would have at least proved Mr. Suydam was dead. Edmonds floundered in indecision and told no one else about his suspicions. After voicing his concerns out loud to his friend, Edmonds felt better. The two men stared at each other. "We have to go to the mayor," Mellick replied.

Mellick, Edmonds, and Cooke hurried to city hall to speak with the newly elected mayor, David W. Vail, who was in charge of the investigation into

Suydam's disappearance. During this time, municipal law enforcement was in its infancy, and police detectives were unheard of. The first detective unit in the U.S., created in Boston, was still six years away. Investigations fell to the city and its citizens.

The mayor listened as Edmonds recounted his story. His reaction was immediate. They would go confront Robinson posthaste. Vail came up with a plan. The four men would converge on the house from different directions, in case Robinson attempted to make his escape.

They met up at Robinson's house and went inside without knocking. The sound of a house still under construction—the banging of hammers, sawing of wood, and the metallic scrape of trowels slathering mortar against brick— greeted them. Robinson came down the stairs at the sound of the men entering his home. They stared up at him as he descended the stairs.

The mayor addressed Robinson. "Do you have a private room?" he asked. "We wish to speak to you alone." Robinson, with a studied casualness, led the group upstairs to the sitting room. Once inside, the interrogation began without ceremony, led by Vail.

"When was the last time you saw Mr. Suydam?"

"Oh, about six weeks ago."

"Where?"

Robinson hesitated for a moment before speaking. "I saw him as I was passing around the corner of Alexander Moore's on Church Street."

"You haven't seen him since then?"

"No."

"Haven't you paid Mr. Suydam a bond and mortgage which you owed since that time?"

"Oh no," Robinson said, "I paid the bond and mortgage about a week after they were given."

"I understand you're in possession of the bond and mortgage that Mr. Suydam held against you," interjected Mellick. "We would like to see it." Robinson left the room and returned a few minutes later with a document and handed it to Mellick. "This isn't the bond," said Mellick, looking up at Robinson. "This is an insurance policy." Robinson apologized. He returned with another piece of paper, which was the mortgage. "What about the bond?" asked Mellick. Robinson retrieved the bond.

Mellick studied the paperwork. The bond was dated March 23, 1840, payable five years after that date. There was no endorsement of receipt attached. Someone had torn off the names and seals from the paper. Mellick handed the documents to the mayor who studied them, then continued his questioning. "How did you pay Mr. Suydam?" The mayor asked.

"Three hundred in gold and the rest in state bank money."

"Where did you get the money to pay him?"

"I'm not obliged to tell you that," Robinson responded.

"I suppose that's true," Vail said. "I don't know about you, but anyone else here who got $700 or $800 together could say where it came from."

"I've had the money here for about eighteen months,"

"Then why did you give Mr. Suydam a bond and mortgage for $780 last March if you had the money in the house at the time?"

"Oh, I don't know. I thought I might need the money to finish the house, so I chose not to pay it."

"You know you're under suspicion for murdering Abraham Suydam. We have examined all the witnesses who had been with or seen Mr. Suydam on the day he disappeared. We even sent to Philadelphia for one. I presume you have no objection to go to Squire Conover to be examined?"

"No, I don't mind, if that's what you want."

"I will keep these papers," said the mayor, indicating the bond, mortgage, and insurance.

"Very well." Robinson slipped on his coat and led the way down the stairs and out of the house. The small group of men made their way to the justice's home, a quarter of a mile distant.

Once there, Justice Conover questioned Robinson. He repeated his story with a few changes. It could have been a month and not six weeks since he had seen Mr. Suydam. He described how only two weeks after signing the paperwork, he had paid off the mortgage at Suydam's mansion. Only he and Suydam were in the back parlor the evening when he paid it off in gold and banknotes, Robinson said. Under questioning, Robinson claimed he had paid off the mortgage early after hearing that Suydam had swindled another working man.

"I wanted to get out of Mr. Suydam's clutches," he said. "I heard Mr. Hoagland had built a house and when it was two-thirds done Mr. Suydam wouldn't let him have any more money."

Robinson continued to refuse to say where he got the money. "It's my own business where I got the money," he told the justice. "I worked and earned it and have had it set aside for eighteen months."[2]

Asked why he had even bothered to get a mortgage if he had money of his own, Robinson answered that when Suydam proposed to sell him the lot, he thought it made sense to take him up on the offer. "I thought I'd hold on to what I had and get all that I could, in case I got sick, or something," Robinson said. Robinson had not finished the house yet. He laid the cellar floor about two weeks earlier, he said.

The questioning continued. They asked him about the pocket watch several people had seen him flashing around town. He said he had bought it in New York months ago. While they interrogated Robinson, a dozen men converged on his house to look for clues. They found the front door locked. "Let's break it down," someone said and there was a murmur of agreement, but Joseph

Danberry noticed that one window was unlocked. He slid it open and slipped inside. He unlocked the back door and the rest of the men came rushing in. They began a room-to-room search for any evidence of a murder. A few men guarded the doors to prevent a growing mob from coming inside and wrecking the place.

The mayor, the city marshal, John Hoagland, and Robinson returned to the house to fetch the gold watch and some other papers, entering through the back basement door. Robinson noticed the others staring at a hole in the back corner of the cellar where someone had pulled up two planks of wood.

"I dug that to get sand for the masons," he told them unprompted.

"How long has this floor been laid?" the mayor asked.

"A long time," Robinson answered. "This is where I've been living."

Just then, a curious neighbor, Charles Smith, arrived with Peter's brother, William; they headed downstairs to the cellar and found Robinson and the others there.

The mayor, noticing the floor looked as if it had been newly laid, turned to Robinson. "Peter, you had better submit to having this floor taken up and examined at once."

"If you take up the floor, the beams have been constructed so that the whole house will fall down,"

The men laughed at his ridiculous statement. "We all know better than that," the mayor said. "The house won't fall by taking up the floor."

Peter's brother, William, spoke up. "There's nothing there. I laid the floor myself."

"Peter, the suspicions against you greatly increase by any delay," the mayor said. "You'd better consent to having this floor taken up."

"But if it's taken up, the floor will be damaged and I'll never be able to lay down another as good."

The mayor looked dumbfounded. "Peter, whatever damage you sustain, if we find nothing, will be indemnified to you," he told Robinson.

The construction workers, too curious to do their jobs, stood staring at the unfolding scene, unable to believe their employer might be a killer. The mayor turned to a carpenter standing nearby. "Can this floor be taken up and re-laid?" The mayor asked him.

"Without too much trouble," the man said.

The mayor turned back to Robinson, "Peter, you must let us examine the house."

"Maybe you should begin with the roof and take down the whole house," Robinson said. "Just don't remove my floors."[3]

Robinson's wife, Ann, came down at the sound of raised voices, and Robinson asked her to fetch the watch for the mayor. She had just gotten back from visiting relatives and was confused and frightened. She stared uncomprehendingly at her husband before she turned and went upstairs to get the watch. She handed it to the mayor. It was an attractive, slim French women's watch with an attached key. The mayor slipped it into his pocket as evidence.

Robinson went upstairs with the mayor and marshal to get more paperwork before returning to the justice's house. Down in the cellar, Smith, Robinson's neighbor, questioned the carpenter. "When was the floor laid?"

"It was just laid," the carpenter answered. "Mr. Robinson put it down himself before I arrived. He worked on it most of the night this past Wednesday."

That was all the impetus they needed. The men first searched the hole Robinson had dug for sand, but it turned up nothing. Smith then searched the cellar's front room. He noticed quicklime on the floor, which was commonly used to speed up a body's decomposition, but was also used in making cement. He opened a closet and peered in. There was nothing of interest. Smith found an ax and an adz, an ax-like woodworking tool, which he set aside as potential evidence. With Robinson gone and unable to stop the men, they then took up the floor.

Working by candlelight in the dark cellar, Smith and Danberry found the narrowest plank and pried it up. They had gotten four planks up when a cat leaped out, scaring them. The cat looked around and then jumped back into the hole. They were dumbfounded and could not figure out how a cat had gotten in there. Had the cat been buried for days, or had it discovered a way in under the flooring? This tantalizing detail may have helped inspire Poe's other famous short story, "The Black Cat," which he wrote the same year as "The Tell-Tale Heart," in 1843.

Another man, Ephraim Randolph, began helping take out the floor. They used the ax and the adz to rip away the rest of the wood planks piece by piece, a dozen in all, to reveal the dirt subfloor beneath.

Smith, walking on the now exposed ground, felt a spot that was softer than the rest of the hard-packed subfloor. He called the other men over. Randolph stuck his hand into the loosely packed ground and started feeling around. His hand touched something slimy. He recoiled until he realized it was just a cabbage stalk that someone had tossed there.

Smith picked up a spade and shoved it into the soft earth. About 15 inches down, he felt something. He pushed his hand deeper and grabbed hold of some cloth. His fingers grasped and searched. It was a leg. He continued hunting around with his hand. "I'd take an oath that there's a body down there," he told the other men. Danberry shoved his hand in and felt what he believed was the seam of a man's pantaloons. Randolph did the same in his turn and agreed it was a body.

They began to dig, each taking a turn with the shovel. About 4 feet down, they could make out the shape of a body. At this depth, the earth was muddy and bog-like. Randolph shoved his hand in again, caught hold of something, and yanked. Out popped an arm he had grabbed by a cold claw-like hand. They cleared more dirt until they had completely revealed the corpse. It was on its left side with the legs drawn up in a fetal position. The 3-foot-long space had been too short for the body to be stretched out. It was still dressed except for a hat, and someone had tossed a coat over it.

They shouted that they had found a body. Someone ran to get the mayor and give him and the others the news. Robinson's demeanor did not change when he heard that they had found a body in his cellar or when the city marshal arrested him for murder.

Mayor Vail returned to Robinson's house and oversaw the removal of the corpse. Danberry pulled the coat off the body and examined it. It had been turned inside out as if someone had rifled through it. He then brushed away the damp earth from the face. "It's Mr. Suydam," Danberry said.

They pulled the body out of the makeshift grave legs first and set it on the ground. Blood and water poured out of the remains. The smell of the decomposing body overwhelmed Randolph, who felt sick and ran outside to get some air. The others stood staring at the body. They could see a deep gash in the back of the head and two more at the crown.

It was likely Poe picked up on both the gruesome aspects of Suydam's burial and Robinson's calm demeanor during the investigation that were extensively reported in the nation's newspapers, helping to solidify some of the details in the short story he would write less than two years later.

Vail and the others picked up the body and pushed their way through the large crowd milling around outside of the house. They formed a solemn procession through the gloomy street lit only by torchlight and headed for the courthouse just down the road. When anyone spoke, it was in a low tone, as befit the somber occasion.

At the courthouse, James Newall, the city coroner, impaneled a coroner's jury made up of the men who had searched Robinson's house. They quietly watched Doctors William Van Deursen, Ephraim Smith, and J. T. B. Skillman examine Suydam's body, which they had washed and laid out on a table under flickering candlelight. That there were three doctors present was proof of Suydam's standing in the community.

The doctors restricted their examination to the head. They first looked at the deepest wound at the back of the head. The scalp had been torn away, and it appeared a blunt instrument, a hammer, or perhaps the back of an ax, had made the injury. The doctors agreed the two wounds at the top of the head were made by a sharp weapon, most likely an ax or an adz. They noticed there was a skull fracture beneath a 4-inch long gash near the crown. The force of the blow had rammed bone fragments into the brain. Either of these wounds would have been fatal, the physicians agreed. The third wound that extended towards the eyes had not fractured the bone.

Dr. Van Deursen, who had known the victim for years, then sliced through the skin of Suydam's forehead just above the nose and continued around until he had reached the point at which he started and peeled back the flesh to reveal the shattered skull beneath. There was a spider's web of cracks radiating out from the wounds. The doctors found no evidence Suydam had put up a fight against his attacker, leading them to believe the killer had surprised him.

The coroner's jury concluded:

> Abraham Suydam came to his death by a blow or blows inflicted on his head by some person or persons unknown and that the body was found under the floor of a house owned and occupied by Peter A. Robinson.[4]

Suydam's body was then carried to his home, where his grieving family waited for his return.

The next day, Danberry and Smith returned to Robinson's house for a more thorough search after the frenzied excitement of the previous night. Their primary goal was to find Mr. Suydam's hat. Instead, they found blood spatter on the bottom of the cellar door's frame. Danberry, a cooper who knew wood like an intimate friend, cut the framing away and discovered more bloodstains the color of iron that had seeped under the frame. It appeared someone had recently planed the casing to hide more stains. Smith found a few spots of blood on the wall and on the floor. He also found a few stains along the entryway to the cellar. The walls and stairs leading down to the basement had a fresh coat of garish yellow-orange paint.

In the cellar, they found a carpet scrap soaked with blood. The stain on the carpet was about the size of a human head. Smith took it upstairs, dipped a rag in water, and ran it across the fabric. When he wrung it out, it ran red.

The same day, Robinson appeared for his preliminary hearing before Justice Conover. The marshal took Robinson's two brothers, William and James, and his wife, Ann, into custody as potential accomplices.

The justice sent someone to the bank to learn what they could. Carmen, the cashier, recalled that Suydam had withdrawn a note he held against Robinson for $75 a day or two before going missing and that he had planned to collect on it.

During the hearing, Robinson owned up to having the note and gave it to the court. Things were not looking good for the prisoner. Both his brothers testified. James, the youngest, admitted Peter had asked him to torch his unfinished house, offering him $50 if he would do it. He turned Peter down. William told the court he had gone to Peter's on Thanksgiving Day, but his brother refused to let him in.

The news of Suydam's murder spread across the city, sparking talk of lynching Robinson before he went to trial. Nothing came of this talk. Robinson's demeanor did not help his cause. He sat through the hearing stone-faced. Afterward, as the guards took him back to his cell, he groused, "supposing I did kill Mr. Suydam, they can't prove it."

While Robinson's preliminary trial was underway, across town, they were burying Suydam. Thousands of citizens solemnly made their way through the

Suydam residence to view the body before it was interred. The funeral was standing room only. They came to say farewell to one of New Brunswick's wealthiest and most prominent citizens. His friends considered him mild and amiable, strict in his religious principles, with a demeanor calculated to inspire respect.

While Rev. Dr. Howe gave the eulogy, an undercurrent of anger and violence against Robinson simmered below the surface of those in attendance. There seemed to be almost constant talk of lynching him for the murder, but no one did. Instead, the days and weeks ticked off as the case moved through the court system while Robinson languished in jail. Robinson had an unflagging belief that he would beat the rap and go free.

After Robinson's arrest, rumors of his past circulated, grim tales of death, theft, and double-crosses that would make it into the newspapers hungry for salacious details about the alleged killer.

Robinson was a skilled carpenter down on his luck. He was not originally from New Brunswick, and this may have helped fuel the malicious stories since he had a murky past, at least in the opinion of his fellow citizens.

He was born in November 1808 on Chambers Street in lower Manhattan to a poor family. His alcoholic father left his wife when Robinson was young, and the boy ran wild through the litter-strewn streets of the city. When he was twelve, his mother hired him out to a New Jersey woodworker to learn chair-making, but Robinson did not get along with his short-fused master. When the man tried to whip him for some minor offense, the two scuffled, and in the fracas, someone knocked a lamp over and set the barn on fire. From there, his mother apprenticed him to a cabinetmaker in Manhattan. Instead of learning the trade or receiving any schooling, Robinson spent his time with rowdy neighborhood firemen who were little better than gangsters and would often fight other fire companies over the right to put out fires. Robinson at least learned to read and then fueled his imagination through books about pirates and sea adventures.

One day while hanging around the docks on the East River, he saw a sign on the deck of a ship indicating it was sailing for the newly gained territory of East Florida. Robinson boarded and spoke to the captain about joining the crew. The captain refused to take him on as a sailor but invited the teenager along as one of the many workmen needed for a timbering operation. Robinson joined up and sailed down the East Coast, headed for what he hoped would be a grand adventure. It turned out to be a hard slog filled with death, disease, biting insects, venomous reptiles, sweltering heat, and cruel overseers. He moved to St. Augustine, the capital of East Florida, for a time before returning to New York, leaving a pregnant girlfriend down south. He moved to New Brunswick in his twenties and was soon getting by as a carpenter; met his wife, Ann, who was working as a cook at a hotel; and settled down to raise a family.

Among the worst lies the local gossips spread was that Robinson had poisoned two of his children, dispatched his own sister, and murdered an itinerant peddler and a competing carpenter. It seemed the Robinson family's tragedies were being dredged up with a darker bent added to them. William Attree, *The New York Herald*'s crime reporter, recounted to his readers the rumors he had gathered while in New Brunswick. Attree was one of the best reporters around and was equally well-known for his vices—liquor and prostitutes (at least until his marriage in 1838). The Robinson case was the kind of story *The Herald*'s readers loved and Attree obliged.

In the summer of 1839, two of Robinson's three children suddenly died within a few weeks of each other. They sent for a doctor after the eldest child, a boy of eight, took sick. His mother said he had eaten jimsonweed, also known as devil's snare, a toxic plant of the nightshade family. The doctor found the boy writhing in pain in bed. He could not save him. The other child, a girl of four, died under similar circumstances not long after.

Peter's older sister, Susan, went missing after attending a church service and was last seen alive in the company of her brother, according to New Brunswick's gossips.

Attree told his readers about a "well-known" peddler who regularly passed through New Brunswick until he mysteriously disappeared after lodging at Peter's house. "A week or two after the peddler disappeared, Peter's wife was seen with his little box and was selling the trinkets it contained. How true this is we know not," wrote Attree.

The Herald reporter also alleged Peter brought home a carpenter from New York City who also vanished after staying at his house. The Robinsons soon moved, and the next tenants claimed the basement stank so badly they could not use it for a year. "These are a few of the charges that are brought with or without sufficient foundation thereof," Attree concluded.

It was not just Robinson's past that everyone scrutinized. While in jail awaiting trial, the jailer allowed a steady stream of gawking locals to look at the prisoner as if he were a zoo animal. The constant trooping in and out by onlookers exhausted the jailer, who was constantly opening and closing the front door.

Worse yet, the authorities had forbidden Robinson's wife and family from visiting him in jail. Strangers surrounded Robinson, but he was alone. His moods swung from lashing out in anger, yelling and screaming and tearing apart his jail cell to abject despondency. Sometimes he would quietly sit in his room and meet with the various pastors who came to pray with him.

The prisoner spent his time chatting with the jailer, James Cowenhoven, when he brought him his meals cooked by the jailer's wife. Cowenhoven was mild-mannered and treated his wards less like prisoners than like unwanted guests.

While Robinson refused to speak about the murder to most people, he would sometimes broach the subject with Cowenhoven, his story wavering between total innocence and hints that he knew more than he was willing to divulge just then.

It was a cold and damp January morning when Hoagland, the New Brunswick city marshal, was at the jail meeting with the sheriff and jailer. He was on his way out when Robinson called to him. Hoagland walked over to Robinson's cell, a small first-floor room with a barred window that looked out onto a field. The prisoner wanted to talk.

"I've always been a hard worker and find it very hard to be confined," Robinson, who was in chains, began before rushing on. "I didn't kill Mr. Suydam, but I know who did."

"Don't say anything that will criminate you, Peter."

"I did wrong by not telling you who committed the murder."

"It's not too late yet if you know."

"If anyone else was concerned, you may tell me, but I don't want to hear about anything involving you."

Robinson recounted his version of Suydam's death. About 10 a.m. on Thanksgiving Day, Suydam came to Robinson's house. They shook hands and Suydam remarked that Robinson was getting along very well with his house. "Yes, I'll soon have it finished off." The two men sat down at the kitchen table and continued chatting. Suydam asked if a local tavern keeper—Robinson refused to divulge the name to the marshal during their conversation—had come by. Robinson answered that the man had not.

A few minutes later, the tavern keeper arrived and sat down beside them at the table. Robinson excused himself and went to the cellar to saw wood for a fire. After sawing a handful, he was coming up the stairs when he saw Suydam sprawled out on the back parlor floor. He was so frightened the wood fell from his arms.

Just then Robinson's brother, William, knocked on the front door. Robinson told him to go away as he was worried that he might get his brother in trouble. The unnamed man then handed Robinson the bond, mortgage, and gold watch. "These are of value to you," the mysterious killer said before taking another handful of paperwork off Suydam's body that he kept. He forced Robinson to help him bury the body in the basement.

"I expect to see this man at jail in the next two weeks," Robinson told the marshal. "He's already been to my window twice. If he doesn't come back, I'll tell you who he is."

"Whatever information you have about this man you should tell me."

"I don't see how I could."

"Those papers you say he took might lead to his detection."

"I'm sure they're destroyed by now. If I'd destroyed the papers he gave me, I'd never have been suspected."

"Did Mr. Suydam bleed much?"

"No, very little."

"Didn't you hear any noise while you were down in the cellar?"

"No, the first thing I saw was the body."

"You know, I intended to come by your house on Thanksgiving Day to serve you a summons."

"What time?"

"About half-past ten."

"I wish to the Lord you had. You would have seen the dead body lying on the floor."[5]

The conversation ended and Hoagland left. This strange story kept playing in the marshal's mind. He did not tell anyone else about it.

A few days later, Robinson told the jailer a similar story although he changed some details. In this version, the man came to Robinson in November and asked to use his house for a secret meeting. The gentleman paid Robinson and asked him to send his wife, Ann, away so he could have the house to himself. Suydam showed up and Robinson went downstairs to saw wood. When he came back upstairs, he saw the body and the man holding a carpenter's mallet in his hand. The killer dragged the body down into the cellar and threatened to give Robinson "some of the same sauce" if he did not help him bury the body. Suydam groaned, and the man struck him in the head with a spade, finishing him off. He and Robinson washed the blood from the floors, the prisoner told the jailer.

"If this is true, you should tell the sheriff and have this man arrested," Cowenhoven responded Robinson refused to give him the man's name but revealed enough details so that the jailer suspected a respectable and well-known tavern keeper. Robinson said the man had visited him at the jail and promised to get him an excellent lawyer and to give him $100. Cowenhoven stationed a guard at the cell window, but no one showed up. They even set up a trap to catch the alleged mastermind. Cowenhoven stretched a thin length of twine from his office to Robinson's cell. The prisoner would yank the string if the mystery man showed up and the jailer would rush over and capture him. Robinson never pulled the string, and nothing came of the jailer's suspicions concerning the barman. Robinson's court date was quickly approaching.

On March 12, the grand jury indicted Robinson for murder. At the courthouse, he pleaded not guilty as he stood between his attorneys, Edward Wood, a local lawyer who had been in the business for a decade, and David Graham, Jr., a high-powered New York defense attorney, law author, and professor.

Graham submitted a motion to have the trial postponed until the next court term, several months away, because there was no way his client would get a fair trial with all the "excitement existing" against Robinson. The court denied the motion and the state attorney general, who was handling the case, fixed the trial date for the following Tuesday. Graham was a heavyweight. He had written the bible on defending cases before the New York Supreme Court. Two years earlier, he became the first professor of law at New York University. Even so, Graham would have an uphill battle to save Robinson from the gallows.

17

A Sheep as a Lamb

William Attree pushed his way into the courthouse facing Bayard Street in downtown New Brunswick for the first day of Robinson's trial that began on Wednesday, March 17, 1841.

Attree was the star crime reporter for *The New York Herald,* one of the new New York City penny papers, which was owned and operated by James Gordon Bennett. Ten years earlier, Bennett had covered the Knapp murder trials for the *Courier and Enquirer,* the same newspaper where Attree got his start.

Bennett's reporting at the Knapp trials helped kick off the national press' obsession with criminal cases that came into its own with the birth of the penny papers. The publishers of these cheap tabloid newspapers were not interested in businessmen looking for the type of financial reports found in "The Wall Street papers," as Bennett derogatorily called them. Instead, the papers aimed for the working class and newly emerging middle class and focused on sensationalistic crimes and human-interest stories. Bennett believed a newspaper's function was "not to instruct but to startle and amuse."

Poe too would soon make a splash in the *Herald*'s rival newspaper, *The Sun,* with his balloon hoax, a series of pieces he wrote about a fictitious balloon trip from America to Europe presented as a genuine story that was a tremendous sensation in 1844.

Attree was glad to be in his element, considering the other stories he had to write for Bennett, including covering Manhattan high society. The year before, Bennett forced him to dress in a suit of armor to report on a fancy-dress ball at the new Fifth Avenue mansion of Henry Brevoort, a rich and powerful member of old-money Manhattan society. Attree clanged around in the ill-fitting costume while mingling with the rich New Yorkers he despised.

The courthouse was brand new and Robinson's case was the inaugural trial. Attree entered the short hallway that led to the expansive courtroom, a handsome, nearly square space, open to the street on three sides. He craned his neck to look at the ceiling, divided into nine compartments and ornamented in the center by intricate scrollwork and supported by four massive Doric columns. Turning his attention away from the space, he focused on the large unruly crowd surrounding him. There were all sorts, ages, and classes. Based on their clothing, he surmised that some were canal boatmen, other farmers, common laborers, tradesmen, mechanics, and schoolboys. He noticed a distinct absence of women and African Americans. The make-up of the crowd reminded him of something the English poet Leigh Hunt had written about a city street and a pig driver— "Such a set of ungainly faces I have seldom seen."

At the front of the courtroom, Chief Justice Joseph Coerten Hornblower presided, flanked by Associate Justices Peter P. Runnion and Josiah Ford. Hornblower, with his thin, hawk-like face, slender frame, and wire-rimmed glasses, looked like a New England schoolteacher and ran his courtroom in the same disciplinarian manner. The proceedings began with Hornblower throwing out the defense's motion to quash the indictment based on a technicality. Defense attorneys David Graham and Edward Wood planned to renew their motion to quash the indictment if the jury convicted Robinson. It was not much, but it was a thread of hope in a fairly open-and-shut case. Attree knew Graham personally. The lawyer had defended Attree's boss, Bennett, three years earlier in a civil suit brought on by a reporting error made by Attree.

George P. Molleson, the state attorney general, led the prosecution. A hometown boy, Molleson had been a state assemblyman three times and was the former district attorney for Middlesex County. John Vandyke, his successor as DA, assisted him.

The court brought in forty-eight potential jurors and asked them a series of questions. "Have you heard anything of the case, as to have made up your mind?" Hornblower asked the men. He followed up with "Do you feel a bias or prejudice for or against the prisoner at the bar?"

One of the first potential jurors, John Wait, a plainspoken and distrustful type, replied, "I am one of the kind of men who don't believe one half of what I read in the newspapers, sir." The courtroom erupted in laughter.

"This is no place for levity or laughter," Hornblower shouted, his pale complexion coloring in anger. "I'll commit the first man to the jail whom I can fix my eye on who I find laughing." The courtroom went quiet and the jury selection continued.

Graham, knowing that there was a strong bias in the community against his client, was ruthless in his search to get Robinson an impartial jury. He challenged nearly all the potential jurors for cause based on prejudice or even if they had merely read about the case in the newspapers. Chief Justice Hornblower became frustrated with Graham's insistent questioning. He asked one of the potential jurors whether he believed everything he read in the papers.

"Yes, pretty much everything," the man responded.

"But did you ever read or hear about the moon story?" asked the judge, referencing the infamous hoax that had appeared in *The Sun* newspaper back in 1835 about flying men and other wild and fanciful creatures who lived on the moon.

"Believe I did."

"Did you believe that?"

"Well, I might, if it was proved in part."

"Did you believe that there were men with wings like angels because it was in the papers?"

"Well, I had no evidence to the contrary."

"Did you believe these stories about Robinson in the same way; or do you believe a thing merely because you read it in a newspaper?"

"Well, that's all the reason most of us have for believing anything. For most people read nothing else and know nothing but what they get from the newspapers."

At this point, Graham stepped in. "What better reason could he have, if the court please?"[1] Hornblower, incensed, decided the gullible citizen would not make a good juror, after all.

Out of forty-eight men, only five became jurors. The court would have to round up more citizens to get a full jury. Hornblower called a recess, giving Attree ample time to study the defendant. Robinson wore a dark-green jacket with a velvet collar, black pants, and a silver vest, an outfit Attree found to be tasteful. He guessed the defendant was about twenty-five (he was actually a decade older) and stood 5 foot 9 inches. The reporter found him to be "well made, not stout," but thought his "cast of countenance very unpleasant." The prisoner's skin had a dirty, pale brownish-yellow look about it, as if he had been sick. His hair was bushy, brown, and cut short. His eyes were light grey. Attree studied Robinson's face. He had a pug nose, a low forehead, and a weak chin. Attree concluded:

> His chin and the lower part of his face are so small they appear to be deformed ... He's repulsive. The organs of combativeness and destructiveness seem to be fully developed. This would be a curious study for a phrenologist.[2]

That afternoon, after a succession of potential jurors told the court they had made up their minds that Robinson was guilty, they finally got twelve men who claimed they could be fair and had not made up their minds either way as to the defendant's guilt or innocence. The court went through nearly 100 men to get an impartial jury.

As Attree watched the proceedings, he kept getting distracted by the sound of peanut shells hitting the floor like a hard rain pelting a roof. The new courthouse was being treated like a Bowery theater by the massive crowd of onlookers. The smell of peanuts and fetid air nearly made him sick.

Finally, by 8 p.m. the judge impaneled the jury and the day's work was done for the court but not for Attree. He still had to write up the story and get it to his editor for the next day's paper.

The next morning, the court gave Attree and the other reporters better accommodation, but it peeved Attree to learn they would not be providing paper, ink, or pens. The courts in New York did.

Everyone turned to watch the defendant enter the courtroom, flanked by two guards and followed by an unruly knot of mischievous-looking boys who had trailed Robinson all the way from the jail into court. To Attree, the defendant looked dejected, unlike the day before, and wondered if it was because Robinson's wife was present in court with their boy. Ann wore what looked like mourning clothes, as if her husband was already dead and buried.

When Robinson saw his wife and child, he begged Graham to make them leave. "It's more than I can bear," he told the lawyer. "I'd rather die a hundred deaths than have them here while the trial is going on." Graham spoke with Robinson's wife, and she and their boy left.

The prosecution called a succession of witnesses who had taken part in the search of Robinson's house and the discovery of Suydam's body. The attorney general showed the jury the adz and ax found at Robinson's house (no one ever determined they were the murder weapons), and Dr. William Van Deursen gave a graphic description of the victim's wounds.

Robinson's defense attorney, Graham, tried to elicit inconsistencies from the prosecution's witnesses, but they were a solid bunch and he made little headway. The best he could do was get the doctor to admit there was no way of knowing whether Suydam's wounds were made before or after death. Graham also tried to muddy the waters by having his client stand up for the jury to show how much taller he was than Suydam had been—3 or 4 inches. The doctor said that even though it was a "straight blow" a man who was Robinson's height "might have given such a blow." Graham then got the doctor to admit that Suydam could have gotten the scrapes and bruises on his face during a "personal scuffle." Van Deursen added that they could have been "caused by a fall on the face or dragging down stairs."

The day ended with the testimony of the Edmonds, father and son, who had first suspected, then accused Robinson of the murder. The best Graham could do with James Edmonds was get him to admit Robinson was always an "industrious, hardworking man."

The next day, Friday, March 19, began with the continued testimony of Jacob Edmonds, James' father, who under cross-examination admitted that Robinson complied with all of his accusers' demands. Robinson willingly turned over whatever they asked and submitted to an examination before Justice Conover before his arrest. Graham was trying to show the jury that Robinson's demeanor was that of an innocent man with nothing to hide.

His questions were the breadcrumbs he hoped the jury would follow all the way to a not-guilty plea, or at least a lesser charge that could save his client from being hanged.

Robinson seemed indifferent to his situation. He laughed at the crowd of boys who pushed and shoved each other, vying for the best view of "Old Pete." His emotions only got the better of him once when he shouted at Jacob Edmonds during his testimony, daring him to look him in the eye. The court erupted with gasps and angry murmurings until Judge Hornblower restored order.

During the trial, he would often drum his fingers on the table and turn to the nearest reporter and comment on the case. "I wish it was over," he told a journalist sitting nearby. "I'd rather be condemned than be in suspense."

Henry Evans, the Newark silversmith, took the stand and identified Robinson as the customer who had come into his shop to trade a men's gold pocket watch for a slimmer women's version. Evans said he had also engraved silver spoons with the initials P.A.R. The prosecutor pointed out that these initials could well stand for Peter and Ann Robinson. "I haven't no doubt that the prisoner is the man," Evans told the court. Suydam's jeweler also testified and identified the gold watch as belonging to the murdered banker.

The afternoon session was even worse for Robinson. The prosecution called his brother, William, to the stand. William recounted how on Thanksgiving Day, his brother had refused to let him into his house when he stopped by before church. Peter later showed up at his brother's home and was laughing about refusing to let him in. William also testified to nailing down the floor in the basement on December 5, two days after Suydam had disappeared. Peter laid the floor before William got there, he told the jury.

"My brother was whimsical and peculiar to me at times and often wouldn't speak to me for days together," William said under cross-examination. It was not the most laudatory of statements.

James Robinson, Peter's other brother, entered the courtroom and proceeded to the stand. The onlookers murmured from the gallery and angled to get a better view of both the witness and his older brother, who he was about to testify against. James began:

> I saw my brother Thanksgiving Day … He came to my house soon after Thanksgiving and spoke about his own new house. He said he wanted to tell me something and that I was not to tell. He wanted me to go to his house with him and prepare it and set it on fire. I asked him what his reason was for so doing. He told me he had the horrors about the house being finished and if it was burnt he could get the insurance. I told him that he ought not to be discouraged as the house was so near done. He offered me fifty dollars if I would go there and do it. He said it could be done by a slow match. I told him somebody might see us and that if he wanted it done, he'd have to do it himself.[3]

James also testified to seeing a newly dug spot in the ground when he helped his brother bring in boards for the cellar floor. "It was about the same spot where the body was found," he told the court.

Peter laid down the floor by himself on the Sunday after Thanksgiving and painted the floor, stairs, and entry with a garish yellow paint, James recounted. "I have known him to work on a Sunday before, but never on his own house," he said.

Under cross-examination, James testified that Peter later told him he was only joking about burning down the house. "I only wanted to see what you would do for $50," Peter had told him.

That night, back at the jail, Robinson exploded. He raved and stomped around his cell before falling into an intense depression. The jailer asked him what was wrong. Robinson said he could not believe his brother, James, had testified against him. Edmonds and the other witnesses were lying, he said. "I'm condemned to die," he screamed. "If there is a heaven and Mr. Edmonds is going there, I don't want to go."

As the trial went on, the prosecution provided more damning testimony. John Brush, who spoke to Robinson on the steamboat in early December, recounted their conversation. What Brush thought was an innocent chat about Robinson's mortgage took on new and ominous relevance. Their chance meeting was the day before Suydam's murder.

A string of witnesses told similar stories of encounters with Robinson that now appeared very sinister. Henry Molleson, a fellow carpenter, who was not related to the attorney general prosecuting the case, testified:

> Peter Robinson came on the third of December to where I was at work … He said he had been to church. I asked him if he had any work and he replied that he didn't want any, as he had plenty of money to live on til spring. He showed me a roll of bills about the size of three of my fingers. It probably had twenty or thirty bills in it. He told me, I think, that he got the money from his employers.[4]

A week later, Molleson ran into Robinson, who had gone to New York. Molleson asked if he had heard anything of Suydam during his travels. Robinson said he had not.

"Mr. Suydam's disappearance is very mysterious," Molleson remarked. Robinson did not answer but pulled out a gold watch just as he turned to leave. "Look what an establishment I have got," the witness recalled Robinson telling him. "It's gold and belongs to Mr. Suydam. It took me to knock him down for it. In fact, I'm wearing some of his clothes now."

An audible gasp arose from the courtroom. Robinson's comment had shocked Molleson, but he did not respond or tell anyone else what his friend had said.

Alexander Watson, a carpenter who had worked on Robinson's house, testified that he was there on December 12, a week after Suydam disappeared. He went into the basement and found Robinson shoveling sand from a hole for a mason who was mixing up mortar. "That's quite handy," Watson said of the hole.

"Yes, here was where I was going to poke Suydam," Robinson answered. "But I had no time to do it." Watson did not respond to his boss' morbid joke. Under cross-examination, Watson said he thought Robinson was trying to be funny. "He said it laughingly." The defense attorney asked Watson if he had seen any bloodstains in the basement or on Robinson's workbench. "If there had been any blood on it, I would have seen it," the witness answered.

The prosecution wrapped up its case and the defense began by presenting more than half a dozen character witnesses who all swore Robinson had always been a sober, hardworking, and honest man. Even the mayor, Vail, who had been instrumental in the investigation and arrest of Robinson, admitted that he had "never heard [Robinson's] integrity questioned for a moment. His general reputation was that of a sober, honest, industrious man," before adding, "previous to this matter." The defense did not have much else to work with, but Graham gave it his best shot.

Attree believed the jury would only take an hour to find Robinson guilty.

Graham's final summation on Wednesday, March 24, was eloquent and riveting. The attorney picked apart the prosecution's case piece by piece, pointing out inconsistencies in witness testimony and highlighting the statements of the witnesses—including the mayor—who spoke of his client's stellar reputation as a sober and hardworking citizen. When Graham finished, the courtroom erupted in shouts, ballyhoos, and a loud and sustained applause. While the crowd was on the side of the prosecution, they had fallen under the spell of Graham's forceful and articulate speech. The chief justice was having none of it; Hornblower growled:

> Stop this noise … If people want to evince anything of this nature, they had better go to a theater, and not to a court of justice. This occasion is a most solemn one; and this is the first time I ever saw any such feeling exhibited in the state of New Jersey during forty years' practice; and it is highly disgraceful to the county of Middlesex.[5]

The attorney general gave his summation, Judge Hornblower then explained the pertinent law, and the jury left to deliberate.

While the jury discussed the case, Attree had a quick conversation with the prisoner. Robinson wanted one of the portraits he had seen several courtroom sketch artists drawing of him during the trial. "I see a good many fellows here taking likenesses of me," Robinson told Attree as he scanned the courtroom. "I would like one. I think I ought to have one."

"I'll try to get you one, Peter."

"I had a very handsome one once. I gave $30 for it. It was quite small. It had me, my wife, and my two children in it, but it was stolen from me when I went to jail. I'll never see it again." Robinson went quiet for a minute, then continued. "I shall be condemned, I suppose. Then there'll be another opportunity for some of you to write books about me, but I think I ought to share the profits."

"Yes," Attree answered.

"If I'm condemned, you'll see no difference in me. I shall be just as cheerful as I am now. I may as well be hung for a sheep as a lamb. And with all they can say, they can't say one word against my character. They can't say I haven't always been a sober, honest, and industrious man."

"Ay," Attree responded.

"But if I had a good lawyer at first, I should have been better off. But my first lawyer came to me in prison and the first thing he said to me was 'Make your peace with God.' What kind of a way was that? Make your peace with God. That was no way for a lawyer to set," he said with bitterness.

The jailer cut off the conversation and shooed Attree back to his seat. The jury was coming out. It was 9.10 p.m. when the jury quietly took their seats. Their deliberations had been so short that Robinson's attorneys who had briefly stepped out did not even make it back in time to hear the verdict. The verdict was guilty.

When Robinson learned his fate, the blood drained from his face, but he showed no other emotion. Attree had been correct in his prediction on the outcome of the case, but not the time the jury needed to deliberate. He had guessed an hour, but it had taken half that time.

The reporter was also insightful enough to have planned for a late night in court. The last train to New York had just left when the jury announced the verdict. Attree had a horse waiting outside the courthouse, saddled and ready to go. As soon as they read the verdict, he dashed off the pertinent details, rushed outside, leaped onto the horse, and rode to the next station on the train's route to send his dispatch back to Bennett at *The Herald* office in Ann Street for the next morning's paper. Thanks to his quick thinking, *The Herald* was the only New York City paper with the news of Robinson's guilty verdict the next morning.

Back in court, as Robinson was being led out, one juror shouted: "How do you feel now?"

"First rate," the prisoner said. He was smiling.

18

GRISWOLD

First it was sickness, then it was a banking crisis. Poe could not win. His hoped-for magazine kept getting derailed. Originally scheduled for February 1841, Poe's continuing illness pushed publication until March. Just as he was gathering enough subscriptions and promised contributions from various writers, the Philadelphia banks suspended business amid the continued turmoil wrought by President Andrew Jackson. His war with the federal banking system in the 1830s led to a long-lasting bank panic and depression that ebbed and flowed all the way into 1843, six years after Jackson had left office.

The economic instability forced Poe to put aside his plans and pick up a steady source of income. He accepted a position at *Graham's Magazine* as the book review editor at $800 a year (equivalent to about $20,000), and a vague promise by the publisher, George Rex Graham, to help Poe with his own magazine within a year.

Graham was a self-made man who went from cabinetmaker to lawyer to successful publisher in less than five years. In 1839, he bought *The Gentleman's Magazine* from Burton—the periodical that had fired Poe—and merged it with his own, *The Casket*.

"As a stern, just and impartial critic Mr. Poe holds a pen second to none in the country, and we have the confident assurance, that with such editorial strength as the Magazine now possesses, the literary department of the work will be of the very highest character," Graham wrote in *The Saturday Evening Post*, in announcing Poe's joining the new magazine. Graham was also the editor and part-owner of that newspaper.[1]

Poe's writings, both fiction and critical essays, were once again on the national stage, and he took full advantage of the position. That spring, the magazine published his story "The Murders in the Rue Morgue." The story introduced Poe's detective, C. Auguste Dupin, and the modern detective genre to the world. The story made a big splash and received accolades from several East Coast newspapers. Poe's star was rising.

In the following months, he reviewed such literary hard-hitters as Henry Wadsworth Longfellow, Nathaniel Hawthorne, and Charles Dickens, of whom he said, "Mr. Dickens, through genius, has perfected a standard from which Art itself will derive its essence, its rules."[2] Poe and Dickens would meet in person the next year and continue a written correspondence after Dickens returned to England regarding his attempt to help Poe find an English publisher.

His personal fondness for Dickens did not prevent Poe from criticizing Dickens' work, *The Old Curiosity Shop*. Poe questioned the author's grip on reality, writing that "the rumors in respect to the sanity of Mr. Dickens, which were so prevalent during the publication of the first numbers of the work, had some slight, some very slight foundation of truth."[3]

Poe's inability to hold back would soon earn him a reputation as a ruthless and hard-hearted critic. Poe was amassing an extensive list of powerful enemies who would haunt him in this life and beyond.

One spring afternoon that year, Poe met with Rev. Rufus Wilmot Griswold to chat about literature. Poe had learned Griswold was working on an anthology on American poetry, *The Poets and Poetry of America*, and he was hoping Griswold would include him. In his simple and elegant but threadbare attire and with his soft Virginia accent, Poe contrasted with Griswold, a New Englander originally from Rutland, Vermont, who was suave, erudite, and always fashionably dressed.

With his thinning hair and chinstrap beard, he looked older than Poe, even though he was six years younger. Griswold, a failed Baptist clergyman, had done well as a freelance writer and editor. He had worked at some of New York's better newspapers and magazines, including Horace Greeley's *The New Yorker*, before settling in Philadelphia for a second time. He had briefly moved to Boston before returning to work at *The Daily Standard* newspaper in Philadelphia. He loved talking literature and politics and was well-versed in both subjects. His large grey eyes would light up and his broad forehead crease in concentration as he hammered home a point he wanted to make.

Their first meeting went well, and Poe sent Griswold several of what he considered his best works, including "The Haunted Palace," an early poem that he was especially proud of. Perhaps it was his pride in the piece, or just his unfortunate obsession with plagiarism, that led him to tell Griswold in the letter accompanying the poems that Henry Wadsworth Longfellow, a rising star among New England's writing circle, had plagiarized Poe's work for his poem "The Beleaguered City." Poe wrote that he had published "The Haunted Palace" in a Baltimore journal in 1839 and then "embodied it in a tale called 'The House of Usher'" later that year:

Here it was, I suppose, that Prof. Longfellow saw it; for, about 6 weeks afterwards, there appeared in the South. Lit. Mess: a poem by him called "The Beleaguered City", which may now be found in his volume ... The identity in tide is striking; for by the Haunted Palace I mean to imply a mind haunted by phantoms—a disordered brain—and by the Beleaguered City Prof. L. means just the same. But the whole tournure of the poem is based upon mine, as you will see at once. Its allegorical conduct, the style of its versification & expression—all are mine.[4]

No one could dissuade him from this belief. Poe's obsession with plagiarism would soon creep into his literary criticism, nearly overwhelming it, and have lasting implications. For now, Poe had to wait for the anthology to come out to learn which poems, if any, Griswold would choose.

19

SENTENCE

At 11.30 a.m. on Thursday, March 25, the court was called to order. A massive crowd thronged the courtroom, hoping to catch a glance of the infamous Mr. Robinson as Judge Hornblower handed down his fate. The guards brought the prisoner in, looking pale and haggard. His lips were dry and cracked.

The crowd, while immense, seemed less agitated than the previous day. Attree believed that had the jury found Robinson not guilty, the onlookers would have hanged Robinson from the nearest tree. The women of New Brunswick were the most strenuous in their convictions on this point, Attree found.

Judge Hornblower took his seat and the bubbling of voices from the gallery quieted.

"Peter Robinson," intoned Hornblower, as the prisoner stood up. "You stand before this court convicted by the verdict of the jury of the murder of Abraham Suydam, in the first degree. Have you aught to say other than what, by yourself and by your counsel, you have already said, why the court should not proceed to pronounce judgment upon you?"

"I have nothing to say," responded the prisoner, his lips quivering. Then, Hornblower spoke:

> Peter Robinson, after a full, fair, and impartial trial with a jury selected by yourself out of a large number of your fellow citizens, and by the aid of efficient, honorable, and able counsel, who have left nothing unsaid or undone in your behalf which become them, or which honorable men ought to have said and done in your behalf, you have been convicted of the willful, foul, malicious, deliberate, and premeditated murder of Abraham Suydam, by which conviction you are doomed to suffer the awful punishment of death.[1]

Loud crying began in the gallery, but the justice continued.

Mr. Suydam was your neighbor, your fellow citizen, and for aught that we know, or that has appeared to the court on the trial, he was your benefactor. He had conveyed to you a lot of land; he had advanced you money to build a comfortable dwelling thereon for yourself and your family. In consequence of what he had advanced to you, and for the security of the proper payment to him of his money, you had furnished him with a bond and mortgage on that property. With these securities on his person, and in his possession, on the morning of the third of December, and, as we have reason to fear, in pursuance of a previous arrangement made by you with him, he left his home and the bosom of his family, and entered your house, never to return to that home and that family alive. It is evident that but a few minutes elapsed after he entered your house, before you cruelly murdered him, and then robbed your victim of his money, his watch, and the papers which he had about his person; and there at the bloody scene of the murder, you dug the unhallowed grave; and within the walls of that building, erected by his money, you sought to conceal his mangled corpse.[2]

The justice went on, telling the prisoner that while he committed this "cold-blooded murder" he had been "unmindful of the just and holy God" whose eye had been upon him during the killing and "through time and through eternity." Hornblower then pronounced the sentence of death:

The outraged majority of the law demands your life, and nothing else will satisfy it. You may affect an indifference to all of this; You may reject the Bible and the minister of Christ and those consolations which they may seek to offer you, but God knows your heart. You cannot deceive God. His eye is upon you as it was when you struck the fatal blow—as it has been ever since—as it will be until the moment when the breath ceases to animate your body—and it will follow you to another world; and his wrath will rage against you through the unwasting ages of eternity. It is considered by the court that you be taken from the jail and you be hung by the neck until you are dead, and may God have mercy on your soul.[3]

The courtroom was still except for the continued sobbing coming from several women in the gallery. A palpable sense of anguish filled the space and sucked the air from the room. The townspeople who had clamored for Robinson's death now wavered in the reality of the moment. Robinson seemed to be the only one who was unfazed. He stood still, his face betraying no feelings, his muscles rigid. The justice, himself overcome with emotion, said nothing for several minutes before ordering the prisoner removed from court. The crowd rushed forward for a glimpse of the condemned man. He grinned at the crowd as two guards led him from the room. As he passed the sheriff, Robinson smiled and told him, "Now, remember you must share the fees with me that you get from hanging me."

Back in his cell, his arms and legs once again in irons, Robinson joked with the jailer. "As I'm a carpenter, I think I ought to be employed to help build my own gallows, and I could build my own coffin, and give my wife the money," he told Cowenhoven. "All I ask is a snug platform and a strong rope." His wife and his six-year-old son came to visit under close supervision. The jailer thoroughly searched Ann before he allowed her in. A guard was with the family the entire time.

Attree returned to New York and the basement on Ann Street where Bennett ran his burgeoning newspaper business. The reporter got back to roaming the halls of justice, digging up juicy crime stories. He made a few return trips to New Brunswick to see how Robinson was making out the closer it came to his execution date.

A week before the execution, Attree spent the day with Robinson and found that he had become obsessed with the idea that doctors and phrenologists would dissect, study, poke, and prod his body after his death. The sheriff swore that would not happen since it had not been part of the judge's sentence against the prisoner. Robinson had asked that someone watch over his grave to prevent the resurrectionists—body snatchers paid by anatomists for fresh corpses—from digging up his body.

During their time together, Attree learned more about Robinson's past, or at least his criminal past, which was what Attree, and his readers, were really interested in. Besides the accidental barn-burning when he was still a child, Robinson gleefully recalled how he broke into his neighbor's cellar to steal salt pork. The man came down the stairs and Robinson hid behind a barrel, intending to bash his head in if he got the chance. Instead, the man's candle blew out, so he went back upstairs, and Robinson escaped.

Robinson continued his pattern of mood swings that had been evident throughout his time in jail. Attree thought his temperament was "as various and uncertain as the weather." The prisoner met with several clergymen, prayed, and quietly read the Bible, then he would fly into a rage because his tea was not strong enough or his family was not doing a good enough job dealing with his affairs. Other times he would crack jokes, gallows humor hinting at a confession he had not yet made.

The sheriff sent in a barber to trim Robinson's hair so he would look his best while hanging from the end of a rope. Robinson seemed to take it all in stride. As the barber worked, Robinson chatted agreeably. "I think me and General Jackson are the two greatest men now living in the United States," Robinson said.

The barber took the bait. "Why so?"

"Because he put his veto to the United States Bank and I put my veto to the Farmers and Mechanics Bank." Robinson laughed at his little joke about Andrew Jackson's fight against the Second National Bank in the 1830s that ended with its destruction and eventually led to a financial crisis known as the Panic of 1837. Suydam, Robinson's victim, had been the president of the Farmers' and Mechanics' Bank.

Now that Robinson's wife, Ann, was allowed to see her husband, she came often. On one visit, she asked her husband to tell the authorities whether he had an accomplice or if he had acted alone and to "clear your wife and child in the eyes of the world from all suspicion that they knew anything about it."

Instead of addressing her question, Robinson asked her how it was going with the disposing of his property, including his carpentry tools. He wanted to help support her and their son before he died. He became preoccupied with this idea and exploded when one of his brothers sold the tools at a lower price than he believed they were worth. "I'd rather go to hell headlong, then see my tools sold under price," he raged.

There were moments of tenderness as well. Attree watched as Robinson's six-year-old son came for a last visit before being taken to live with his mother's family in Newark. The boy ran over to his father, who showed the first sign of warmth Attree had seen from him. The two hugged and sat together, talking quietly. A few minutes after the boy left, Robinson suddenly blurted out, "Oh no, I didn't wish him goodbye. I shall never see him again in this world." Attree was unmoved as he had heard that Robinson physically abused his two older children. He would beat them and had once locked them in the house for an entire day with no food. Then there were the stories about how those two children, a boy and a girl, had died suddenly less than a year earlier under mysterious circumstances. Robinson threw himself to the ground and continued to cry, his chest heaving, his wailing filling the cell.

As the reporter sat listening to Robinson sobbing, he looked out the window and caught sight of a young girl, maybe twelve or thirteen, running through the neighboring field covered in spring blooms—snowdrops, daisies, and crocuses. The girl collected them and put the flowers into her raven hair that fell in ringlets down her neck. Attree turned to look at Robinson, who sat on the floor, his arms and legs chained to an iron bolt, his hair matted, his eyes listless and glazed as he stared blindly into space. The reporter thought about the contrast between Robinson and the innocent child who "bounded with almost fairy lightness" and wondered what lessons someone could draw from it. He wrote:

How brief a space had passed since for him, perchance, then light in heart and limb, the world and its mysterious ways were bland, bright, and golden, like the early gleams of morning ... He has not numbered more than half the days allotted in this life by God to man, and all is darkness, desolation, and night.[4]

20

THE SUNKEN EYE, THE PALLID CHEEK

On the evening of April 13, 1841, Attree furiously scribbled as Robinson's words came rushing out. He couldn't believe his luck. Attree had been coming to the jail to visit Robinson regularly. He had built a rapport with the prisoner, and Robinson had confessed to him a little at a time.

With less than forty-eight hours before Robinson's hanging, the prisoner unburdened himself completely to Attree.

The reporter again was in the right place at the right time. He had come to New York from his hometown of Brighton, England, in 1832 and landed a newspaper career in the penny press, which suited his writing style and temperament that leaned towards black humor, the cynically comic, and biting criticism.

Five years before covering the Robinson trial, he had gone to Texas during their bid for independence from Mexico, joined the fight as an express rider, and was there to report on the massacre at the Alamo for three different New York papers. He felt he had done his part for the cause and even helped advance Davy Crockett's legend.

Then there was the sad case of Helen Jewett when he was still writing for *The Transcript*. Jewett was a beautiful dark-haired prostitute who had become a fashion plate, celebrity, and confidante to some of New York's most important men. Attree wrote about her savage murder in April 1836 by another Robinson. Richard P. Robinson, her nineteen-year-old killer. He was a shipping clerk from a respectable New England family. Robinson had carried on a tempestuous affair with Jewett for ten months before slamming a hatchet into her head and setting her on fire out of jealousy. Attree was livid that a jury acquitted him of the killing.

Like the murderer, Attree had also been a client, but more than that, the hard-nosed crime reporter had become sentimentally attached to her. It was the loss of Jewett that spurred on his adventures in Texas. Now he was back in New York and at a fast-growing penny paper covering the "horribles," a beat that was proving to be popular with New York's readership. Sitting in Robinson's cell in

New Jersey, he listened intently as the killer rambled on about being broke and owing Suydam and everyone else in town money for a house that had become an albatross around his neck.

It was unusual for Attree to be writing down his subject's words as they spilled out. He was famous for having a photographic memory. He typically waited until he was back at the office to put anything down on paper, but this was not a typical situation. This was the confession of a cold-blooded murder:

> Everyone to whom I owed a few dollars was after me to sue or to get me to give my furniture for the debt. I did so. I did all that I could. I was driven nearly crazy by all these debts. I hadn't a friend on earth to whom I could go and borrow five dollars, so I let them take my furniture, until there was scarcely anything left in the house and I was ashamed to let anyone come into it to see how poor we really was and how bad off.[1]

Robinson broke down then, the tears streaming down his face as he recounted how he tried to work off what he owed but could not earn enough to support his family:

> All the money I had in the world was buried into that house and I had worked so hard at it that I thought if I had to lose it after all, because I couldn't pay the interest and the mortgage that I'd just as soon risk my life and lose that with it.[2]

The tiny jail cell was oppressive. Besides the prisoner and Attree, Rev. Hamble Leacock, an Episcopalian minister of West Indian descent, was there to offer what aid he could to Robinson before the prisoner met his fate at the end of a rope. Cowenhoven, the jailer, was also present.

In the days before Robinson's $75 note came due to Suydam, he desperately tried to raise the money. Robinson went to see one of his clients who owed him for the work he had done on his home. The man told him he could not pay him for at least a week.

Robinson's brother who had promised to help him out never came up with the cash. Robinson went to New York, bringing his wife and child along, to see if any of his friends or relatives there could help. Robinson recalled:

> I was disappointed in raising money … On Wednesday, December 2, I put my wife and child on board the Newark steamboat and told her to stay there at her sister's until I could put up the doors in the house I had built. I then took passage on the steamboat Raritan for this place. After I arrived here, and took my supper at my brother William's, I walked around the town and called upon a number to whom I was indebted and told them it was impossible to raise any money to pay them. They threatened prosecution against me. The same evening, about eight o'clock, I called

on Mr. Suydam at his dwelling. This day was the first that I contemplated the act, which has brought me where I now am.[3]

Robinson knocked on Suydam's door. Suydam answered, surprised to see one of his clients on his doorstep at such a late hour on the day before Thanksgiving. "I have company," he said coldly. Robinson remained on the doorstep:

> If you don't mind going to the bank tomorrow and get the note you hold against me and call at my house and bring the rest of the papers, I can settle with you. I have $300 in gold. I can pay off the note and the balance can go towards the bond and mortgage.[4]

Suydam seemed surprised. Robinson explained that the money was his wife's and that she insisted on paying it herself. He told Robinson he would see come by the house the next day.

After leaving Suydam's, Robinson returned to his brother William's house. He told no one of his plans. That night, the realization of what he was about to embark on made him restless. Robinson did not like sleeping at his own place without his family there, so he stayed over at William's. That night, he barely slept.

The next morning, Robinson dragged himself out of bed. It was Thanksgiving Day. He ate breakfast with his brother and left the house about 9 a.m. He stopped by Cornel's grocery store for dried corn to feed his chickens.

Back at the house he could not afford to finish, he tossed the corn in the yard and watched the chickens scuttle about and peck at the food. He felt like he was in a trance as he went about his chores. The knowledge of his plan whirred away in the back of his mind constantly. Would he actually go through with it?

He went down to the cellar and chopped wood. The ax sliced through log after log as he lifted and swung, lifted and swung, lifted and swung. He hauled the wood upstairs and built a roaring fire in the back parlor.

He sat at the table, waiting. Finally, the sound he had been expecting and dreading arrived. It was 10.30. There was a loud knocking at the door, but why was it coming from the back door? Robinson had planned for Suydam to arrive by the front of the house. There was a hatchet near the entrance he had planned to use. Suydam rapped on the door again. Robinson slowly got up from his chair and answered the door with a sense of the inevitability of what he was about to do. The banker came in and Robinson, without his noticing, locked the door behind him. They greeted each other and sat down by the fire. "I have to apologize. I didn't have a pen nor ink so my wife had to go out and get them," Robinson said.

He asked if Suydam would not like to see how the work had been progressing in the cellar. With nothing better to do since they needed a pen and ink to finish their business, Suydam agreed. He went down first, with Robinson following behind him on the narrow cellar stairs.

Robinson picked up a heavy wooden mallet and followed Suydam through the basement. He steadied his nerves for the kill but could not do it. The banker seemed oblivious. They went back upstairs. Robinson softly thumped the mallet against his palm, feeling the weight of it. They stood by the fire and continued discussing the house. Suydam was getting restless. It had been fifteen minutes since he arrived. "My wife is taking quite a long time," Robinson remarked.

"I believe I'll take a walk around the neighborhood and then come back," Suydam said, moving towards the back door. He put on his hat and nearly reached the doorway—his hand was on the doorknob—when Robinson swung the mallet and caught him in the back of the head, crushing his hat with the force. Suydam fell heavily to his knees, stunned but still conscious. He attempted to stand, but Robinson swung the heavy wood mallet again and Suydam fell to the ground, knocked senseless. Robinson—panting, the adrenaline surging through him—laid the mallet down. He had killed Mr. Suydam. He had really done it.

He staggered to the front door and locked it. He had forgotten to lock it earlier. Anyone could have walked in. He went down to the cellar and began digging a grave. The sweat poured out with his exertion. He stopped suddenly. He could not leave the body upstairs. He had to bring it down. As he rounded the stairs, he stopped short. Suydam was on all fours, attempting to stand. Blood covered his face and hands and dripped heavily to the floor. Suydam looked up then and saw Robinson staring at him. "Peter, oh Peter," he gurgled and said the words again. Robinson was losing his will to continue and knew that if Suydam begged for his life, he would spare him. Instead, Robinson grabbed the mallet from the floor and swung with all his might, landing the blow with a sickening thud, like a melon dropped from a high window. Suydam was dead. Robinson began rifling through his pockets and finally found the papers he'd been looking for—the papers that had led him to this moment.

He dragged the body down the stairs by the feet and into the cellar. He left it there while he looked for something to cover the windows while he worked. He found paper curtains that he tacked up to the basement window. Upstairs, he put curtains up at the sidelight of the front door. He stripped off the sheet from the bed to cover a window that looked in on the cellar stairs.

He returned to the basement and got back to digging the hole next to where the body lay. His muscles strained as he dug 4 feet into the hard-packed earth. Finally done, Robinson went through his victim's pockets one last time. He found a fat roll of bills, a penknife, and a few shillings. That was when he noticed the watch-chain. He pulled it out. It was a handsome gold pocket watch. He slipped it into his own pocket, feeling the weight and poshness of it. Suydam would not be needing it. Robinson looked at his work and decided he needed to make the hole wider and a little deeper. He flung the dirt with his spade onto Suydam's head and body. He could not stand to look at it. He heard an unearthly noise then. He flinched and moved away from the sound. The noise continued— Suydam was alive.

Robinson crawled out of the hole and stood on the mound of dirt covering Suydam's head, hoping to smother him and the unearthly groans coming from the dying man. He groaned louder. Robinson could not take it anymore and slammed the edge of the spade into Suydam's head, feeling the tool sink into his skull. The noises stopped finally. Robinson, breathing heavily, hopped back into the hole and quickly finished digging the grave. He pulled himself out, picked up the body, and dumped it in, head first. It was easy. He felt so strong. However, he had miscalculated Suydam's height and had to wedge the legs into a fetal position to make them fit. He dumped the dirt onto the body and filled the hole, tamping down the earth as best he could.

Robinson rubbed the dirt from his hands as he made his way up the stairs. He needed to clean the blood from the floor. He was just getting started when someone knocked at the back door. His heart jumped. If someone saw this mess, it would all be over. "Who is it?"

"It's me, Peter." It was William.

Robinson could not let his brother in. He could not let William get involved. "You can't come in. I've got the horrors. I wouldn't even let Annie in if she were here." William tried again to get in the house but eventually gave up, knowing his brother's peculiarities. When he heard his brother leaving, Robinson breathed easier.

He began wiping up the pools and streaks of blood and the bloody handprints left when Suydam tried to stand but could not. There was not that much blood, maybe a pint or two. Robinson noticed there were not even any bloodstains on his shirt and pants, though the bottoms of his shoes had some blood on them. He went into the yard and retrieved several buckets of water from the well to wipe away the evidence. He sloshed the water on the floor and wiped everything clean.

Afterward, Robinson sat down to have a look at the various papers he had taken from Suydam. There was the mortgage, the bond, the insurance policy, and an agreement between Robinson and the mason working on the house. Suydam had paid the mason $210, which was accruing interest. Robinson tossed the agreement into the fire but kept the other papers related to the house.

Just then, there was another knock at the back door. Robinson held his breath. The knocking continued. "If this person comes in, I'm going to kill them," he thought. "I could kill twenty men if they should come in one by one."

The knocking stopped. Robinson let out his breath and got back to sorting through the paperwork. Besides the documents relating to him, Suydam had bonds worth about $16,000. Robinson took it all upstairs to the front room. He pried up a floorboard near the hearth and tossed in the bonds. He put the papers related to the house in a tool chest along with the gold watch. Robinson left the house and walked down to the canal and hurled the penknife into the river.

The next day, Robinson noticed some blood he had missed in his rush to clean up the evidence. He planed the floor to remove some stubborn stains and scraped the walls clean of evidence, even spots of blood no bigger than a pinhead, and then painted the floor and the stairs going down to the basement and a few other areas.

He looked at his work and was proud. It had taken only a few hours between the time he killed Suydam and the cleanup. Yet he was always an excellent worker, fast and efficient. Where another man might only plane, plough, and groove sixteen floor planks, he could do forty-five or more in the same time.

Attree stopped writing. The sun had dropped below the horizon as the shadows stretched across the small cell, hiding the face of the prisoner. Attree handed the written confession to the pastor who read it to Robinson. Cowenhoven, the jailer, watched as Robinson signed the document. The prisoner acknowledged it was "the truth, and nothing but the truth." He handed the confession to Cowenhoven.

Robinson denied the long-swirling rumors of the other murders attributed to him by the gossips of New Brunswick, rumors that made their way into the big New York newspapers, including *The Herald*, and from there around the world. Robinson spoke as Attree once again acted as his scribe:

> Being about to die shortly, and with the thought of eternity before my eyes, and the fear of God on my soul, and knowing that I cannot be forgiven if I die with a lie in my mouth, I, here, this fourteenth day of April, 1841, deny all knowledge of how the peddler Allen, or Randolph [the carpenter] who was killed at Dark Lane a few years since, or my children, came to their death, other than by natural causes ... I also deny knowing what became of my sister Susan.[5]

Susan had married a Southerner and moved to Alabama, according to Robinson. Her family believed she had died of yellow fever, along with her husband, dispelling the rumors that Robinson murdered her. The prisoner signed his name, and Attree and Cowenhoven witnessed the document.

Robinson returned to thoughts of his victim. He mused:

> It's over now, he's dead and I will soon be dead, and we will be better friends in the next world ... I shan't knock him in the head there nor he won't get a mortgage on to me. But he had me down tight while he lived, and that's a fact. I made him loosen his grip on me.[6]

Attree did not respond but prepared to leave. As the reporter gathered his things, Robinson spoke up again:

All I wish you would do for me is to prevail on the sheriff to take me up to the big field opposite my place, so let me have twenty-thousand people to see me go off and then if I could only have a good band of music up from New York to play some lively tunes I should go off contented … But it's hardly a fair shake to shut me up and strangle me in the hole and corner fashion they talk of. Whatever you do, don't let the doctors get a hold of me and make medicine of me.[7]

In the last twenty-four hours of Robinson's life, Attree spent nearly every waking moment with him in his cell, often just the two of them, as the prisoner prepared to die. Robinson kept his cell extremely hot in preparation, he said, for what he would be facing after his death. The jailer indulged Robinson, providing as much fuel for the condemned man as he wanted. Attree sweated profusely in the sweltering room but continued to stay with Robinson. He was willing to forgo comfort for a good story.

Robinson's last day began with the arrival of two men from the Fowler company (later Fowler and Wells), the leading practitioners of the pseudo-science of phrenology, who came to make a plaster cast of the prisoner's head. Phrenologists claimed that by studying the size and shape of the human head, they could determine a person's mental abilities and personality traits.

Attree had sent for the men, believing Robinson would make a worthy subject of study. Robinson heartily agreed, but he insisted that they put his likeness alongside "General Jackson's, General Washington's, and Napoleon Bonaparte's, and Lord Wellington's heads, and all the heads of the great men and great murderers."

The Fowler company's office in Manhattan included a gallery of the plaster casts of the heads of both the famous and infamous.

When the men arrived, Robinson changed his mind and decided he did not want them to take the cast. "You want to hawk it about the streets of New York and cry out 'here's the head of Peter Robinson, the murder, only half a dollar.'" Only after the phrenologists told him they had personally cast the head of Senator Daniel Webster did Robinson agree to have his done.

While all this was going on, a minister, one of several who visited that day, told Robinson he needed to focus on the "awful matter you have to undergo tomorrow."

"Very well," Robinson answered, "I suppose I have to, but it's only me that has to suffer any of it." The minister went on, telling Robinson that Suydam had held a high opinion of him and would have helped him with paying his debts. "Yes, and it was a sad thing, and all for seventy-five dollars, too," Robinson answered. "And, sir, if I'd only known that there was such a thing possible as having a note renewed, I'd a gone to Mr. Suydam, given him $20 and had it renewed, and then he'd been alive right now."

In the evening, Robinson's wife, brothers, and sister-in-law came to see him for the last time. Attree found it painful to watch as the family said goodbye to Robinson while he was in his chains. He looked pale and haggard, his hands cuffed, and his legs in irons. His wife, Ann, broke down when she was told it was time to leave. Her husband seemed unaffected. William and James stayed with their brother throughout the night as Robinson slept fitfully, getting only three hours of sleep. Several ministers returned at around dawn to continue their vigil.

On the morning of April 16, 1841, a carnival-like atmosphere pervaded New Brunswick despite the cold and misty weather that seeped into the bones. The air was electric with anticipation. This was the day Robinson would hang. Horses, buggies, and pedestrians choked the roads into town as everyone surged towards the jail where the execution would take place. The crowd outside the two-story stone jail became livid when they learned the event was a private one requiring a ticket handed out by the sheriff. A 16-foot-tall fence blocked them from getting a view of the action.

The fence surrounded a 6-foot-wide and 25-foot-long enclosure where workers had been busy erecting the gallows for several days, hauling the 12-foot timbers and other enormous pieces of wood used in the death machine's construction.

That morning, it was ready for use. The two main vertical beams stretched towards the sky where a crossbar joined them. A third upright beam held five heavy weights attached to a rope that ran to the crossbar. The scaffold where Robinson was to stand was only 8 inches off the ground. The noose waited for its victim. When the executioner cut the rope that held the weights in place, the force would fling the victim into the air, with the expected result of a broken neck. Yet more often than not, the condemned would slowly suffocate to death.

By 10 a.m., the sun had burned away the mist, giving way to a beautiful early spring day. The sheriff and jailer entered Robinson's cell with the tailor who had sewn the shift Robinson would wear to die in. It was time to go.

Attree had spent several days nearly alone with Robinson. Now, he found himself one of many reporters crowded into the cramped space. The other journalists who had not seen Robinson since his trial could not believe the change he had gone through in the weeks since his conviction. A reporter for the *Newark Daily* wrote:

> The sunken eye, the pallid cheek, and the quivering muscle, showed that a fearful struggle had been going on within … The gaze of the morbid and curious, eager to catch a sight of the culprit, was nothing to him. He had done with the world, and was only anxious to escape from himself, to leap from life to death.[8]

Cowenhoven unlocked Robinson's leg irons and did the same with the handcuffs but was having a hard time with them.

"Mr. Cowenhoven, that's not the right key," the prisoner told him. "You'll have to get the key."

The jailer, somewhat embarrassed, left the room and returned with another key. He unlocked the cuffs. The tailor helped Robinson slip the simple muslin shift over his own clothes—a shirt and pantaloons. A white hood came next. It would cover his face so the onlookers would not have to see his expression at the moment of death.

Robinson insisted on shaking everyone's hand who was there with him. Turning to Cowenhoven, he grabbed his arm. "I hope God will bless you and your family, for you have treated me like a father," Robinson told him.

His arms bound to his sides, they led Robinson from the cell. A priest led the way down the corridor. The sheriff and Cowenhoven flanked the prisoner as they walked. Robinson's gait was firm as he headed to his fate. He took the few steps to the gallows with what seemed a light, carefree manner that onlookers commented on. Sixty people attended the execution, including Attorney General Molleson, District Attorney Vandyke, and Wood, one of Robinson's defense attorneys.

Only 10 feet from the gallows in the jail's section where Cowenhoven and his family lived, the murmuring of women's voices, the clanking of pots as they prepared lunch for the other prisoners, and the high-pitched squeals of children playing made for a strange counterpoint to Robinson's impending death. Several laborers locked up in jail for unpaid debts who knew Robinson watched the execution from the barred windows of their second-story cells.

Once Robinson had reached the scaffold and stood beneath the gallows, the sheriff slipped the hood down over the prisoner's face and adjusted the noose. All was quiet. The sheriff read the death warrant and then swung a hatchet, cutting the rope holding back the massive weights. Robinson flew upwards, drawing his legs up as his body shot into the air. The noose suddenly slipped from around his neck and he crashed to the ground with a heavy thump. The crowd shrieked in unison.

For nearly a minute, Robinson made no sound before he groaned loudly. The city marshal, John Hoagland, helped him back up. While stunned, Robinson slowly got back onto the scaffold by himself. "The Lord have mercy on me," he said, his voice shaky. He kept repeating the phrase while they put the gallows back in order, readjusting the weights and rope. The sheriff once again slipped the noose around the prisoner's neck and then cut the beam rope. Robinson launched into the air. He bounced around at the end of the rope and his body spasmed. He hung there for forty-five minutes before a doctor checked for a pulse and pronounced him dead.

"I want to be sure of it," said the sheriff, letting Robinson hang there for nearly ten more minutes before cutting the body down.

Workers put the body in a pine coffin stained to resemble mahogany. Attree went in for a closer look and decided Robinson did not look too bad for a dead man, although his expression showed that he had suffered during death. His eyes were open and gazed up towards the sky, "as if in supplication."

They carried the casket into the jail where Robinson's family waited to take it away. Beyond the fence, the massive crowd, which was treating the execution like a fair, milled around waiting for news. Two companies of the state militia prevented the rowdies from tearing down the fence to get a view of what was happening inside. The militia arrested one man caught using a crowbar to rip away the fence posts.

Mayor Vail went to see the waiting crowd; he had to shout over the noise:

> I am requested by the sheriff to inform the populace that the execution is over, and the body moved … The military will take the station assigned to them and the populace will please disperse quietly and without hesitation.[9]

The crowd was not happy with the mayor's speech. They had hoped to at least get to look at the murderer's body. Several people hissed and one cried out "down with the sheriff." When the prison gate opened, the crowd surged inside. Several people ascended the barricade and got a hold of the rope used in the execution. They cut it into pieces and tossed them into the crowd for souvenirs.

Attree left and went to find a quiet bar in which to write up his notes, but everywhere he went, boisterous merrymakers crowded him out. He gave up and headed to the train bound for New York City. "The long agony is over," he said to himself as he left New Brunswick for good.

21

ENEMIES?

After a small dinner party on a frigid January evening in 1842, Virginia sat down at the piano to entertain their friends. Even as poor as they often were, Poe scraped together the money to get her a piano and a harp. Her fingers delicately struck the keys and her voice filled the room. The music stopped, her voice suddenly choked by a gurgling in her throat and a wracking cough. Blood flowed onto her white, nearly translucent skin. Poe picked her up and carried her to their bedroom and went to fetch their doctor, who lived all the way across Philadelphia.

They returned together, and the doctor examined Virginia. He uttered the dreaded word "consumption." He doubted she would recover. Consumption, the nineteenth-century term for tuberculosis, was at the time incurable, a virtual death sentence with no reliable course of treatment, besides rest and, if possible, a "change of air" by the sea.

Poe's bright-eyed and animated Virginia looked as if she would not last the night. His relationship with his "dear little cousin," his "sissy," to whom he was passionately devoted, had begun as affection between cousins and blossomed into romantic love while they were living under the same roof with Mrs. Clemm in Baltimore. To see her suffer sent Poe rushing headlong for the bottle to escape the pain.

The morning after Virginia's attack, Poe went to see his boss, Graham. Virginia's condition desperately worried Poe, who felt it was prudent to squirrel away money to help make sure he could properly care for her.

Poe asked Graham for a two-month advance on his salary. Graham turned him down flat and was not nice about it. This treatment enraged Poe, since it was his hard work that had helped boost the magazine's national reputation. Poe's "Autography" articles, a unique series published in *Graham's* between November 1841 and January 1842, was wildly successful and much-discussed across the country. It included signatures of the literati, pseudo-handwriting analysis, and literary gossip.

For weeks, it seemed Virginia, who was just nineteen, could hardly breathe without someone constantly fanning her, either her mother or Poe, as she lay in the tiny room with a ceiling so low it nearly touched her face, the narrow bed seeming to swallow up her tiny frame. She hovered between life and death before she slowly recovered. Two weeks after the aortic rupture, the doctor told Poe he believed Virginia was out of danger, at least for now. Poe knew the disease was a death sentence, yet he continued to hope.

If only Graham had given him even a small percentage in the magazine—as little as 10 percent—Poe would have felt like he could properly care for Virginia. Instead, Graham gave him only a paltry salary. Graham's meddling with Poe's critical reviews was also harming Poe's reputation as a critic. Graham watered down his harsher comments and forced Poe to modify his opinions to praise influential, though subpar, writers.

Graham knew how deeply Poe loved Virginia, witnessing his ministrations first-hand. The publisher believed Poe was experiencing "a sort of rapturous worship of the spirit of beauty which he felt was fading before his eyes."

> I have seen him hovering around her when she was ill, with all the fond fear and tender anxiety of a mother for her first-born—her slightest cough causing in him a shudder, a heart-chill that was visible. I rode out one summer evening with them, and the remembrance of his watchful eyes eagerly bent upon the slightest change of hue in that loved face, haunts me yet as the memory of a sad strain. It was this hourly anticipation of her loss, that made him a sad and thoughtful man, and lent a mournful melody to his undying song.[1]

Graham may have been sympathetic to Poe's preoccupation with Virginia's health, but he had a magazine to run and so turned to Griswold to shore up editing duties as Poe became erratic in his work habits and cantankerous in his behavior. Poe's drinking did not help things.

Their crumbling professional relationship ended in April 1842. Graham did not want to lose Poe, but the situation had become untenable and he let him go. When asked what had happened, Poe concealed the truth. He told friends the parting was over the magazine's content that he felt was too full of "contemptible pictures, fashion-plates, music, and love-tales." Graham, who was living a life of luxury, paid him too little for the countless hours he labored for the magazine, Poe said.

Poe considered his boss a very gentlemanly, although an exceedingly weak man. It stung that it was Griswold who had replaced him as editor. Though he claimed to have no quarrel with either man, he told a friend "I hold neither in especial respect."

Graham continued to see Poe socially, even checking in at Virginia and Poe's cottage to see how they were getting along. Virginia was slowly recovering and

Poe, no longer having to go into an office, could spend more time watching over her as he worked on his stories.

He returned to his on-again-off-again *Penn Magazine* project and hoped to have the inaugural issue out by the first of the year. Poe could not help but resent Graham for never coming through with help for his magazine. Graham was a man of capital and Poe had no money, so he had gone along with the publisher's views while he worked for him, hoping that Graham would bankroll *The Penn Magazine*. "The result has proved his want of faith and my own folly," he wrote to the poet Daniel Bryan. "In fact I was continually laboring against myself."

Poe believed that by raising *Graham's Magazine*'s stature, and its circulation—it went from about 6,000 subscribers to 40,000 while Poe was an editor there—he was all but guaranteeing that Graham would not back him on his own venture.

Amid his professional rupture with Graham, Griswold's anthology, *The Poets and Poetry of America*, came out. When Poe got his copy and leafed through it, he became incensed. Griswold had only included three of his poems—a measly two pages—in the anthology and a smattering of "lukewarm praise" of his talent. Griswold gave Longfellow four pages and many minor poets nearly as much space. Added to this, Poe learned Graham was paying Griswold more than he had paid Poe when he was the editor.

Griswold was suave and nearly sycophantic towards the writers Graham hoped to get as contributors. It made Poe sick. While he and Griswold were civil in person, behind the scenes, they worked against each other.

In June, Poe wrote to his old Baltimore friend, Dr. J. Evans Snodgrass, an editor and physician, denigrating Griswold's anthology. "Have you seen Griswold's Book of Poetry?" he asked. "It is a most outrageous humbug, and I sincerely wish you would 'use it up'."

Poe did not stop there. In a letter to another friend, Poe claimed Griswold had tried to bribe him to "puff" his book:

> I accepted his offer forthwith, wrote the review, handed it to him and received from him the compensation:—he never daring to look over the M. S. in my presence, and taking it for granted that all was right. But that review has not yet appeared, and I am doubtful if it ever will. I wrote it precisely as I would have written under ordinary circumstances; and be sure there was no predominance of praise.[2]

In September, Graham offered Poe his old job back, but Poe turned him down. Griswold was no longer in Graham's favor as he had been only months before. Since coming on board, Griswold's true personality had emerged. He was petty, vengeful, and a back-stabber. Griswold spread malicious gossip about Poe, telling friends in the clannish literary world of the day "shocking bad stories" about him.

Poe and Griswold's relationship waxed and waned. A month later, in November, Poe wrote a favorable review of *The Poets and Poetry of America* in the monthly magazine, *The Boston Miscellany*. In the review, he described Griswold's anthology as "the most important addition which our literature has for many years received" and called Griswold "a man of taste, talent, and tact" even if he did not agree with all the author's choices.

Yet in early 1843, another, unsigned review of Griswold's book came out in the *Philadelphia Saturday Museum* that was brutal, especially the ending, in which the author predicts that Griswold will be "forgotten, save only by those whom he has injured and insulted, he will sink into oblivion, without leaving a landmark to tell that he once existed; or, if he is spoken of hereafter, he will be quoted as the unfaithful servant who abused his trust." Griswold believed Poe was behind the article and while they continued to have a professional relationship, Griswold prayed for a chance to revenge himself against Poe.

22

THE PENNY PAPERS

When Attree died in November 1849, there was little notice outside the tight circle of the New York press concerning the death of the man his fellow reporters and editors had considered one of the best in the business. At the height of his popularity, he was so well known in New York that he was a paid spokesman for a patent medicine company, Sherman's Headache Lozenges, which guaranteed to cure "nervous or sick headaches, heart palpitations, and lowness of spirit," among many other claims.

During Attree's career, he had been stabbed, beaten, sued multiple times, and derided as "Oily Attree" by a rival newspaper that claimed he was a blackmailer who never bathed. Worse than all of this, the industry that had once hailed him for his talents tossed him away in his final years.

After the Robinson trial, Attree continued covering crime and the society pages. He also took on some political reporting, including covering Daniel Webster's speech at the 1840 Whig presidential nominating convention in Richmond, Virginia, when William Henry Harrison ran for president.

In 1842, Attree became the *Herald*'s Washington, D.C. bureau chief covering national politics. After leaving the *Herald*, he would use his prodigious reporting talent to help document New York's Constitutional Convention in 1846, but jobs were getting scarcer for the old newsman. By 1849, Attree's heavy drinking finally caught up with him. He was out of work, broke, and physically and mentally broken. He once explained that his excessive drinking was because of his chosen profession in the newspaper business, which "exhausts the physical powers of a man, as well as his mental energies" requiring "artificial stimulants to recruit his powers."[1]

He ended up in a Manhattan mental hospital and died a few months later leaving his widow, Mary, destitute. The *Herald* gave their old reporter a bittersweet send-off, noting that he was "a man of varied learning, wholly self-acquired" whose "talents were of a high order; and as a writer he was formidable and agreeable."[2]

Besides giving Attree's talents their due, James Gordon Bennett, Attree's old boss who wrote the *Herald* story, mentioned Attree's drinking, alleging that he was his own worst enemy because of his "morbid craving for stimulants." Bennett went on to say Attree's death "was not unexpected. For some years past Mr. Attree was in declining health and within a few months it became evident that his sojourn on earth would be brief."[3]

By the time Attree died, Bennett was at the top of the publishing world after his newspaper, *The Herald*, blew past his two main rival penny papers, *The Sun* and the *Daily Transcript,* thanks in part to its more well-rounded coverage than the competition. Attree was also instrumental in the *Herald*'s early success with his thrilling crime stories. While Bennett's newspaper was heavy on sensationalism, especially crime, it also covered local and national politics in a non-partisan way, international news (with a nationalistic slant), human-interest stories, and also pioneered the society pages, also covered by Attree.

Bennett was nearly forty when he had launched the *Herald* in 1835 after a run of failed attempts at getting others off the ground after leaving his post as an editor at the *Courier and Enquirer* in 1832. Bennett hailed his paper's meteoric rise in its own pages along with gibes at the city's other newspapers. His attacks against the other papers were so vitriolic that three rival editors physically assaulted Bennett over the years. James Watson Webb, his old boss at the *Courier and Enquirer* (where Bennett covered the Knapp murder trials in 1830), thrashed him three times. Bennett had all these altercations written up as news stories since they made good reading. By the time Bennett turned over the running of his newspaper to his playboy son, James, Jr., the *Herald* was the biggest and best-known newspaper in the country.

Unlike Attree's death, Bennett's passing on June 1, 1872, at age seventy-six, was big news, making national headlines, as he quietly succumbed following a short illness. The *Herald* building's flags flew at half-staff that day, but the newspaper kept humming along despite the death of the man who, with the help of an alcoholic British crime reporter, had changed the newspaper business for good.

PART III

ALL THINGS IN HEAVEN AND EARTH

23

TELL-TALE

By November 1842, Poe still could not claw his way from underneath his ever-increasing mound of debt, even with the publication of two books, including one in two volumes; several popular short stories; and his growing national reputation. The money he made from his work was too little to support himself, his wife, and his mother-in-law.

He desperately wanted to get the federal appointment at the custom-house in Philadelphia, to help ease his financial burdens. His friend and fellow writer Frederick William Thomas had suggested the idea. The year before, Thomas had secured himself a good job as a clerk with the U.S. Treasury Department in the nation's capital through his political connections and believed he could do the same for Poe. Thomas had visited Poe in Philadelphia two months earlier, in September, to discuss the possibility. He had set up a meeting with President John Tyler's son, Robert, for the next day in New Jersey. The prospect excited Poe, but he did not show up at the meeting. He sent a letter to his friend Thomas apologizing for missing the appointment. He blamed a chill and fever, which he said overtook him before he could leave for New Jersey.

The federal job had become a holy grail of sorts for Poe, who believed a steady government job with all that entailed would make everything better, maybe even save his sick wife from an early grave.

During Virginia's first illness, Poe had steeled himself to her inevitable passing. As she slowly regained her strength, his heart flooded with the belief she would beat this illness. This pattern continued. Each time Virginia's health faltered, he felt all the agonies of her death, and when she would recover, he desperately clung to the hope that she would live. Poe's intensely sensitive nature heightened these already acute feelings.

Although he fought desperately with his desire to drink, alcohol was a solace of sorts, but with each sip, his sense of self would slip away. A kind of insanity overtook him, and he would have fits of absolute unconsciousness that could last for days. With the return to sobriety, the overwhelming pain and frustration of being able to do nothing for his beloved Virginia came rushing back.

His bouts of intemperance did not stop him from working on his short stories and poetry or his longed-for magazine, which he had renamed *The Stylus*, feeling *Penn Magazine* was too limiting a name since the periodical would not just be regional but national in scope. These activities took up a lot of his time.

He had chafed under the yoke of his earlier magazine publishers and hoped to produce "a well-founded Monthly Journal, of sufficient ability, circulation, and character, to control, and to give tone to, our Letters," he explained to a friend. Poe imagined a 120-page periodical of high but not overly refined taste, which would be boldly printed on good paper, featuring beautifully illustrated and "spirited" woodcuts, but most importantly, would be independent, truthful, and original. He wanted it to go for $5 a year—a good sum for the time (equivalent to more than $100 today); he believed it would make him, and anyone else who got behind it, a lot of money.

It was through his endeavors to gather the work of the country's best writers that he began corresponding with James Russell Lowell, a New England poet who was launching his own literary magazine, *The Pioneer*. *Graham's* had published several of Lowell's poems since Poe became editor, and Poe had praised Lowell in one of his "Autography" entries in *Graham's*, ranking him "at least the second or third place among the poets of America" because of the "vigor of his imagination—a faculty to be first considered in all criticism upon poetry." Lowell had heard through friends that Poe had also praised his poem "Rosaline" among his literary circle.

On November 16, Poe sat down and began a letter to Lowell in his neat hand:

> Learning your design of commencing a Magazine, in Boston, upon the first of January next, I take the liberty of asking whether some arrangement might not be made, by which I should become a regular contributor ... I should be glad to furnish a short article each month—of such character as might be suggested by yourself— and upon such terms as you could afford "in the beginning." That your success will be marked and permanent I will not doubt. At all events, I most sincerely wish you well; for no man in America has excited in me so much of admiration—and, therefore, none so much of respect and esteem—as the author of "Rosaline."[1]

With the lines of communication now open, the two men became fast friends through the mail. Lowell quickly responded and offered to pay $10 (a little more than $300 today) for whatever Poe would send him, especially stories, with the potential for more money if the periodical did well. Lowell's goals for his magazine lined up with the magazine Poe was still desperate to produce. Both focused on publishing the best American authors, eschewing love tales and sketches for more "healthy and manly periodical literature."

A few days before writing to Lowell, Poe had sent off his newly completed story, "The Tell-Tale Heart," to *The Boston Miscellany*, another Massachusetts-based magazine. The editors had published his review of Griswold's poetry anthology, and Poe hoped they would become a steady income stream. Unfortunately, an editor, H. T. Tuckerman, had just come on board, and he rejected it, based on a personal vendetta against Poe. Poe had described Tuckerman in one of his articles as "a correct writer so far as mere English is concerned, but an insufferably tedious and dull one."

When Poe sent the story to *The Miscellany,* he was already thinking about *The Pioneer*, asking that if they were not interested in the story to pass it along to Lowell. Ten days later, Poe still had not heard back from *The Miscellany* and wrote to Lowell, knowing the story was "of the class" he was interested in. He asked his new friend to check up on the status of the story for him.

Unbeknown to Poe, Lowell had already received the story and planned to include it in his first issue, writing to his "true friend" that he had gotten the story from Tuckerman, who had refused to publish it. "Perhaps your chapter on Autographs is to blame," Lowell wrote, adding he "was very glad to get it" for himself. [2]

When Poe finally heard back from Tuckerman, he was happy the editor had rejected "The Tell-Tale Heart." He told Lowell as much in his next letter and said if Tuckerman ever accepted one of his stories, Poe would question what kind of "twaddle" he had written to receive Tuckerman's approval. He quoted the note he had received about the rejection. "If Mr Poe would condescend to furnish more quiet articles he would be a most desirable correspondent," Tuckerman wrote. Poe derided the statement, saying Tuckerman's "quietude" would be the death of *The Boston Miscellany*.

Around this same time, Poe picked up a copy of a Philadelphia paper and was dismayed by what he read. A headline declared that they had solved the Mary Rogers mystery. Poe had written a fictionalized version of the infamous Mary Rogers murder of 1841. "The Mystery of Marie Rogêt," written in 1842, was Poe's attempt to solve the real-life murder of Rogers, an employee of a Manhattan cigar shop who had become something of a local celebrity, known for her beauty and charm. Her decomposed body was found floating in the Hudson River near the shore in Hoboken, New Jersey on July 28, 1841, three days after she left her house on Nassau Street in Manhattan. She had told her fiancé she was going to visit her aunt. Rogers was known as "the beautiful cigar girl" and her case was a sensation that gripped the entire country for months. Poe was not immune to the mystery—or the possibility of tapping into the case's notoriety to elevate his own star.

Poe set his story in Paris and made it a sequel to his already popular story "The Murders in the Rue Morgue," whose main character, Dupin, was a detective, a man of leisure, and a genius. Poe dubbed his new genre "ratiocination" and unknowingly created the modern detective genre.

When writing the sequel, Poe had poured through the newspaper reports of the Rogers' case, including those of William Attree, the same *Herald* reporter who covered the Peter Robinson case. Poe did not like Attree or his newspaper and hid a personal insult against the reporter in his story, comparing him with a character from a Greek tragedy who seeks revenge against his twin brother for having an affair with his wife.

Attree had been writing non-stop about the Mary Rogers case from the time her body had washed up onshore. The *Herald* had been pushing the theory that a gang raped and killed Rogers. Poe, through his main character, Dupin, pinned the crime on a mysterious sailor whom he believed had been Mary's lover and the cause of her earlier disappearance a year before her murder.

Poe believed he had solved the actual Mary Rogers murder through his fictionalized story, but these recent developments in the case had him wondering if, and how, he might have gotten it wrong. He rewrote the story to include the possibility of a botched abortion, which the papers were reporting as the cause of her death. The press based their stories on the deathbed confession of a tavern owner named Fredrica Loss who claimed to have been involved in the illegal abortion that killed Rogers. Police rejected Loss' confession since it contradicted some of the evidence. The murder remains unsolved.

Poe had been perfecting his idea of marrying sensationalism with serious literature to create a new American writing that was popular yet retained high literary standards. As early as 1835, Poe had relied on true crimes as the starting point for his literary works. He based his only play (which he never finished), *Politian*, on the Beauchamp–Sharp case, popularly known as "The Kentucky Tragedy."

In November 1825, Jereboam O. Beauchamp stabbed Kentucky legislator Solomon Sharp to death to avenge his fiancée's honor. The woman, Anna Cook, alleged Sharp had seduced her and fathered her illegitimate child, which was not altogether true. She made Beauchamp promise to murder Sharp before she would marry her new suitor. Poe set his play in sixteenth-century Rome but included the key details of the 1825 case. The published portions of the unfinished play were not well-received, and it changed Poe's career path. From then on, he focused more on short stories.

"The Tell-Tale Heart" followed Poe's writing of "The Mystery of Marie Rogêt," and while it contained elements of both the White and Suydam murders, it would differ greatly from his detective stories.

Poe had other problems to deal with besides the news of the Mary Rogers case. The possibility that he could have gotten things wrong had him questioning everything.

The newspaper also had announced four new federal appointments at the custom-house. One name was Pogue. Poe thought it might be a misspelling of his name since he was up for one of the jobs. He asked around and learned no one named Pogue was up for an appointment.

Thomas S. Smith, the customs collector appointed by President Tyler, had gruffly told him twice before that he would send for Poe when he wished to swear him in. Finally, after hearing nothing for two days, Poe lost his patience and went to the custom-house.

Poe made his way down to Second Street, below Dock Street, to the corner of Elmslie's Alley. He entered through the archway that led to a manicured lawn dotted with trees and then to the three-story, plain-looking federal custom-house. The first story had a marble façade, and the rest was of brick. It did not have the air of a grand federal building except for the allegorical wooden statue of a woman representing "Commerce" carved by the renowned Philadelphia artist William Rush near the building's apex.

He walked up the stairs leading to the front door then took the staircase to the second floor to the principal business room where he found Collector Thomas Smith. "Have you no good news for me yet?" Poe asked, trying to keep the conversation friendly.

"No, I am instructed to make no more removals," Smith snapped, barely glancing at Poe.

Poe, astonished and put off by Smith's tone, said, "I have heard, through a friend, from Mr. Robert Tyler, that he requested that you appoint me."

Smith gave Poe a once over, then asked, a new toughness coming into his manner. "From whom did you say?"

"From Mr. Robert Tyler." Poe hated this pompous man seated before him. "What a scoundrel," he thought.

"From Robert Tyler—hem! I have received orders from President Tyler to make no more appointments and shall make none." When Poe said he had heard otherwise, Smith acknowledged that he had made one appointment since he had gotten his instructions. Smith ended the conversation. Poe, angry and humiliated, went home and immediately wrote to his friend Frederick Thomas in Washington, D.C., relating the interview with Smith and venting his frustration:

> Mr. Smith has excited the thorough disgust of every Tyler man here … He is a Whig of the worst stamp, and will appoint none but Whigs if he can possibly avoid it. People here laugh at the idea of his being a Tyler man. He is notoriously not such. As for me, he has treated me most shamefully. In my case, there was no need of any political shuffling or lying.[3]

Poe asked his friend to bring the issue to the president's son to procure "a few lines" from the president ordering Smith to give Poe a post. "With these credentials he would scarcely again refuse," Poe continued. "But I leave all to your better judgment."

Poe thought the other applicants who had already received positions "low ruffians and boobies—men, too, without a shadow of political influence or caste." He felt the same way about Smith who, if he was a gentleman, would have "perceived that, from the very character of my claim,—by which I mean my want of claim,—he should have made my appointment an early one:"

> It was a gratuitous favor intended me by Mr. Rob Tyler, and Smith has done his best to deprive this favor of all its grace by delay. I could have forgiven all but the innumerable and altogether unnecessary falsehoods with which he insulted my common sense day after day.[4]

Poe felt his longed-for federal job slipping through his fingers and knew he was at the mercy of political hacks who could not comprehend how important this post was for him and his family.

It also seemed his magazine would never get off the ground. His professional dreams had stalled even as his literary reputation ascended that year with the well-received publication of "The Pit and the Pendulum," "The Masque of the Red Death," and "The Mystery of Marie Rogêt." At least he had his sweet wife, Virginia, whose health had improved slightly since that horrible night in January.

When the first issue of *The Pioneer* magazine arrived in January 1843, it greatly impressed Poe. He was also a little jealous, as it was perfectly in line with what he wanted for *The Stylus*, which still had not gotten off the ground. Thankfully, Poe had just convinced Thomas C. Clarke, the publisher of the *Saturday Museum*, a weekly Philadelphia newspaper, to join with him in producing Poe's new magazine that he now hoped to get out by July.

Reading through *The Pioneer*, Poe was also deeply grateful to see Lowell's mention of him in his article about seventeenth-century playwright Thomas Middleton, in which Lowell favorably compares Poe's "powerful imagination" in describing the thoughts of a murderer to that of both Middleton and Poe's contemporary, the poet Thomas Hood. It was a nice compliment and in a letter that Poe sent to Lowell a few weeks later, he thanked him for it and for the $10 he received for publishing "The Tell-Tale Heart" in the magazine.

Poe's story and Lowell's *The Pioneer* both received national recognition. The New York newspaper *Brother Jonathan* called "The Tell-Tale Heart" a "very wild and very readable" story "that is the only thing in the number that most people would read and remember."

Another New York City paper, the *New York Daily Tribune*, called Poe's story "strong and skillful." The subject, though, put off the reviewer, Horace Greeley, the paper's editor, with its "over-strained and repulsive analysis of the feelings and promptings of an insane homicide." Greeley praised Poe's ability to paint "the terror of the victim while he sat upright in his bed feeling that death was near him." he called the scene, "powerful and fearfully vivid."

Several newspapers reprinted Poe's story with no compensation given to the author. In what had become an all too common problem for Poe, even as he was being hailed for his writing, he could barely survive. That same month, *The Saturday Museum* published a full front-page piece on Poe's poetry and an exaggerated biography.

Like Poe's time at West Point, where he cultivated a dark and romantic image by making up his history to suit his needs, he continued to exaggerate and alter his personal story to project the image he wanted the world to see. The paper also featured the prospectus for Poe's *The Stylus*, which the paper's editor had agreed to subsidize.

It looked as if Poe's magazine would finally become a reality. Poe was again contributing to *Graham's Magazine*, which published his poem "The Conqueror Worm" in January and several pieces of literary criticism over the coming months. Still, money was tight. He was only just recovering from his bankruptcy in December, and Virginia's health continued to be shaky.

In the February issue of *The Pioneer*, Poe's poem "Lenore" appeared and the March issue contained his article, "Notes upon English Verse." Poe hoped to continue as a regular contributor for the literary magazine, at least until his own got off the ground. It would be another source of steady income as he pushed ahead with his plans for *The Stylus*.

Yet in late-March, Poe received a letter from Lowell with unwelcome news, the first of many that year. *The Pioneer*, after only three issues, was dead. Lowell had gone to New York for medical treatment for an eye disease he was suffering from and left his business partner, Robert Carter, in charge. While Lowell tried to help run things from afar as he recovered in New York, the magazine suffered and finally went bankrupt. There was worse news. Lowell was broke and would not be able to pay Poe for his contributions, at least until he could get a loan to cover his debts.

Poe wrote Lowell back and told him not to worry about the money. "As for the few dollars you owe me—give yourself not one moment's concern about them," he wrote. "I am poor, but must be very much poorer, indeed, when I even think of demanding them." It was a sweet gesture. It was also overly generous for a writer who could barely afford to feed himself and his family.

The demise of Lowell's literary journal did not bode well for Poe's own magazine. Lowell had some of America's best writers behind his magazine, and it had still failed. How would Poe, who had alienated so many in the literary world through his acidic criticism, have any chance?

In May, Clarke withdrew his financial support for *The Stylus* and Poe was once again without the backing needed to launch his magazine. It was also becoming obvious to Poe that the federal job at the U.S. Custom House would not happen, either.

24

REVENGE

Dr. Joseph Evans Snodgrass was at his Baltimore home on the afternoon of Wednesday, October 3, 1849, when a note, hurriedly written in pencil, arrived at his door:

> There is a gentleman, rather the worse for wear, at Ryan's 4th ward polls, who goes under the cognomen of Edgar A. Poe, and who appears in great distress, and he says he is acquainted with you, and I assure you he is in need of immediate assistance.[1]

It was signed "Yours in haste" by Joseph Walker, a printer Snodgrass knew.

Snodgrass and Poe had known each other in Baltimore when they both wrote for the same paper, and they had corresponded off and on for more than a decade, mostly discussing literature and Baltimore gossip. However, they had not communicated with one another in nearly seven years.

Snodgrass left his house on High Street and hurried through the spitting rain, his cloak pulled tight against the chill, as he traveled the two blocks to Ryan's tavern and inn. The establishment went by several other names, including Gunner's Hall and the Fourth Ward Hotel. Snodgrass knew it as Coath and Sargeant's, after the tavern's previous owners. It was Election Day in Baltimore, and the tavern served as a polling place. There was a sizable crowd of men, some involved in politics, others there to drink.

As a militant temperance advocate and die-hard teetotaler, the doctor was hesitant to enter the establishment but plunged in. He found Poe slumped forward in a chair, his face sweaty and drained of color. Snodgrass noticed his friend was "surrounded by a crowd of drinking men, actuated by idle curiosity rather than sympathy" and had an "aspect of vacant stupidity" that made Snodgrass shudder. "The intellectual flash of his eye had vanished" and a cheap straw hat was perched precariously on his head. Snodgrass believed Poe was completely drunk, which did not shock him. The poet had lost his way after the death of his beloved wife, Virginia, in January 1847. Still, Poe's appearance astounded Snodgrass.

Poe was a fastidious and impeccable dresser. While his clothes were often threadbare, they were always mended, clean, and well-made. Likewise, Poe was precise in his personal hygiene—his hair combed, his chin shaved, and his face washed.

When Snodgrass found Poe, his hair was unkempt, his face dirty, and his clothing did not appear to belong to him. The shapeless sack coat was thin, grimy, faded, and ripped in several places. The pants were ill-fitting and worn through. Poe's trademark black neckcloth was gone, his vest was missing, and his shirt front was badly soiled and wrinkled. Even his boots were wrong. They were of coarse leather and had not been shined in a very long time. Snodgrass believed someone had robbed his friend of his clothing or cheated him in an exchange.

He went to get a room at the inn above the bar for Poe so he could rest while Snodgrass figured out what to do with him. He knew Poe still had relatives in the city. As he went back downstairs to fetch Poe, he ran into Henry Herring, Poe's uncle by marriage, who had arrived after hearing about his nephew's condition. He suggested they take Poe to a hospital and Snodgrass agreed. He sent a messenger to order a carriage while they watched over Poe, who was falling in and out of consciousness.

The carriage arrived out front, and Snodgrass and Herring tried to get Poe on his feet, but he was beyond being able to walk. The men had to carry him through the crowded bar. He was dead weight. Snodgrass felt like he was carrying a corpse. Poe's head lolled, and he mumbled incoherently, angry at being moved from his chair.

They got Poe, barely conscious and still muttering, into the carriage, which went rattling through the streets of Baltimore to Washington College Hospital, less than 1 mile away. They arrived at around 5 p.m. and turned Poe over to Dr. John J. Moran. At twenty-five, Moran was the resident physician in charge of the 200-bed teaching hospital. He and his family lived on the premises of the well-appointed facility.

The doctor put Poe into a private room on the second floor in a ward reserved for patients suffering from alcohol-related issues. After Moran examined the patient, he did not believe alcohol was to blame for Poe's condition. The doctor did not smell any alcohol, and Poe did not appear to be suffering from delirium tremens. Moran noted his "pallid" skin, "slight nausea at the stomach and a strong disposition to sleep." He determined Poe was experiencing some kind of "stupor" of unknown origin, possibly a brain fever. The nurses gave the patient a sponge bath and applied mustard plasters on his feet, thighs, and stomach to help promote circulation. They placed a cool, damp cloth on his head. Moran darkened the room and stationed a nurse at the door. He ordered that no one disturb the writer, who, by then, was a household name thanks to his poem "The Raven," which came out four years earlier.

Eventually, Poe woke, his eyes fluttering open. "Where am I?" he asked, his voice husky. Dr. Moran came in and pulled up a chair next to his patient and took one of his hands in his own. He felt Poe's forehead with his other hand.

He asked the patient questions, hoping to find out what had happened to him and how he had ended up in Baltimore. Poe's answers were incoherent and made little sense. He told the doctor he had a wife in Richmond. In his delirious state, he may have been referring to Sarah Elmira Royster Shelton, a childhood sweetheart who he had just asked to marry him only weeks earlier. The doctor gave up on questioning his patient and left him so he could again sleep.

The next day, Neilson Poe, his cousin, came to the hospital, but Moran turned him away. The doctor insisted that Poe have no visitors for fear any excitement could be too much for him in his weak condition. Neilson left and returned the next day with a change of linen for his cousin and whatever else he thought might help. The doctor again prevented him from seeing Poe.

Poe drifted in and out of consciousness. Moran continued to minister to Poe, who he believed was near death. He attempted to lift his spirits by telling him he was in the care of his friends. Poe became agitated. "My best friend would be the man who would blow my damned brains out with a pistol," Poe responded, putting two fingers to the side of his head.[2]

"Try and be quiet, Mr. Poe; we will do all we can to make you comfortable and relieve your distress." The doctor gave him something to help him sleep and stayed by his side as the patient drifted off. Moran noted his labored breathing, his eyes that darted under their lids, and the intermittent jerking of his body.

Poe again woke and Moran tried to get him to drink a little liquor, which he refused to do. "Mr. Poe, it is very necessary that you should be quiet and free from excitement; you are in a critical condition, and excitement will hasten your death."

"Doctor, I am ill. Is there no hope?"

"The chances are against you."[3]

By early Sunday, October 7, it was over. In his last moments, Poe became quiet and restful before moving his head from his pillow. "Lord help my poor soul," were his last words before his eyes rolled upward until only the whites were visible. His muscles twitched and jerked in one last spasm and he died.

What finally killed Poe at age forty remains a mystery. Dr. Moran put it down to "brain fever," but there was no autopsy and the death certificate has been lost. Over the years, theories including poisoning, cholera, and rabies have been suggested as the cause of death.

The nurses wrapped Poe's body in a shroud made by Mary Moran, the wife of the doctor, who had sometimes sat by Poe's bedside reading scripture to the dying poet. They put Poe's body into a plain unlined mahogany casket paid for by his uncle, Henry Herring, for burial.

On the cold and windy afternoon of Wednesday, October 9, a hearse carried Poe's body through the city's streets, followed by a single carriage. They held the graveside funeral at the Presbyterian Cemetery at Fayette and Greene Streets, in Baltimore. The small group of men, Neilson Poe, Henry Herring, Dr. Snodgrass, and Zaccheus Collins Lee huddled near the open and unlined grave. Lee was a college friend of Poe's and cousin of Robert E. Lee, with a law practice in Baltimore. There were no women in attendance.

Rev. W. T. D. Clemm said a few words before the gravediggers lowered Poe's casket into the hole. Clemm was the minister of the Caroline Street Methodist Episcopal Church in Baltimore and Virginia Poe's cousin.

Neilson could not believe his cousin, with whom he had shared a contentious relationship with, was dead. The last time he had tried to see Poe in the hospital, he was told that the poet was recovering, so when he received the note that he had died, it shocked him.

When the gravediggers began shoveling the earth into the hole, Snodgrass felt ill. Disappointment, disgust, and something like resentment coursed through him at the sound of the dirt and rocks striking the wooden casket—a noise that sounded extremely loud in the somber cemetery. It was as if society's "heartlessness"—something always present at the burial of "the poor and forsaken"—had come alive as "a malign goddess," creating the discordant sounds "as best befitting her own unearthly mood."[4]

They buried Poe near his grandfather, General David Poe, in an unmarked grave. It was not until 1860 that Neilson Poe ordered a gravestone for his cousin, but it was damaged before it could be installed. Poe's grave continued to sit, nameless and overgrown, until 1875 when a Baltimore school teacher, Sara Sigourney Rice, led a fund drive for a proper headstone for Poe, whose literary fame had exploded after his death.

Maria Clemm, who Poe continued to live with in Fordham (now the Bronx) after Virginia's death, was not at the funeral of her beloved "Eddie." She read about his death in a New York newspaper. On the day of Poe's funeral, of which she was unaware, she wrote to Neilson Poe, anxious and desperate for news of what had happened to her son-in-law and nephew. Neilson wrote back two days later.

"I would to God I could console you with the information that your dear Son, Edgar A. Poe is still among the living," he began. "The newspapers, in announcing his death, have only told a truth, which we may weep over & deplore, but cannot change."[5] Neilson apologized for not writing to her but explained that he did not know how to reach her. He described Poe's last days and the funeral.

He told her it was a mystery when and how Poe had arrived in Baltimore, where he had been for the several days he was there, or where he had stayed. He and Herring could not locate Poe's trunk and clothes. "There is reason to believe that he was robbed of them, whilst in such a condition as to render him insensible of his loss," he wrote.[6]

Poe had left Richmond on September 27, heading back to New York City with a stop off in Philadelphia to edit a book of poetry by Marguerite St. Leon

Loud, a wealthy writer. The pay was $100 for what Poe figured would be only three days of work.

He had been in high spirits; had spent part of the summer in Richmond, his hometown, where he had rekindled his relationship with Elmira, who had agreed to marry him; had a successful series of lectures on poetry; and had generated interest in and gotten subscriptions for his planned magazine. The evening before he left, Elmira noticed his pulse felt ragged, and he appeared feverish. Poe complained of feeling sick, and his fiancée thought he seemed morose.

He had not mentioned to anyone that he planned to visit Baltimore, though he may have decided at the last minute to go there to drum up more support for *The Stylus*. He may have tried to see Dr. Nathan Brooks, an editor he knew, to interest him in the magazine. Brooks was away. Where Poe went from there and how he ended up near the tavern in another man's clothes has never been answered.

Poe's life had dramatically changed since January 1843, when "The Tell-Tale Heart" came out. His first big literary success arrived later that year, in June, when he won the grand prize in a Philadelphia newspaper writing contest for his short story "The Gold Bug." He won $100 and had the story printed on the front page of *The Dollar Newspaper*. By 1844, Poe would brag that more than 3,000 copies had been "circulated." It became his most widely read short story during his lifetime.

In 1845, his poem, "The Raven," brought him even more fame, making him a literary celebrity. He capitalized on this with two books, *Tales by Edgar A. Poe* (which contained "The Tell-Tale Heart") and *The Raven and Other Poems*, which brought more renown than money. Poe earned around $699 (equivalent to about $20,000 today) that year, but that did not include paying back various friends, publishers, and others for loans he had previously taken out and for living expenses for himself, Virginia, and his mother-in-law, Maria Clemm.

By this time, he had moved his family to New York City and had gained a financial interest in a weekly magazine, *The Broadway Journal*. In October, he became its sole proprietor, achieving his dream of owning his own magazine. It was short-lived. By January, the magazine collapsed, and he was again set adrift.

Virginia finally succumbed to tuberculosis on January 30, 1847. Her death tore Poe apart and exacerbated his drinking problem. In the next two years, he had failed romances, a suicide attempt, and continued financial strains, along with more literary successes.

By 1845, Poe and Griswold had once again become friendly, and Poe decided the reverend should act as his literary executor in the event of his death. It would be the worst lapse of judgment Poe ever had. When Griswold learned of Poe's death, he quickly wrote up an obituary for *The Daily Tribune*, a leading New York newspaper where he was an editor, and began what would be the first salvo in his war on the reputation of a man whom he had been harboring deep resentment towards for years, going all the way back to 1842.

The article that Griswold did not even put his actual name to, instead using his pen name "Ludwig," appeared on October 9. It began "EDGAR ALLAN POE is dead. He died in Baltimore the day before yesterday. This announcement will startle many, but few will be grieved by it" and only became more venomous from there.

In the piece, Griswold praised Poe's work but trashed him personally, alleging "he had few or no friends," hated humanity, and was a dishonest and unbalanced social-climber. None of this was true, but it did not stop it from being reprinted in several other newspapers across the country. Griswold was also lazy with the obituary, cobbling it together from his earlier pieces on Poe and a passage from a novel by Edward Bulwer-Lytton called *The Caxtons*, that describes a character, Francis Vivian, in unkind terms:

> Passion, in him, comprehended many of the worst emotions which militate against human happiness. You could not contradict him, but you raised quick choler; you could not speak of wealth, but his cheek paled with gnawing envy. The astonishing natural advantages of this poor boy—his beauty, his readiness, the daring spirit that breathed around him like a fiery atmosphere—had raised his constitutional self-confidence into an arrogance that turned his very claims to admiration into prejudice against him. Irascible, envious—bad enough, but not the worst, for these salient angles were all varnished over with a cold repellant cynicism, his passions vented themselves in sneers. There seemed to him no moral susceptibility; and, what was more remarkable in a proud nature, little or nothing of the true point of honor. He had, to a morbid excess, that desire to rise which is vulgarly called ambition, but no wish for the esteem or love of his species; only the hard wish to succeed—not shine, not serve—succeed, that he might have the right to despise a world which galled his self conceit.[7]

While Griswold had included quotation marks around the passage in the original version, in later versions, he did not, making it seem that it was actually about Poe and not the description of a fictitious character. The only positive aspect of Griswold's obituary was the first appearance of Poe's last poem, "Annabelle Lee."

Griswold later admitted to the poet Sarah Helen Whitman, Poe's ex-fiancée, that he had written the obituary and told her "I was not his friend, nor was he mine" but claimed he had not intended the piece to seem harsh.[8] Griswold's continued smearing of Poe's name belied his declaration of innocence to Whitman.

Maria Clemm unwittingly helped this literary assassin when she asked him to edit an edition of her late son-in-law's work less than a week after Poe's death. Griswold insulted Maria Clemm behind her back, saying she had "no element of goodness or kindness in her nature" and was "full of malice and wickedness."[9] To her face, he remained cordial, as he had done with her beloved son-in-law for years.

With Poe's reputation now firmly in his grasp, Griswold spent the next several years systematically destroying it like a torturer taking pleasure in slowly breaking his victim's bones one by one. He twisted the truth and forged letters he used in his memoirs of Poe to make the author look even worse.

These attacks did not go unchallenged by Poe's friends. Shortly after the *Tribune* obituary came out, several letters to the editor and newspaper articles defending Poe appeared. In one, the writer called "Ludwig" a "slanderous hypocrite" whose "statements intended to throw odium and discredit on the character of the deceased are scandalous inventions."[10]

The author and critic John Neal, who had been an early supporter of Poe, called Griswold unfit to be Poe's literary executor and railed against the mistreatment Poe had received even before his death.

Graham, who both Poe and Griswold had worked for, also defended the dead poet, calling him a "polished gentleman, the quiet, unobtrusive, thoughtful scholar, the devoted husband; frugal in his personal expenses, punctual and unwearied in his industry, and the soul of honor."[11]

Since Griswold was Poe's official literary executor, his version of Poe's character stuck. For years afterward, biography after biography repeated Griswold's distorted picture of Poe as the truth.

Griswold died in 1857 from tuberculosis. His body moldered in a public mortuary for eight years before being interred in a plot at Greenwood Cemetery in Brooklyn. No one bothered to put a headstone on it. While Griswold had permanently damaged Poe's reputation, he remains little more than a footnote in Poe's biography remembered more for his antagonistic relationship with a genius than for any positive contributions to the world. By smearing Poe's reputation, he inadvertently made his enemy more famous. To this day, the popular misconceptions swirling around Poe's personality and alleged vices can be attributed to Griswold, yet they only add to Poe's mystique.

"The Tell-Tale Heart" was published at least a dozen times in newspapers and magazines across the United States, in England, and in Canada during Poe's lifetime, without him seeing any money for it besides the original $10 Lowell had given him when it was first published in 1843. It would become one of his best-known short stories and continues to have a life more than 170 years after the death of its author. Among the sources that Poe used to create his masterpiece, the two murderers, Richard Crowninshield and Peter Robinson, live on in some small way too.

ENDNOTES

PREFACE

1   This detail is from a display accompanying Poe's childhood bed at the Edgar Allan Poe Museum in Richmond, VA.

2   Poe, E. A., "The Tell-Tale Heart," in Lowell, J. R. and Carter, R. (eds), *The Pioneer: A Literary and Critical Magazine* Vol. 1 no. 1 (Boston: Leland and Whiting, January 1843), pp. 29–31.

CHAPTER 2

1   Knapp, J. J., *Trials of Capt. Joseph J. Knapp, Jr. and George Crowninshield, Esq: For the Murder of Capt. Joseph White of Salem, on the Night of the Sixth of April 1830* (United States: Charles Ellms, 1830), p. 29.

2   *Ibid.*, pp. 8–10.

3   Knapp, J. F., "A Report of the Evidence and Points of Law, Arising in the Trial of John Francis Knapp, for the Murder of Joseph White, Esquire," (Salem: W. & S. B. Ives, 1830), p. 27.

4   *Ibid.*, p. 15.

5   *The Salem Gazette*, April 1830 (Phillips Library at the Peabody Essex Museum collections; Salem, Mass.: Essex Institute, 1830).

6   "The Committee of Vigilance minutes" (Phillips Library at the Peabody Essex Museum collections; Salem, Mass.: Essex Institute, 1830).

7   Knapp, J. F., *op. cit*, pp. 17 and 40.

CHAPTER 3

1   Poe, E. A. and Ostrom, J. W. (ed.), Letter to John Allan, January 3, 1831, "Letters: Chapter I," *The Letters of Edgar Allan Poe: Vol. I: 1824–1845* (The Edgar Allan Poe Society of Baltimore, 1966), p. 41.

CHAPTER 4

1   Knapp, J. F., "A Report of the Evidence and Points of Law, Arising in the Trial of John Francis Knapp, for the Murder of Joseph White, Esquire (Salem: W. & S. B. Ives, 1830), p. 36.

2   *Ibid.*, pp. 35–36.

3   *Ibid.*, p. 36.

CHAPTER 5

1 Winans, J. A. and Bradley, H. A., *Daniel Webster and the Salem Murder* (United States: Lawbook Exchange, 2007), p. 77.
2 *Ibid.*
3 *Ibid.*
4 Knapp, J. J., "The confession of John Jenkins Knapp" (Phillips Library at the Peabody Essex Museum collections; Salem, Mass.: Essex Institute, 1830).
5 Knapp, J. J., Trials of Capt. Joseph J. Knapp, Jr. and George Crowninshield, Esq: For the Murder of Capt. Joseph White of Salem, on the Night of the Sixth of April 1830 (United States: Charles Ellms, 1830), p. 6.
6 Knapp, J. J., "The confession of John Jenkins Knapp."
7 *Ibid.*
8 *Ibid.*
9 *Ibid.*

CHAPTER 6

1 Poe, Edgar Allan. "Edgar Allan Poe letter to John Allan - June 28, 1830." Edgar Allan Poe Society of Baltimore.
2 *Ibid.*

CHAPTER 7

1 "Trial of George Crowninshield," *The Salem Gazette* reprinted in *The Evening Post* (New York: November 18, 1830).
2 *Ibid.*
3 *Ibid.*
4 Knapp, J. F., "A Report of the Evidence and Points of Law, Arising in the Trial of John Francis Knapp, for the Murder of Joseph White, Esquire" (Salem, W. & S. B. Ives, 1830), p. 5.
5 Shaw, L. C. J., "An Address delivered before the Bar of Berkshire, by Lemuel Shaw C. J., September term 1830, at Lenox," Mass.Gov.org.
6 Emerson, R. W., Carlyle, T., and Norton, C. E., *The Correspondence of Thomas Carlyle and Ralph Waldo Emerson, 1834–1872* (Boston: Osgood and company, 1883), p. 260.

CHAPTER 8

1 Winans, J. A. and Bradley, H. A., *Daniel Webster and the Salem Murder* (United States: Lawbook Exchange, 2007), p. 34.
2 Knapp, J. F., "A Report of the Evidence and Points of Law, Arising in the Trial of John Francis Knapp, for the Murder of Joseph White, Esquire" (Salem: W. & S. B. Ives, 1830), p. 15.
3 Pray, I. C., *Memoirs of James Gordon Bennett and His Times* (United States: Stringer & Townsend, 1855), p. 119.
4 Winans and Bradley, *op. cit.*, p. 80.
5 Knapp, *op. cit.*, p. 56.
6 Winans and Bradley, *op. cit.*, p. 97.
7 "Crowninshield—The Murder and Suicide." *The NY Courier and Enquirer* reprinted in *The Republican Monitor* (Morrisville, NY. August 10, 1830. NYS Historic Newspapers).
8 *Ibid.*
9 *Ibid.*

CHAPTER 9

1 Gibson, T. W., "Poe at West Point." *Harper's New Monthly Magazine.* (Harper: United States, 1867), pp. 754–756.
2 *Ibid.*
3 Quinn, A. H., *Edgar Allan Poe: a Critical Biography* (Baltimore: Johns Hopkins University Press, 2008), pp. 171–172.
4 Gibson, T. W., *op. cit.*, pp. 754–756.

CHAPTER 10

1 Knapp, J. F., "A Report of the Evidence and Points of Law, Arising in the Trial of John Francis Knapp, for the Murder of Joseph White, Esquire" (Salem: W. & S. B. Ives, 1830), p. 10.
2 *Ibid.* p. 31.
3 *Ibid.* p. 29.
4 Winans, J. A and Bradley, H. A., *Daniel Webster and the Salem Murder* (United States: Lawbook Exchange, 2007), p. 147.
5 *Ibid.*, p. 151.
6 *Ibid.*, p. 156.
7 *Ibid.*, p. 216.
8 "Salem Murder," *The Salem Register* as reprinted in the *Vermont Republican and American Journal* (Windsor, Vermont. January 1, 1830).

CHAPTER 11

1 "Supreme Judicial Court: Trial of Joseph J. Knapp, jun," *The Salem Gazette* as reprinted in the *Hartford Courant* (November 16, 1830).
2 Knapp, J. J., *Trials of Capt. Joseph J. Knapp, Jr. and George Crowninshield, Esq: For the Murder of Capt. Joseph White of Salem, on the Night of the Sixth of April 1830* (Charles Ellms: *United States,* 1830), p. 18.
3 *Ibid.*
4 *Ibid.*, p. 31.
5 *Ibid.*, p. 31.
6 "Salem Murder," *The Salem Register* as reprinted in the *Vermont Republican and American Journal* (Windsor, Vermont: January 1, 1830).
7 West, J., *The Arbiters of Reality: Hawthorne, Melville, and the Rise of Mass Information Culture* (United States: Ohio State University Press, 2008), pp. 34–35.

CHAPTER 12

1 Winans, J. A. and Bradley, H. A., *Daniel Webster and the Salem Murder* (United States: Lawbook Exchange, 2007), p. 229.
2 Dickens, C., *The Works of Charles Dickens* (United Kingdom: Chapman and Hall, 1908), p. 153.

CHAPTER 13

1 Poe, E. A. and Ostrom, J. W. (ed.), Letter to John Allan, January 3, 1831 "Letters: Chapter I," *The Letters of Edgar Allan Poe: Vol. I: 1824–1845* (The Edgar Allan Poe Society of Baltimore, 1966), p. 39.
2 *Ibid.* p. 40.
3 *Ibid.* p. 41

4   *Ibid.* p. 42.

5   Quinn, A. H., *Edgar Allan Poe: a Critical Biography* (Johns Hopkins University Press: Baltimore, 2008), p. 321.

6   Poe, E. A. and Ostrom, J. W. (ed.), *op. cit.*, p. 43.

CHAPTER 14

1   Attree, W., "Trial of Robinson" *New York Herald* (New York: March 18, 1841), p. 1.

2   Thanksgiving was not a national holiday celebrated on the fourth Thursday of the month until 1941.

3   Attree, W., *op. cit.*

4   Attree, W., "Trial of Robinson," *New York Herald* (New York: March 22, 1841), p. 1.

5   *Ibid.*

6   *Ibid.*

CHAPTER 15

1   Thomas, D. R. and Jackson, D. K., *The Poe Log: A Documentary Life of Edgar Allan Poe, 1809–1849* (Boston: J.K. Hall, 1987), p. 272.

2   Poe, E. A., Letter to William E. Burton (June 1, 1840. Edgar Allan Poe Society of Baltimore).

3   Poe, E. A. and Ostrom, J. W. (ed.), Letter to William Poe, August 14, 1840. "Letters: Chapter IV," *The Letters of Edgar Allan Poe: Vol. I: 1824–1845* (The Edgar Allan Poe Society of Baltimore, 1966), p. 141.

CHAPTER 16

1   "Two Old Letters Tell of Apprehension of Murderer of Local Bank President," *The Daily Home News* (New Brunswick: March 7, 1926; Courtesy of the New Brunswick Free Public Library).

2   *Ibid.*

3   "Murder of Mr. Suydam," *New York Express* as reprinted in the *York Gazette* (York, Pennsylvania: December 22, 1840), p. 3.

4   "The New Brunswick Tragedy." *Newark Daily Advertiser* as reprinted in the *Pilot and Transcript* (Baltimore. December 19, 1840).

5   Attree, W., "Trial of Robinson," *New York Herald* (New York. March 22, 1841), p. 1.

CHAPTER 17

1   Attree, W., "Trial of Robinson," *New York Herald* (New York. March 18, 1841), p. 1.

2   *Ibid.*

3   Attree, W., "Trial of Robinson," *New York Herald* (New York. March 20, 1841), p. 1.

4   Attree, W., "Trial of Robinson," *New York Herald* (New York. March 22, 1841), p. 1.

5   Attree, W., "Trial of Robinson," *New York Herald* (New York. March 25, 1841), p. 1.

CHAPTER 18

1   Thomas, D. R. and Jackson, D. K., *The Poe Log: A Documentary Life of Edgar Allan Poe, 1809–1849* (Boston: J.K. Hall, 1987), p. 320.

2   Poe, E. A. and Harrison, J. A., *Literary criticism* (United States: G. D. Sproul, 1902), p. 141.

3   *Ibid.*, p. 143.

4   Poe, E. A., Letter to Rufus Wilmot Griswold (May 29, 1841. Edgar Allan Poe Society of Baltimore).

CHAPTER 19

1 Attree, W., "Trial of Peter Robinson," *New York Herald* (New York: March 26, 1841), p. 2.
2 *Ibid.*
3 *Ibid.*
4 Attree, W., "Peter Robinson—His approaching Execution—His Confessions," *New York Herald* (New York. April 12, 1841), p. 2.

CHAPTER 20

1 Attree, W., "Peter Robinson in Prison—His Confessions—The Manner in Which he Murdered Mr. Suydam," *New York Herald* (New York. April 15, 1841), p. 1.
2 *Ibid.*
3 *Ibid.*
4 *Ibid.*
5 *Ibid.*
6 *Ibid.*
7 *Ibid.*
8 Attree, W., "Peter Robinson's Last Moments," *New York Herald* (New York. April 16, 1841), p. 2.
9 "Execution of Peter Robinson," *New York Daily Chronicle* as reprinted in the *Edenton Sentinel and Albemarle Intelligencer* (Edenton, North Carolina. May 1, 1841), p. 1.

CHAPTER 21

1 Minto, W., "Edgar Allan Poe," *Littell's Living Age* (United States: E. Littell & Company, 1880), p. 693.
2 Quinn, A. H., *Edgar Allan Poe: a Critical Biography* (Baltimore: Johns Hopkins University Press, 2008), p. 353.

CHAPTER 22

1 Cohen, P. C., *The Murder of Helen Jewett: The Life and Death of a Prostitute in Nineteenth-century New York.* pp. 245. United Kingdom: Vintage Books, 1999.
2 Bennet, J. G., "Death of Mr. William B. Attree," *New York Daily Herald* (New York, November 20, 1840), p. 2.
3 *Ibid.*

CHAPTER 23

1 Poe, E. A., Letter to James Russell Lowell. November 16, 1842 (The Edgar Allan Poe Society of Baltimore).
2 Mckee, G., "A New Letter from Poe to Lowell on the Pioneer," in *The Edgar Allan Poe Review,* Vol. 20, No. 1 (University Park, Pennsylvania: The Penn State University Press, 2019), p. 32.
3 Quinn, A. H., *Edgar Allan Poe: a Critical Biography*, p. 362.
4 *Ibid.* p. 363.

CHAPTER 24

1 "The Mysterious Death of Edgar Allan Poe." Edgar Allan Poe Society of Baltimore: General Topics: The Mysterious Death of Edgar Allan Poe, 19 January 2014.

2 Moran, J. J., "Official Memorandum of the Death of Edgar A. Poe," *Baltimore Sun* (Baltimore, October 29, 1875), p. 1.

3 *Ibid.*

4 Snodgrass, J. E., "Edgar A. Poe's Death and Burial," *New York Reformer* (Watertown, NY, July 26, 1855), p. 2.

5 Quinn, A. H., *Edgar Allan Poe: a Critical Biography,* pp. 642–643.

6 *Ibid.* p. 363.

7 *Ibid.*, p. 647.

8 "Edgar Allan Poe and Rufus Wilmot Griswold." The Edgar Allan Poe Society of Baltimore, eapoe.org/geninfo/poegrisw.htm

9 *Ibid.*

10 Quinn, A. H., *op. cit.*, p. 654.

11 Moran, J. J., *A Defense of Edgar Allan Poe*, p. 52.

BIBLIOGRAPHY

"A Crime Recalled," *San Francisco Chronicle* (San Francisco, California: August 20, 1888), p. 3, newspapers.com/image/27556904/?terms=
%22John%2BFrancis%2BKnapp%22%2Bhanging

"A New Book by Dickens," *Washington Times* (Washington, D.C.: February 27, 1898), p. 18, newspapers.com/image/80789128/

"Atrocious Murder," *The New York Currier* as reprinted in the *Pilot and Transcript* (Baltimore: December 17, 1840), p. 2.

"Attree," *Wayne County Herald* (Honesdale, Pennsylvania: February 14, 1849), p. 2, newspapers. com/image/362463718/?terms=%22William%2BH.%2BAttree%22

"Biographies of the Secretaries of State: Daniel Webster," Office of the Historian. U.S. Department of State, history.state.gov/departmenthistory/people/webster-daniel.

"COMMONWEALTH v. JOHN FRANCIS KNAPP," masscases.com/cases/sjc/26/26mass496.html.

"Crowninshield—The Murder and Suicide," *The NY Courier and Enquirer* reprinted in *The Republican Monitor* (Morrisville, NY. August 10, 1830), nyshistoricnewspapers.org/lccn/
sn83031470/1830-08-10/ed-1/seq-2/#sequence=0&proxdistance=5&county=&phrasetext=
&andtext=&date1=01%2F01%2F1830&city=&date2=
12%2F31%2F1832&searchType=advanced&from_
year=1830&proxtext=Knapp&dateFilterType=range&sort=date&SearchType=prox5&index=
19&to_year=1832&rows=20&words=Knapp&lccn=&am+p=&ortext=&page=9

"Death of an Outcast," *The Daily Tobacco Plant* (Durham, North Carolina: August 15, 1888), p. 2, newspapers.com/image/71645259/?terms=%22George%2BCrowningshield%22

"Death of James Gordon Bennett," *Chicago Tribune* (Chicago: June 3, 1872), p. 5, newspapers. com/image/349748839/?terms=%22James%2BGordon%2BBennett%2BSr.%22%2Bobituary

"Death of Mr. William B. Attree," *New York Daily Herald* (New York, November 20, 1840), p. 2, newspapers.com/image/466618449/?terms=%22william%2Battree%22

"Death of Mr. Wm. H. Attree," *The Brooklyn Daily Eagle* (Brooklyn, N.Y. November 20, 1849), p. 2, newspapers.com/image/50251004/?terms=%22William%2BH.%2BAttree%22

"Death Recalls Murder of 1840," *The Courier News* (Bridgewater, New Jersey. March 29, 1911), p. 2.

"Execution of John F. Knapp," *The Essex Register* as reprinted in
The Evening Post (New York: October 4, 1830), newspapers.com/
image/39628051/?terms=%22J.F.%2BKnapp%22%2Bexecution

"Execution of John Francis Knapp," *The Boston Courier* as reprinted in *The Torch Light and Public Advertiser* (Hagerstown, Maryland. October 7, 1830), newspapers.com/
image/39378137/?terms=%22John%2BFrancis%2
BKnapp%22%2Bhanging

"Execution of Peter Robinson," *New York Daily Chronicle* as reprinted in the *Edenton Sentinel and Albemarle Intelligencer* (Edenton, North Carolina: May 1, 1841), p. 1, newspapers.com/
image/64242096/?terms=%22Peter%2BRobinson%22%2B%22Abraham%2BSuydam%22

"Execution of Peter Robinson," *New York Tribune* (New York: April 17, 1841), p. 2, newspapers.
    com/image/78136004/?terms="Abraham%2BSuydam"%2Bfuneral
"Execution of Peter Robinson," *Public Ledger* (Philadelphia. April 17, 1841), p. 1, newspapers.
    com/image/40140754/?terms=%22Peter%2BRobinson%
    22%2Bnew%2Bbrunswick%2Bexecution
"James Gordon Bennett," *New York Daily Herald* (New York: June 5, 1872), p. 4, newspapers.
    com/image/329688016/?terms=%22James%2BGordon%2BBennett%2BSr. %22%2Bobituary
"Joseph J. Knapp," *The Horn of the Green Mountains* (Manchester, Vermont: December 28,
    1830), p. 3, newspapers.com/image/355386331/?terms=%22J.J.%2BKnapp%22%2Bexecution
"Knapp's Escape," *Fall River Monitor* (Fall River, Massachusetts: September 18, 1830), p. 3,
    newspapers.com/image/590098489/?terms=%22mary%22%2Bsalem%2Bknapp
"Knapp's Execution," *Fall River Monitor* (Fall River, Massachusetts: October 2, 1830),
    newspapers.com/image/590098496/?terms=
    %22John%2BKnapp%22%2Bhanging
"Murder of Mr. Suydam," *New York Express* as reprinted in the *York
    Gazette* (York, Pennsylvania: December 22, 1840), p. 3, newspapers.com/
    image/551023029/?terms=%22Justice%2BConover%22%2B%22New%2BBrunswick%22
"Mysterious," *The Baltimore Sun* (Baltimore: December 10, 1840), p. 4, newspapers.com/
    image/364985375/?terms=%22Abraham%2BSuydam%22
"Obituary, Chief Justice Hornblower," *The New York Times* (New York: June 14, 1864),
    nytimes.com/1864/06/14/archives/obituary-chiefjustice-hornblower.html
"One Hundred Years Ago." *The Gazette and Daily* (York, Pennsylvania. December 20, 1940), p. 6.
"Robinson's Trial," *Trenton State Gazette* and reprinted in the *Monmouth
    Enquirer* (Monmouth, New Jersey. March 25, 1841), p. 2, newspapers.com/
    image/376106379/?terms=%22Peter%2BRobinson%22%2B%22Abraham%2BSuydam%22
"Salem Murder," *Roanoke Advocate* (Halifax, North Carolina: January 13, 1831), newspapers.
    com/image/66294584/?terms=%22mary%22%2Bsalem%2Bknapp
"Salem Murder," *Vermont Advocate and State Paper* (December 27, 1830), p. 3,
    newspapers.com/image/489849200/?terms=%22mary%22%2Bsalem%2Bknapp
"Salem Murder." *The Salem Register* as reprinted in the *Vermont Republican
    and American Journal* (Windsor, Vermont: January 1, 1830), newspapers.com/
    image/490087723/?terms=%22J.J.%2BKnapp%22%2Bexecution
"Salem," *The Freeman's Journal* (Cooperstown, N.Y.: January 17,
    1831), nyshistoricnewspapers.org/lccn/sn83031222/1831-01-17/ed-1/
    seq-1/#sequence=0&proxdistance=5&county=&phrasetext=&andtext=&date1=
    01%2F01%2F1830&city=&date2=12%2F31%2F1832&searchType=advanced&from_
    year=1830&proxtext=
    Knapp&dateFilterType=range&sort=date&SearchType=prox5&index=17&to_
    year=1832&rows=20&words=Knapp&lccn=&am+p=&ortext=&page=19
"Samuel Sumner Wilde," mass.gov/person/samuel-sumner-wilde.
"Sentence of J. J. Knapp, Jr.," *The Salem Gazette* as reprinted in *The Evening Post* (New York:
    November 19, 1830), p. 2, newspapers.com/image/39628501/?terms=%22J.J.%2BKnapp%22
"Sentence of J. J. Knapp, Jun." *The Evening Post* (New York: November 18, 1830), p. 2,
    newspapers.com/image/39628486/?terms=%22J.J.%2BKnapp%22
"Sherman's Camphor," *The Sunbury Gazette* (Sunbury, Pennsylvania. December 10, 1842), p. 4,
    newspapers.com/image/511600545/?terms=%22W.H.Attree%22%2BPoe
"Speech Costs Senator His Seat." U.S. Senate (December 12, 2019), senate.gov/artandhistory/
    history/minute/Speech_Costs_Senator_His_Seat.htm.
"Stole From His Employer," *The Boston Globe* (December 14, 1887),
    p. 1, newspapers.com/image/430790129/?terms=%22George%2BCrowninshield%22
"Supreme Judicial Court: Trial of Joseph J. Knapp, jun." *The Salem Gazette* as
    reprinted in the *Hartford Courant* (November 16, 1830), newspapers.com/
    image/233790555/?terms=%22J.J.%2BKnapp%22
"The Committee of Vigilance minutes," Phillips Library at the Peabody Essex Museum collections
    (Salem, Mass.: Essex Institute, 1830)
"The Murder," *The Salem Gazette* reprinted in *Burlington Weekly Free Press* (Burlington, Vt.:
    October 25, 1830), newspapers.com/clip/24831844/crowninshield/

"The Mystery of Edgar Allan Poe's Death (U.S. National Park Service)," *National Parks Service* (U.S. Department of the Interior), nps.gov/articles/poe-death.htm.

"The New Brunswick Tragedy." *Newark Daily Advertiser* as reprinted in the *Pilot and Transcript* (Baltimore: December 19, 1840), newspapers.com/image/325993957/?terms=%22Justice%2BConover%22%2B%22New%2BBrunswick%22

"The Rambler Writes of the Old Belmont House," *The Evening Star* (Washington, D.C. December 8, 1918), p. 59, newspapers.com/image/332642259/?terms=%22Nathaniel%2Bphippen%2Bknapp%22

"The Salem Trial," *The Boston Commercial Gazette* as reprinted in *The United States Gazette* (Philadelphia, August 13, 1830), newspapers.com/image/605066560/?terms=%22J.F%2BKnapp%2

"The Trial of John Francis Knapp," *Vermont Gazette* (Bennington, Vt.: August 24, 1830), newspapers.com/image/518517129/?terms=%22Captain%2BJoseph%2BWhite%22

"Today's Document," *Tumblr.com* (26 October 2014), todaysdocument.tumblr.com/post/100945836306/usnatarchives-october-is-american-archives.

"Trial of George Crowninshield," *The Geneva Gazette* (Geneva, N.Y.: December 22, 1830), nyshistoricnewspapers.org/lccn/sn83031114/1830-12-22/ed-1/seq-1/#sequence=0&proxdistance=5&county=&phrasetext=&andtext=&date1=01%2F01%2F1830&city=&date2=12%2F31%2F1832&searchType=advanced&from_year=1830&proxtext=Knapp&dateFilterType=range&sort=date&SearchType=prox5&index=8&to_year=1832&rows=20&words=Knapp&lccn=&am+p=&ortext=&page=18

"Trial of George Crowninshield," *The Salem Gazette* reprinted in *The Evening Post* (New York: November 18, 1830), newspapers.com/image/39628486/?terms=%22J.J.%2BKnapp%22

"Trial of Joseph J. Knapp," *The National Gazette* (Philadelphia, Pennsylvania: November 15, 1830), newspapers.com/image/346634550/?terms=%22J.J.%2BKnapp%22

"Trial of Peter Robinson," *New York Commercial Advertiser* as reprinted in *The Charleston Daily Courier* (Charleston, South Carolina: March 25, 1841), p. 2.

"Trial of Robinson at New Brunswick," *Public Ledger* (Philadelphia. March 23, 1841), p. 1, newspapers.com/image/40140666/?terms=%22Justice%2BConover%22%2B%22New%2BBrunswick%22

"Trial of Robinson at New Brunswick," *Public Ledger* (Philadelphia. March 23, 1841), p. 1, newspapers.com/image/40140666/?terms=%22Justice%2BConover%22%2B%22New%2BBrunswick%22

"Trial of Robinson For the Murder Of Mr. Suydam, At New Brunswick, N.J.," *Alexandria Gazette and Virginia Advertiser* (Alexandria, Virginia. March 27, 1841), p. 2, chroniclingamerica.loc.gov/lccn/sn85025007/1841-03-27/ed-1/seq-2/

"Tuesday Evening," *The Evening Post* (New York. June 4, 1844), newspapers.com/image/32694728/?terms=%22William%2BH.%2BAttree%22

"Two Old Letters Tell of Apprehension of Murderer of Local Bank President," *The Daily Home News* (New Brunswick. March 7, 1926; Courtesy of the New Brunswick Free Public Library).

Armiento, A. B., "Poe in Philadelphia," in Phillips, P. E. (ed.), *Poe and Place* (Palgrave Macmillan, 2019), pp. 133–136.

Attree, W., "The Extraordinary Case of Peter Robinson, The Murderer," *New York Herald* (New York: March 27, 1841), p. 1; "Peter Robinson—His approaching Execution—His Confessions" *New York Herald* (New York: April 12, 1841), p. 2; "Peter Robinson in Prison — His Confessions — The Manner in Which he Murdered Mr. Suydam," *New York Herald* (New York: April 15, 1841), p. 1; "Peter Robinson the Murderer," *New York Herald* (New York: April 13, 1841), p. 2; "Peter Robinson's Life and Confessions," *New York Herald* (New York: April 14, 1841), p. 2; "Peter Robinson's Last Moments," *New York Herald* (New York: April 16, 1841), p. 2; "Peter Robinson's Last Moments—His Execution—Breaking of the Rope," *New York Herald* (New York: April 17, 1841), p. 2; "Peter Robinson in Prison." *New York Herald* (New York: April 16, 1841), p. 2; "The Trial of Peter Robinson," *New York Herald* (New York: March 18, 1841), p. 1; "Trial of Robinson," *New York Herald* (New York: March 19, 1841), p. 1; "Trial of Robinson," *New York Herald* (New York: March 22, 1841), p. 1; "Trial of Peter Robinson," *New York Herald* (New York: March 23, 1841), p. 1; "The Trial of Peter Robinson," *New York Herald* (New York: March 24, 1841), p. 1; "The Trial of Peter Robinson," *New York Herald* (New York: March 25 1841), p. 1.

Baldwing, J. F., *Regulations for the U. S. Military Academy at West Point, New York* (United States: 1873), google.com/books/edition/_/bSk3jqWL3E4C?hl=en&gbpv=1

Bandy, W. T., "Dr. Moran and the Poe-Reynolds Myth," *Myths and Reality*, (Baltimore: The Edgar Allan Poe Society, 1987), pp. 26-36, eapoe.org/papers/psbbooks/pb19871d.htm

Beale, H. J., *A Selection of Cases and Other and Other Authorities Upon Criminal Law* (Harvard Law Review Publishing Association, 1907), pp. 634-635.

Biographical Directory of the U.S. Congress: Retro Member details. Biographical Directory of the United States Congress (ccessed May 14, 2020), bioguide.congress.gov/scripts/biodisplay. pl?index=r000063.

Booth, R., *Death of an Empire: the Rise and Murderous Fall of Salem, America's Richest City* (New York: Thomas Dunne Books, 2011), pp. 39; 67; 93; 120; 134–138; 160–162; 210–211; 214–216; 241–245; 258–260; 281–283.

Byrd, R. C., *The Senate, 1789–1989: Classic Speeches, 1830–1993* (Washington, D.C.: Government Printing Office, 1994), senate.gov/artandhistory/history/common/generic/Speeches_ WebsterToHayne.htm

Campion, N. R., "Who Was Sylvanus Thayer?" (Thayer School of Engineering at Dartmouth, Dartmouth College, accessed May 14, 2020), engineering.dartmouth.edu/magazine/who-was-sylvanus-thayer.

Caraman, L., "The Urge to Tell vs. the Need to Conceal: Confession as Narrative Desire in Poe's 'The Black Cat,' 'The Tell-Tale Heart' and 'The Imp of the Perverse." *American and British Studies Annual*, vol. 7 (December 2014), pp. 98–108; 120–130, researchgate.net/publication/282869583_ The_Urge_to_Tell_vs_the_Need_to_Conceal_ Confession_as_Narrative_Desire_in_Poe's_The_ Black_Cat_The_Tell-Tale_Heart_and_The_Imp_of_the_Perverse.

Caswall, H., *The Martyr of the Pongas: Being a Memoir of Hamble James Leacock, Leader of the West Indian Mission to Western Africa* (United Kingdom: T.N. Stanford, 1857), books.google.com/books?id=wTFlAAAAMAAJ&pg=PA56&lpg= PA56&dq=%22rev.+H.J.+Leacock%22&source=bl&ots=lu_ IGvveeb&sig=ACfU3U19kDTgcahKOsMyfQmgNqFZDzS3SQ&hl= en&sa=X&ved=2ahUKEwjhpP7dpYfkAhVlu1kKHeMaA9A Q6AEwB3oECAQQAQ#v=onepage&q=robinson&f=false

Clayton, W. Woodford, *History of Union and Middlesex Counties*. p. 496-511. Philadelphia: Everts & Peck, 1882.

Cohen, P. C., *The Murder of Helen Jewett: The Life and Death of a Prostitute in Nineteenth-century New York* (United Kingdom: Vintage Books, 1999), pp. 245–247.

Colman, H., *European Life and Manners: In Familiar Letters to Friends* (United Kingdom: Charles C. Little and James Brown, 1849), books.google.com/ books?id=qsM8KsQBbK8C&pg=PA1&source=gbs_toc_r&cad=4#v=onepage&q&f=false

Crouthamel, J. L. and Jackson, A., "James Gordon Bennett, the 'New York Herald', and the Development of Newspaper Sensationalism," *New York History* Vol. 54, No. 3 (Cooperstown, N.Y.: July 1973), pp. 298. jstor.org/stable/23169403?read-now= 1&refreqid=excelsior%3A43a02195f05db1ef1711c055197e27ef&seq=2#page_scan_tab_contents

Crowninshield, R., Letter from Richard Crowninshield to his sister (Phillips Library at the Peabody Essex Museum collections; Salem, Mass.: Essex Institute, 1830).

Curtis, C. P., "The Young Devils and Dan'l Webster." *American Heritage* (May 1, 2020), americanheritage.com/young-devils-and-danl-webster#1.

Dickens, C., *The Works of Charles Dickens* (United Kingdom: Chapman and Hall, 1908), pp. 153–160, books.google.com/books?id=ebfBZo-dODoC&pg=PA153&lpg=PA153&dq=charles+ dickens+%22an+american+in+europe%22colman&source=bl&ots=BKoLRfC6hX&sig=ACfU3 U2MAG8DHz6X159N_-44MRwPPTqBuQ&hl=en&ppis=_ c&sa=X&ved=2ahUKEwiUhMuDwdnoAhVghHIEHYcpDOIQ6AEwAXoECAkQLw#v =onepage&q=charles%20dickens%20%22an% 20american%20in%20 europe%22colman&f=false

Edgar Allan Poe National Historic Site, *Edgar Allan Poe And His Tumultuous Romances* (U.S. National Park Service, 2016), nps.gov/articles/poeromances.htm

Edgar Allan Poe Society of Baltimore, "Poe's Memorial Grave" (2016), eapoe.org/balt/poegrave. htm; *Tales—The Tell-Tale Heart* (2020), eapoe.org/works/info/pt043.htm; "Edgar Allan Poe's Appearance, Etc." (25 January 2011), eapoe.org/geninfo/poeapprn.htm; "Edgar Allan Poe and

Rufus Wilmot Griswold" (January 22, 2009), eapoe.org/geninfo/poegrisw.htm; "The Mysterious Death of Edgar Allan Poe" (19 January 2014), eapoe.org/geninfo/poedeath.htm; "Poe's Memorial Grave—Miss S. S. Rice" (2016), eapoe.org/balt/poesrice.htm; eapoe.org/geninfo/poethrsn.htm.

Emerson, R. W., Carlyle, T., and Norton, C. E., *The Correspondence of Thomas Carlyle and Ralph Waldo Emerson, 1834–1872* (United States: Ticknor, 1884), p. 260, books.google.com/books?id= lM8bAQAAIAAJ&pg=PA267&lpg=PA267&dq=thomas+carlyle+to+emerson+letter+daniel+webster&source=bl&ots=5_Eb-u2afm&sig=ACfU3U2JR5_2Ad8Bxk04gyvRfy5qATO84w&hl=en&ppis=_c&sa=X&ved=2ahUKEwjkmt-wj6LoAhUkiOAKHbwuA0AQ6AEwAHoECA0QAQ#v=onepage&q=daniel%20webster&f=false

Farrell, J. M., "Pretrial Publicity in 1830 Salem: Daniel Webster, New England News, and the Knapp-White Trial," *Journalism History* Vol. 44, No. 4 (Winter 2019), pp. 233–240.

Finneman, T., "Farrell Podcast: Salem, Murder, and the Press," *Journalism History* (December 20, 2018), journalism-history.org/2019/01/22/farrell-podcast-salem-murder-and-the-press/.

Fowler and Wells Phrenological Character Readings, Ephemera, and Printed Material, 1840–1910, dla.library.upenn.edu/dla/ead/ead.html?q=fowler&id=EAD_upenn_rbml_PUSpMsColl1418&

Gibson, T. W., "Poe at West Point," *Harper's New Monthly Magazine* (United States: Harper, 1867), . pp. 754–756.

Gilderlehrman.org, "Great Speech of the Hon. Daniel Webster At Richmond.... [On Silk] Gilder Lehrman Institute of American History" (2020), gilderlehrman.org/collection/glc05862

Groneman, B., *Eyewitness to the Alamo* (United States: Taylor Trade Publishing, 2001), pp. 46–49.

Hancock, H. I., *Life at West Point; the Making of the American Army Officer: His Studies, Discipline, and Amusements* (New York: G.P. Putnams Sons, 1911), pp. 193–200, books.google.com/books?id=YXsYAAAAYAAJ&pg=PA193&lpg=PA193&dq=west+point+summer+encampment&source=bl&ots=CZEGhgHIt6&sig=nuDhkCRl-CTmTkumqF8K_Oz7n3o&hl=en&ei=yLqWSfbrBp6DtweRmJCcCw&sa=X&oi=book_result&resnum=6&ct=result#v=onepage&q=west% 20point%20summer%20encampment&f=false

Harrison, J. A., *Life of Edgar Allan Poe* (United States: Thomas Y. Crowell, 1903), pp. 79–92.

Haveman, H. A. and Kluttz, D. N., "Copyright Law, Cultural Conceptions of Authorship, and the American Magazine Industry." Law.berkeley.edu (October 23, 2013), p. 10, law.berkeley.edu/files/csls/HavemanPaper4Nov.pdf.

Hayes, K. J. (ed.), *The Cambridge Companion to Edgar Allan Poe* (Cambridge: Cambridge University Press, 2002), p. 84.

Herley, S., "Rial Side: Part of Salem in 1700," *Historical Collections of the Essex Institute* (United States, Essex Institute, 1919), pp. 71–73, books.google.com/books?id=GWJno5a-8cAC&pg=PA71&lpg=PA71&dq=cherry%2Bhill%2Bfarm%2Bwenham%2Bwhite%2Bmurder&source=bl&ots=GA8jYXGXYS&sig=ACfU3U0cVfw-fU2LC64cdSDw6yFcZSSoJw&hl=en&-ppis=_c&sa=X&ved=2ahUKEwiRrurxpIHoAhWBmOAKHZtFAbQQ6AEwAXoECAoQAQ#v=onepage&q=cherry%20hill%20farm%20wenham%20white%20murder&f=false.

Hervey, A., *Israfel: The Life and Times of Edgar Allan Poe* (N.Y.: George EL Doran Company, 1926), pp. 184–217; 227–268; 417–465; 841–847, eapoe.org/papers/misc1921/hva26112.htm#fn0355

Hurd, D. H., *History of Essex County, Massachusetts* (Boston: J. W. Lewis & Co., 1887), p. 146, archive.org/stream/historyessexcou00hurdgoog/historyessexcou00hurdgoog_djvu.txt

Ireland, R. M., "Privately Funded Prosecution of Crime in the Nineteenth-Century United States," *The American Journal of Legal History* Vol. 39, No. 1 (Oxford University Press, January 1995), pp. 45–46; 48, jstor.org/stable/845749?read-now=1&seq=5#page_scan_tab_contents

Johnson, T., "Cadet Edgar Allan Poe," *American Heritage* (June 1976), americanheritage.com/cadet-edgar-allan-poe#2

Jones, J., *When Charles Dickens & Edgar Allan Poe Met, And Dickens' Pet Raven Inspired Poe'S Poem "The Raven"* (2016) openculture.com/2016/10/charles-dickens-edgar-allan-poe-met.html

Judd, O. B. (ed.), "Deaths," *The New York Chronicle* Vol. 1 (New York: Holman & Gray, 1849), p. 339.

Katz, W. J., *Humbug! The Politics of Art Criticism in New York City's Penny Press* (United States: Fordham University Press, 2020), pp. 35; 40–41.

Knapp, A. M., *The Knapp Family in America* (Boston: Fort Hill Press, 1909), pp. 31-32, archive.org/details/knappfamilyiname01knap/page/n39/mode/2up/search/Phippen

Knapp, J. F., "A Report of the Evidence and Points of Law, Arising in the Trial of John Francis Knapp, for the Murder of Joseph White, Esquire. Before the Supreme Judicial ... Pam. vol.," *Hathi Trust Digital Library* (Salem, W. & S. B. Ives, 1830), babel.hathitrust.org/cgi/pt?id=hvd.32044019037472&view=1up&seq=27.

Knapp, J. F., *Second trial of John Francis Knapp by a new jury: recommenced at Salem, August 14, 1830, for the murder of Capt. Joseph White, before the Supreme Judicial Court of the Commonwealth of Massachusetts, at a special session, commenced at Salem, July 20, 1830* (Boston: Dutton and Wentworth, 1830), pp. 7–9.

Knapp, J. J., *Confession of Joseph Jenkins Knapp* (Phillips Library at the Peabody Essex Museum collections. Salem, Mass.: Essex Institute, 1830); *Trials of Capt. Joseph J. Knapp, Jr. and George Crowninshield, Esq: For the Murder of Capt. Joseph White of Salem, on the Night of the Sixth of April 1830* (United States: Charles Ellms, 1830).

Knapp, N. P., *Select Sermons of the Late Rev. N.P. Knapp: Rector of Christ Church, Mobile, Ala* (United States: Herman Hooker, 1855), books.google.com/books?id=aDARAAAAIAAJ&pg=PR3&lpg=PR3&dq=ellen+lee+knapp&source=bl&ots=zAI6IJ9Qo8&sig=ACfU3U22c6wV38W7rMqtLh--kgWaVz4dOg&hl=en&ppis=_c&sa=X&ved=2ahUKEwj0g9Wp0tfoAhU0lnIEHanYBzcQ6AEwAHoECAsQKKQ#v=onepage&q=ellen%20lee%20knapp&f=false

Kopley, R., "A Tale by Poe," *Edgar Allan Poe's the Tell-tale Heart and Other Stories* (United States: Facts On File, Incorporated, 2014), pp. 173–176.

Lai, A., "The Experiment That Shocked the World," *Helix Magazine* (Science in Society, Northwestern University research center for science outreach and public engagement, August 2, 2017), helix.northwestern.edu/article/experiment-shocked-world.

Lawrence, J. C. "A Theory of the Short Story," *The North American Review* Vol. 205, No. 735 (Cedar Falls, Iowa: University of Northern Iowa, February 1917), pp. 274–286, jstor.org/stable/25121469?seq=2#metadata_info_tab_contents

Lawson, J. D., "The Trial of George Crowninshield as an Accessory in the Murder of Joseph White, Salem. Massachusetts, 1830," *American State Trials: A Collection of the Important and Interesting Criminal Trials which Have Taken Place in the United States, from the Beginning of Our Government to the Present Day: with Notes and Annotations* (United States: Thomas Law Book Company, 1917), pp. 640–670, books.google.com/books?id=Cow8AAAAIAAJ&pg=PA640&lpg=PA640&dq=george+crowninshield+trial&source=bl&ots=inBM0IruDc&sig=ACfU3U3p8A0XQrq8Il9al7JePEjT0S1b8A&hl=en&ppis=_c&sa=X&ved=2ahUKEwitlt2W5LTlAhWNhOAKHbfaB404ChDoATABegQICRAB#v=onepage&q=george%20crowninshield%20trial&f=false

Leach, J. G., *Memoranda Relating to the Ancestry and Family of Hon. Levi Parson Morton, Vice-president of the United States (1889–1893)* (N.p.: Printed at the Riverside Press, 1894), p. 29, books.google.com/books?id=dBk5AAAAMAAJ&pg=PA29&lpg=PA29&dq=was+perez+morton+related+to+marcus+morton&source=bl&ots=qinlGwGpq&sig=ACfU3U0Pc0HnmpnSqjf6lyNU8YIiBE7kNQ&hl=en&sa=X&ved=2ahUKEwjUjfHh2cjkAhXJVN8KHQi7BT0Q6AEwAnoECAgQAQ#v=onepage&q=Perez&f=false

Lee Family Digital Archive, Letter from Nathaniel Phippen Knapp to Ellen McMacken Lee Bedford Knapp, July 20, 1853, leefamilyarchive.org/9-family-papers/174-nathaniel-phippen-knapp-to-ellen-mcmacken-lee-bedford-knapp-1853-july-20.

Lehuu, I., *Carnival on the Page: Popular Print Media in Antebellum America* (United Kingdom, University of North Carolina Press, 2000), pp. 26–27.

Ljungquist, K. P., "Poe's 'Autography': A New Exchange of Reviews," *American Periodicals* Vol. 2 (Columbus, Ohio: Ohio State University Press, Fall 1992), pp. 51–63, jstor.org/stable/20771015

Lowell, J. R., *Edgar Allan Poe Society Of Baltimore—Editions—The Pioneer (Prospectus)* (2015), eapoe.org/works/editions/mpnr001p.htm

Lowell, J. R. and Carter, R. (eds), *The Pioneer: A Literary and Critical Magazine* Vol. 1 no. 1 (Boston: Leland and Whiting, January 1843), pp. 29–31; 37; 61, archive.org/details/pioneerliteraryc01lowe/page/30/model/2up?q=tell-tale

Mabbott, T. O., *Collected Works of Edgar Allan Poe* Vol. 1 (Cambridge: Harvard University Press, 1969), pp. 350–374; 789–797; 799–847.

Macon Telegraph (Macon, Georgia: August 11, 1888), p. 2, newspapers.com/image/591125725/?terms=%22George%2BCrowninshield%22

Magistrale, A., Frank, F. S., and Poe, E. A., *The Poe Encyclopedia* (United Kingdom: Greenwood Press, 1997), pp 62; 74. books.google.com/books?id=TevIJKwqWPMC&pg=PA74&lpg=PA74&dq=Wm.+T.+D.+Clemm+poe&source=bl&ots=3wafM4RRoM&sig=ACfU3U1HkBH7FMEISu7FZcApTmgWM1fWrQ&hl=en&sa=X&ved=2ahUKEwjWyrKU2InpAhVKgnIEHYbfABgQ6AEwAXoECAwQAQ#v=onepage&q=Wm.%20T.%20D.%20Clemm%20poe&f=false

Marti, D. B., "The Reverend Henry Colman's Agricultural Ministry," *Agricultural History* Vol. 51, No. 3 (Agricultural History Society: Winter Park, Florida, July 1977), pp. 524–539, jstor.org/stable/3741721?read-now=1&refreqid=excelsior%3A0bacb2576131865c062cb406a36b523e&seq=1#page_scan_tab_contents

Martineau, H., *Retrospect of Western Travel*, Vol. 1 (London: Saunders and Otley, 1838), pp. 280–282.

McAllister, J., "Essex County Chronicles: A 'Mighty Blusterer' to Some, Salem's Putnam Was a Legal Icon," *The Salem News* (Salem, Massachusetts: April 26, 2010), salemnews.com/opinion/essex-county-chronicles-a-mighty-blusterer-to-some-salems-putnam-was-a-legal-icon/article_36e70aa8-ec4e-5190-adf4-989c06839429.html.

Mckee, G., "A New Letter from Poe to Lowell on the Pioneer" *The Edgar Allan Poe Review*, Vol. 20, No. 1 (University Park, Pennsylvania: The Penn State University Press, 2019), pp. 27–45. jstor.org/stable/10.5325/edgallpoerev.20.1.0027

Meyers, J., *Edgar Allan Poe: His Life and Legacy* (New York: Cooper Square Press, 1992), pp. 126–127.

Miller, J. (Warden), Letter to Nathaniel Knapp, June 6, 1830 (Phillips Library at the Peabody Essex Museum collections. Salem, Mass.: Essex Institute, 1830).

Mindich, D. T. Z., *Tuned Out: Why Americans Under 40 Don't Follow the News* (United Kingdom: Oxford University Press, USA, 2004).

Minto, W., "Edgar Allan Poe," *Littell's Living Age* (United States: E. Littell & Company, 1880), pp. 690–699.

Moran, J. J., *A Defense of Edgar Allan Poe* (Washington, D.C.: William F. Boogher, 1885), eapoe.org/papers/misc1851/jjm18850.htm; "Official Memorandum of the Death of Edgar A. Poe," *Baltimore Sun* (Baltimore: October 29, 1875), p. 1, eapoe.org/papers/misc1851/18751029.htm

Mott, F. L., "A Brief History of Graham's Magazine," *Studies in Philology* Vol. 25, No. 3 (Chapel Hill, North Carolina: University of North Carolina Press, July 1928), pp. 362–374, jstor.org/stable/4172007?read-now=1&refreqid=excelsior%3A70d3ee7a2c0edc997145c8fe6db3fa81&seq=1#page_scan_tab_contents

New Brunswick Junior Chamber of Commerce, "The 1927 Illustrated Official Book of New Brunswick" (New Brunswick: Junior Chamber of Commerce, 1927).

Nj.gov., *State Of New Jersey* (2020), nj.gov/oag/oag/ag_1841-1844_mollesson_bio.htm

Onion, R., 2013. "'A Terrible Evil': Edgar Allan Poe Writes About His Wife's Illness And Death," *Slate Magazine* (2013), slate.com/human-interest/2013/05/edgar-allan-poe-a-letter-to-a-fan-in-which-he-tells-the-story-of-virginia-poe-s-death.html

Online Books Page, "Colman, Henry, 1785–1849" (University of Pennsylvania), Accessed May 17, 2020, onlinebooks.library.upenn.edu/webbin/book/lookupname?key=Colman, Henry, 1785-1849.

Ostrom, J. W., "Edgar A. Poe: His Income as Literary Entrepreneur," *Poe Studies*, Vol. XV, No. 1 (Baltimore: John Hopkins University Press, June 1982), pp. 1–7, eapoe.org/pstudies/ps1980/p1982101.htm.

Palmer, J. C. R., *Explanation: or 1830; being a series of facts connected with the life of the author, from 1825 to the present day* (Printed for the author, Boston: 1831).

Palmer, J., "Harvard University Alumni Necrology (1851–1863)," USGenWeb Archives—census wills deeds genealogy (Boston: J. Wilson & Son), files.usgwarchives.net/ma/suffolk/towns/cambridge/obits/harvard.txt.

Pearl, M., "A Poe Death Dossier: Discoveries and Queries in the Death of Edgar Allan Poe: Part I," *The Edgar Allan Poe Review*, Vol. 7, No. 2 (University Park: Penn State University Press, 2006) pp. 4–29.

Pearson, E., "The Murder of Captain White," *Vanity Fair* vol. 25–26 (United States, Condé Nast, 1926), pp. 62; 84; 86, books.google.com/books?id=aX87AQAAIAAJ&pg=PA84&lpg=PA84&dq=knapp%2Bsalem%2Bmurder%2Bbandits&source=bl&ots=BK15rzIYph&sig=ACfU3U3fXtNQYDXqc_

Ii76Wh3OVbFu7aUg&hl=en&sa=
X&ved=2ahUKEwiq5PDS2bHpAhUHZd8KHbhaD8cQ6AEwAnoECAgQAQ#v=
onepage&q=knapp%20salem%20murder%20bandits&f=false.

Peirce, C., *A Meteorological Account of the Weather in Philadelphia: from January 1, 1790, to January 1, 1847, Including Fifty-Seven Years; with an Appendix Containing a Great Variety of Interesting Information ...*, (Lindsay & Blakiston, 1847), pp. 232–233.

Pickersgill, H. E. and Wall. J. P., *History of Middlesex County, New Jersey, 1664–1920* (New York: Lewis Publishing Company, 1921), pp. 267.

Picton, T., *Fun and Fancy in Old New York: Reminisces of a Man About Town* (Maryland: Wildside Press LLC, 1996), pp. 76–77.

Poe, E. A. and Harrison, J. A., *Literary criticism* (United States: G. D. Sproul, 1902), pp. 145–150, books.google.com/books?id=BcBEAAAAYAAJ&pg=PA150&lpg=PA150&dq=
%E2%80%9CMr.+Dickens,+through+genius,+has+perfected+a+standard+
from+which+Art+itself+will+derive+its+essence,+its+rules.
%E2%80%9D&source=bl&ots=JecSi65aLT&sig=ACfU3U3ZCv3rEpqaxg3LqsZ56O75tZPO-
g&hl=en&sa=X&ved=2ahUKEwjowOuW3vLoAhXPhHIEHaXjC8UQ6AEwBHoECAkQKQ#
v=onepage&q=%E2%80%9CMr.%20Dickens%2C%20through%20genius%2C%20has%20
perfected%20a%20standard%20from%20which%20Art%20itself%20will%20derive%20
its%20essence%2C%20its%20rules.%E2%80%9D&f=false

Poe, E. A. and Kennedy, J. G. (ed.), *The Portable Edgar Allan Poe* (United States: Penguin Publishing Group, 2006), pp. 482–484.

Poe, E. A. and Mabbott, T. O., *Collected Works of Edgar Allan Poe* (The Belknap Press of Harvard University Press, 1979), pp. 787–790.

Poe, E. A. and Ostrom, J. W. (ed.), *The Letters of Edgar Allan Poe*. Vol. 1. (New York: Gordian Press, 1966), pp. 1–50; Letter to John Allan (February 21, 1831) from "Letters: Chapter I," *The Letters of Edgar Allan Poe — Vol. I: 1824-1845* (1966), pg. 43; Letter to William Poe (August 14, 1840) from "Letters: Chapter IV," *The Letters of Edgar Allan Poe—Vol. I: 1824–1845* (1966), pg. 141, eapoe.org/works/ostlttrs/pl661c01.htm#pg0043

Poe, E. A., "Edgar Allan Poe letter to John Allan—June 28, 1830," eapoe.org/works/letters/p3006280.htm; "Edgar Allan Poe to John Allan—February 4, 1829 (LTR-009)," (February 4, 1829), eapoe.org/works/letters/p2902040.htm; "Review of New Books," *Graham's American Monthly Magazine of Literature, Art, and Fashion* (United States: G.R. Graham., 1841), pp. 248–251, books.google.com/books?id=6dURAAAAYAAJ&pg=PA248&lpg=PA248&dq=%E2%80%A6the
+rumors+in+respect+to+the+sanity+of+Mr.+Dickens,+which+were+so+prevalent+during+
the+publication+of+the+first+numbers+of+the+work,+had+some+slight,+some+very+slight+
foundation+of+truth.%E2%80%9D&source=bl&ots=-ZI_q88LEe&sig=
ACfU3U1JCfXXYI48eQ72UOr3aElaSyvcnQ&hl=en&sa=X&ved=2ahUKEwjW5KuJ3_
LoAhUBmXIEHbwfBVAQ6AEwAHoECAUQKQ#v=onepage&q=%E2%80%A6the
%20rumors%20in%20respect%20to%20the%20sanity%20of%20Mr.%20Dickens%2C%20
which%20were%20so%20prevalent%20during%20the%20publication%20of%20
the%20first%20numbers%20of%20the%20work%2C%20had%20some%20slight%2C%20
some%20very%20slight%20foundation%20of%20truth.%E2%80%9D&f=false; "The Tell-Tale Heart," poemuseum.org/the-tell-tale-heart; Letter to John Allan (January 3, 1831), eapoe.org/works/letters/p3101030.htm; Letter to Rufus Wilmot Griswold (May 29, 1841), eapoe.org/works/letters/p4105290.htm; Letter to William E. Burton (June 1, 1840), eapoe.org/works/letters/p4006010.htm

Pollard, R. S., "Against the Law and Beyond the Evidence," *ABA Journal* 63 (February 1977): 205–7, books.google.com/books?id=soQPrs_VQc4C&pg=PA210&dq=joseph+knapp+trial+confession&hl=en&sa=X&ved=2ahUKEwi1sfWw_p_
pAhWigXIEHbTEDJYQ6AEwAnoECAIQAg#v=onepage&q=joseph%20knapp%20trial%20
confession&f=false

Pray, I. C., *Memoirs of James Gordon Bennett and His Times* (United States: Stringer & Townsend, 1855), pp. 182–185, books.google.com/
books?id=7HwqAAAAMAAJ&pg=PA182&lpg=
PA182&dq=%22William+H.+Attree%22&source=bl&ots=DvxG7I--DF&sig=ACfU3U1Nks-
gcqpVOVUyEsON8cCGNv28tw&hl=en&sa=X&ved=2ahUKEwip4PfcvfzoAhUhYTUKHUDfC
_4Q6AEwCHoECAoQAQ#v=onepage&q=%22William%20H.%20Attree%22&f=false

Quinn, A. H., *Edgar Allan Poe: a Critical Biography* (Baltimore: Johns Hopkins University Press, 2008), pp. 81–96; 118–122; 138–185; 263–404; 519–58; 615–641.

Reynolds, D. S., *Beneath the American Renaissance: The Subversive Imagination in the Age of Emerson and Melville* (New York: Knoff, 1988), pp. 231–234.

Robbins, J. A., "George R. Graham, Philadelphia Publisher," *The Pennsylvania Magazine of History and Biography* Vol. 75, No. 3 (Philadelphia: University of Pennsylvania Press, July 1951), pp. 279-294, jstor.org/stable/20088271?read-now=1&seq=2#page_scan_tab_contents

Russell, J. R., *The Pioneer: A Literary and Critical Magazine* (Boston: Leland & Whiting, January 1843).

Seilhamer, G. O. and Jenkins, H. M., *Memorial History of the City of Philadelphia: Special and biographical* (United States: New-York History Company, 1898), books.google.com/books?id=zOwLAAAAYAAJ&pg=PA114&lpg=PA114&dq=119+South+Front+Street,+in+Carpenters%E2%80%99+Hall,+and+on+Second+Street+belo w+Dock+Street&source=bl&ots=-TIUfpEEP9&sig=ACfU3U0ieb1kLq2A 7wQ6chE6EHetA8SxEw&hl=en&ppis=_c&sa=X&ved=2ahUKEwiohrrF- p7mAhWNxVkKHYr8CaYQ6AEwAXoECAwQAQ#v=onepage&q=119%20South%20 Front%20Street%2C%20in%20Carpenters%E2%80%99% 20Hall%2C%20and%20on%20Second%20Street%20below%20Dock%20Street&f=false

Seitz, D. C., *The James Gordon Bennetts, Father and Son, Proprietors of the New York Herald* (Indianapolis: The Bobbs-Merrill Company, 1928), p. 69.

Semtner, C., "Charles Dickens Meets Edgar Allan Poe—Poe Museum Blog," (2012). Available at: thepoeblog.org/charles-dickens-meets-edgar-allan-poe/; "The Other Poe" (June 12, 2014), thepoeblog.org/the-other-poe/; "Rufus Wilmot Griswold-Poe's Literary Executor—Poe Museum Blog" (2014). Available at: thepoeblog.org/rufus-wilmot-griswold-poes-literary-executor/

Shaw, L. C. J., "An Address delivered before the Bar of Berkshire, by Lemuel Shaw C. J., September term 1830, at Lenox," mass.gov/person/isaac-parker.

Smith, G., Strangehistory.org (2020). Available at: strangehistory.org/cms/index.php?option=com_ content&view=article&id=96

Snodgrass, J. E., "Death and Burial of Edgar A. Poe," *Life Illustrated* (New York: May 17, 1856), p. 24, eapoe.org/papers/misc1851/18560517.htm; "Edgar A. Poe's Death and Burial," *New York Reformer* (Watertown, NY, July 26, 1855), p. 2, eapoe.org/papers/misc1851/18550726.htm; "The Facts of Poe's Death and Burial," *Beadle's Monthly* (New York: May 1867), pp. 283–287, eapoe.org/papers/misc1851/18670300.htm

Starr, L. M., "James Gordon Bennett—Beneficent Rascal," *American Heritage* Vol. 6, Issue 2 (February 1955), americanheritage.com/james-gordon-bennett-beneficent-rascal

Strahan, D., "Washington Square North and Mall Street, Salem, Mass" (Lost New England, January 5, 2019), lostnewengland.com/2019/01/washington-square-north-and-mall-street-salem-mass/.

Strong, J. and McClintock, J., *Cyclopaedia of Biblical, Theological, and Ecclesiastical Literature* (United States: Harper, 1894), p. 977, books.google.com/books?id=tac8AAAAYAAJ&pg=PA977&lpg=PA977&dq=Cleaveland+john+ payne+The+Cyclopedia+of+Biblical,+Theological, +and+Ecclesiastical+Literature.+James+Strong+ and+John+McClintock&source=bl&ots=WY9ywkM9XI&sig=ACfU3U1W13FOH7bcd0qL7_ Jn6gvA5Ixn5A&hl=en&sa=X&ved=2ahUKEwjV_ N2V7rrpAhUOg3IEHSDxDCgQ6AEwAXoECAoQAQ#v=onepage&q=Cleaveland%20 john%20payne%20The%20Cyclopedia%20of%20Biblical%2C%20Theological%2C%20 and%20Ecclesiastical%20Literature.%20James%20Strong%20and%20John%20 McClintock&f=false

Sumner, W. H., *A History of East Boston: With Biographical Sketches of Its Early Proprietors, and an Appendix* (United States: Higginson Book Company, 1858), pp. 34; 428–434; 670–671. books.google.com/books?id=StCjWnfopIIC&pg= PA443&lpg=PA443&dq=east+boston+stephen+white&source=bl&ots=3tDjCe5Cod&sig=ACf U3U304hEpLtqkJJT3ayyYpWousk-i_Q&hl=en&ppis=_c&sa=X&ved=2ahUKEwjNsauBkdnoA- hWBlXIEHRZSCIMQ6AEwCHoECAsQKQ#v=onepage&q=east%20boston%20stephen%20 white&f=false

Takahashi, R., "Edgar Allan Poe's Terror of the Relationship: 'Madness' in 'The Tell-Tale Heart.'" *Semanticscholar.org*, pdfs.semanticscholar.org/2fc8/697f71c42fcd65cfa82cd9886a577d156ca9. pdf.

Tally, R. T., *Poe and the Subversion of American Literature: Satire, Fantasy, Critique* (London: Bloomsbury Publishing, 2014), pp. 83–91.

The National Gazette (Philadelphia, Pennsylvania, March 12, 1841), p. 2, newspapers.com/image/346359886/?terms=%22Peter%2BRobinson%22%2B%22Abraham%2BSuydam%22

The Salem Gazette (April 1830. Phillips Library at the Peabody Essex Museum collections. Salem, Mass.: Essex Institute: 1830).

Thomas, D. R. and Jackson, D. K., *The Poe Log: A Documentary Life of Edgar Allan Poe, 1809–1849* (Boston: J.K. Hall, 1987), pp. 111–143; 247–313; 315–390; 393–446; 783–854.

Todd, C. B., *In Olde New York: Sketches of Old Times and Places in Both the State and the City* (United States: Grafton Press, 1907), pp. 69–71, books.google.com/books?id=0VEdAAAAMAAJ&pg=PA69&lpg=PA69&dq=%22William+H.+Attree%22&source=bl&ots=oCFFeADM0D&sig=ACfU3U1Fd3UsRJUrxnYMUsm5Oouo HUYGDw&hl=en&sa=X&ved=2ahUKEwjqyt3p1__jAhWEdd8KHW3eDv84ChDo ATACegQICBAB#v=onepage&q=attree&f=false

Trial, Confession, and Execution of Peter Robinson, for The Murder of Abraham Suydam, Esq, of New Brunswick, N.J. (New York: The Reporter, 1841).

Tucher, A., *Froth & Scum: Truth, Beauty, Goodness, and the Ax Murder in America's First Mass Medium* (Chapel Hill, North Carolina: University of North Carolina Press, 1994), pp. 27; 121; 214.

Tucker, B., Letter from Benjamin Tucker to N.D. Gay. Phillips Library at the Peabody Essex Museum collections (Salem, Mass.: Essex Institute, 1830).

U.S. Customers Service, "Our 198th Year," Collectors of the Port of Philadelphia: the United States Customs Service (United States: The Service, 1987), books.google.com/books?id=BRCvLA6QzR0C&pg=PA7&lpg=PA7&dq= philadelphia+custom+house+1840+smith&source=bl&ots=WNRX-2cfLT&sig=ACfU3U 3fHwD8IqtiV0Z0Y5_tFyJGzCFi8A&hl=en&ppis=_c&sa=X&ved=2ahUKEwjH0KS3gJ_ mAhWsxVkKHaW-CEcQ6AEwBnoECBQQAQ#v=onepage&q=philadelphia %20custom%20house%201840%20smith&f=false

Undine, *Poe And Charles Dickens* [online] (2012), worldofpoe.blogspot.com/2013/03/poe-and-charles-dickens.html>.

Vermont Enquirer (Norwich, Vermont: December 30, 1830), p. 4, newspapers.com/image/526423239/?terms=%22Captain%2BJoseph%2BWhite%22

Wagner, E. J., "A Murder in Salem" (Smithsonian Institution, November 1, 2010), smithsonianmag.com/history/a-murder-in-salem-64885035/.

Walker, I. (ed.), *Edgar Allen Poe* (United Kingdom: Taylor & Francis, 2013), pp. 132–133.

Walker, I., "The Poe Legend," *A Companion to Poe Studies* (United Kingdom: Greenwood Press, 1996), pp. 20–36.

Walker, L., "The Murder of Captain Joseph White: Salem, Massachusetts, 1830," *The ABA Journal*, Vol. 54 (May 1968), pp. 462–466, books.google.com/books?id=Nbo3ZyldHpkC&pg=PA464&lpg= PA464&dq=%22franklin+dexter%22+attorney+massachusetts+ 1830&source=bl&ots=i91zYJJAOl&sig=ACfU3U2O5EWxoXmy ENzdtksEoy4vjgZ_Bw&hl=en&sa=X&ved=2ahUKEwjO- uz2wsPkAhXktlkKHfpcAcsQ6AEwA3oECAUQAQ#v=onepage&q=%22franklin%20 dexter%22%20attorney%20massachusetts%201830&f=false

Wallis, J. J., *The Depression of 1839 to 1843: States, Debts, and Banks* (University of Maryland, National Bureau of Economic Research, Paper 133, April 2001).

Webster, D., "The Murder of Captain Joseph White." *Legal arguments and speeches to the jury. Diplomatic and official papers. Miscellaneous letters* (N.Y.: Little, Brown, 1853), pp. 44–49; "The Murder of Captain Joseph White," *Masterpieces of Modern Oratory* (United States: Ginn, 1906), pp. 53–65.

West, J., *The Arbiters of Reality: Hawthorne, Melville, and the Rise of Mass Information Culture* (United States: Ohio State University Press, 2008), pp. 4; 23–36.

Winans, J. A. and Bradley, H. A., *Daniel Webster and the Salem Murder* (United States, Lawbook Exchange, 2007), pp. 15; 18–21; 24–25; 31; 34–40; 66–67; 96–98; 100–159; 225–232.